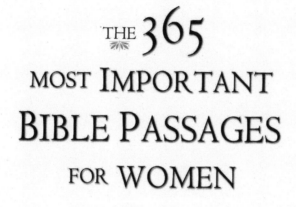

THE 365
MOST IMPORTANT
BIBLE PASSAGES
FOR WOMEN

THE 365

MOST IMPORTANT

BIBLE PASSAGES

FOR WOMEN

*Daily Readings and Meditations
on Becoming the Woman
God Created You to Be*

Copyright © 2011 GRQ, Inc.

FaithWords
Hachette Book Group
237 Park Avenue
New York, NY 10017

Visit our website at www.faithwords.com.

Scriptures noted AMP are taken from the Amplified® Bible, Copyright © 1954, 1958, 1962, 1964, 1965, 1987 by The Lockman Foundation. Used by permission.

Scriptures noted CEV are taken from the Contemporary English Version. © 1991, 1992, 1995 by American Bible Society. Used by permission.

Scriptures noted ESV are taken from The Holy Bible, English Standard Version, © 2001 by Crossway Bibles, a division of Good News Publishers. Used by permission. All rights reserved.

Scriptures noted GOD'S WORD are taken from God's Word®. Copyright © 1995 God's Word to the Nations. Used by permission of Baker Publishing Group. All rights reserved.

Scriptures noted GNT are taken from the Good News Translation® (formerly Today's English Version), Second Edition. Copyright © 1992 American Bible Society. All rights reserved.

Scriptures noted MSG are taken from The Message: The New Testament in Contemporary English. Copyright © 1993, 1994, 1995, 2000, 2001, 2002. Used by permission of NavPress Publishing Group.

Scriptures noted NASB are taken from the NEW AMERICAN STANDARD BIBLE®, © Copyright The Lockman Foundation 1960, 1962, 1963, 1968, 1971, 1972, 1973, 1975, 1977, 1995. Used by permission.

Scriptures noted NIV are taken from the HOLY BIBLE, NEW INTERNATIONAL VERSION®. NIV®. © 1973, 1978, 1984, by International Bible Society. Used by permission of Zondervan. All rights reserved.

Scriptures noted NLT are taken from the Holy Bible, New Living Translation © 1996, 2004. Used by permission of Tyndale House Publishers, Inc., Wheaton, Illinois 60189. All rights reserved.

Printed in the United States of America

First Edition: April 2011

10 9 8 7 6 5 4 3 2 1

FaithWords is a division of Hachette Book Group, Inc.
The FaithWords name and logo are trademarks of Hachette Book Group, Inc.

Library of Congress Cataloging-in-Publication Data

ISBN 978-0-446-57500-3

Manuscript: Karen H. Whiting
Editor: Diane Stortz
Design: Whisner Design Group

People are like stained-glass windows.
They sparkle and shine when the sun is out,
but when the darkness sets in,
their true beauty is revealed only
if there is a light from within.

—Elisabeth Kübler-Ross

The fact that I am a woman does not make
me a different kind of Christian, but the fact that
I am a Christian does make me a different kind
of woman. For I have accepted God's idea of me,
and my whole life is an offering back to Him
of all that I am and all that He wants me to be.

—Elisabeth Elliot

CONTENTS

Introduction 19

Significance

You Are Important... 22
Reason for Respect 23
Gemstones... 24
Wanderer Turned Community Builder............................ 25
Mother's Grief Stirs a King 26
A Little Flame Burst.. 27
Words Matter 28
Welcome to the Family... 29
Called to Significance... 30
Time to Act Significantly... 31
Significant Work 32
Walk with Dignity.. 33
Accept Opportunities 34
Expect Prosperity... 35
Leaving a Legacy.. 36
Never Too Old.. 37
Significant Women.. 38
Striving for Position.. 39
Transforming Bad Intentions 40
Big Mysteries.. 41
Powerful Woman... 42
Fullness of Life... 43
Dignity for the Sick... 44
Who Is Insignificant? 45
Real Worth 46
Traditions Build Identity.. 47
Purpose with Power.. 48
Significant Answer to Prayer... 49
Daddy's Little Girl 50
Heavenly Joy 51

Relationships & Communication

Impressions.. 54
Let's Dine Together 55
God's Ideal Relationships 56
An Understanding Heart.. 57

Contents, continued

Leaven—Ingredient of Heaven 58

Love the Unlovable 59

Empathy among Friends 60

Encouraging Friendships 61

Swift Settlements 62

Internal Divisions Ruin Relationships 63

What Causes Fights? 64

Friends Defend Friends 65

Praying for Family 66

Supportive Family 67

Close-Knit Family 68

To Love, Honor, and What? 69

Strong Marriages 70

Don't Be the Bad Woman 71

Always a Daughter 72

In-Law Relations 73

In-Law Advice 74

Great Leadership 75

Follow Your Leader 76

It's Your Choice 77

Choose God First 78

Forever Together 79

Angels among Us 80

Little Children, Big Angels 81

Covenant Relationship 82

The Gift of Words 83

Powerful Words 84

Gossip or Information? 85

Seasoned Conversation 86

Conversation Peace 87

Deep, Living Words 88

Slow to Speak 89

Communicating with Integrity 90

A Bit of Control 91

Voice Recognition 92

A Farmer's Tale 93

The Real Meaning 94

Words from the Heart 95

Dogged Conversation 96

Effective Prayer 97

Contents, continued

A Little Whisper 98
Great Discovery 99
Echoes of Nature 100
Burning Lips 101
Enlightening Words 102
Angelic Voices 103
Skywriting 104
Fear of Speaking 105
Shining Speakers 106
Pleasant Words 107
Bringing Out the Best 108
Strange Proposal 109
Voicing Concern 110
The Wrong List to Be On 111
Consequences 112
Be Still and Know God 113

Understanding Men

Competing Boys at Heart 116
Did He Really Listen? 117
God, Is That You? Really? 118
Gone Fishin' 119
Loyalty among Guys 120
Men and Courage 121
A Guy Party 122
Mourning Lost Friendship 123
Authoritative Tone 124
Not Man Enough 125
Loud Rejection, Private Weeping 126
The Way to a Man's Heart 127
Pursuit 128
Beloved Mother and Wife 129
Picturing Marriage 130
Wandering Eyes 131
Cover-Ups 132
Boomerang 133
Did I Do That? 134
Fairness 135
Perspectives on Flowers 136
Misplaced Faith 137

CONTENTS, CONTINUED

A Man of Integrity 138
The Romantic Lover... 139
Finding a Congenial Wife 140
Why Don't They Listen?... 141
Pride or Integrity? 142
Diplomatic Arguments.. 143
Moved by Hospitality 144
Pleasing Your Man 145
Secret Missions.. 146

Choices

Unpredictability of Life.. 148
The Price of Curiosity 149
Beneficial Living 150
Morning Attitudes 151
Maximizing Potential.. 152
Mary's Response.. 153
Costly Choices 154
Prayer Releases Power 155
Choose to Love.. 156
Timely Choices 157
Precious Knitting 158
Children Are Gifts... 159
Choose Fullness of Life... 160
Stay on Track... 161
A Great Dish.. 162
Double Shifts... 163
Choosing Life 164
Creative, Responsible Living 165
The Answer Is Blowin' in the Wind............................... 166
New 'Tudes 167
Patterns and Repetitions 168
Laziness Invites Calamity 169
Never Lost... 170
Passion and Purity.. 171
Angry Enough to Kill... 172
Tastefully Visible.. 173
Generosity Triumphs... 174
Divine Appointment.. 175
Choose Hospitality 176

The True Giver 177
Choosing to Stay 178
Talents and Careers 179

Stress & Community

Facing Troubles 182
Let Not Your Heart Be Troubled...................................... 183
Stop Stressing, Start Asking.. 184
Against God's Will 185
Pity Parties.. 186
Yielding to Nagging.. 187
Discerning Cons 188
Same Old Problems, Better Hope 189
Lurking Green Monsters.. 190
Murder in the Family.. 191
Rape and Revenge 192
Not Guilty, but Jailed.. 193
Restoring Lost Years 194
Not Your Battle 195
Marital Strife 196
No Comparison... 197
Temporary Troubles.. 198
Clinging to Promised Comfort.. 199
Opposition.. 200
Conflicts and Biting Words 201
Self-Image Makeover.. 202
The Real Struggle 203
Start with Self-Improvement 204
Complete Trust 205
Expressing Emotions 206
Letting Go of Fear.. 207
Blind Obedience 208
Speechless before God 209
Vain Envy 210
Deep-Down Cleansing.. 211
Victory at Last.. 212
All Are Welcome... 213
Devoted Community... 214
Community Grapevine... 215
Community Traditions... 216

Contents, continued

Encouragement Builds Community 217
Neighborliness 218
Town Parade 219
Getting Along 220
Harmony 221
Peace-Driven Life 222
Accepting Others 223
Social Justice 224
Enthusiasm Is Contagious 225
Open to Debate 226
U-Turned 227
Facing the Bullies 228
A Richer Life 229
Serving the Community 230
Together without Envy 231
Comm-Unity 232
Unity Begins with Two 233
Children Unite a Community 234
Children Belong 235
Look Who's Moving In 236
Community Revival 237
Grateful Reactions 238
Tears for the Treasured City 239
Boomerang Living 240
Community Prayer Gets Results 241
A Generous Church Community 242
Let's Party, Girlfriends 243

Beauty & Health

Spa Treatments 246
Lookin' Good 247
No More Bad-Hair Days 248
Pedi-Cure 249
Beauty Secret 250
Purely Beautiful 251
Time and Beauty 252
Better Than Pilates 253
Luminaries 254
The Truth about Good Health 255
Word Famine 256

Beauty by God.. 257
Outwardly Unattractive 258
Adorned by God 259
Healthy Food Contest... 260
The Value of Rest 261
The Beauty of God's Love... 262
Unfailing Energy.. 263
Food for Health.. 264
Beautiful Gifts 265
Beautiful Feet... 266
That Time of Month 267
Splendidly Clothed 268
Get Moving... 269
Healing Touch Any Day.. 270
Reaching Out for Healing 271
Less Stress with Sharing... 272
Don't Show Off.. 273
Wellspring of Life.. 274
Bold Friends Promote Healing 275

Hope & Contentment

Promises of Hope 278
Timely Hope... 279
Loftier Thoughts 280
Expect Change... 281
Hope for Peace 282
Knock at Night... 283
No-Tears Living 284
Hope after Failure... 285
Rescue from Debts... 286
Anchored in Hope 287
Reason to Laugh.. 288
Hope-Filled Traditions 289
Colors of Hope... 290
Messiah's Mission 291
Hope Springs from God-Given Dreams........................... 292
Hidden Face, Hopeful Words... 293
From Despair to Mountaintop 294
Happy Days Ahead.. 295
Guiding Light 296

Contents, continued

Banners Up 297

Creation's Rebirth.. 298

A Gleam in His Eye.. 299

Kindness Changes Hearts... 300

Festive Times 301

A Face Aglow.. 302

Collecting Lasting Treasures 303

Book of Fame.. 304

Gone with the Wind 305

More Precious Than Gold.. 306

Hopeless without God 307

Focus for Contentment... 308

Renewed Thinking 309

Developing Confidence... 310

I Am What I Am... 311

Peace of Mind 312

Good House Building 313

Unlimited Help.. 314

Ups and Downs of Life 315

Seasons of a Woman's Life 316

Celebrations and Rest.. 317

Discontent and Envy.. 318

Material Obsessions... 319

Order and Contentment 320

Be Happy for Others.. 321

Wild Music.. 322

Roller Coaster from Pain to Joy... 323

Contented Harmony... 324

Music Soothes the Savage 325

Humble Prayers Bring Contentment 326

Beautiful in Time 327

The Heart of Security 328

A Generous Lord 329

Share Cheerfully 330

Carefree Living 331

Feeling Doubly Good 332

You Will Smile Again 333

Heart's Desires Fulfilled 334

Can-Do Thinking... 335

CONTENTS, CONTINUED

Divine Discontent.. 336
Get Fired Up!... 337

Faith & Love
Doubts and Proofs... 340
Believe, for I Told You So... 341
Toppled by Obedience 342
Believing the Message 343
Eager Faith 344
Listen with Faith.. 345
Faith for Needs.. 346
Predictions That Stir Faith 347
Seeds of Possibilities.. 348
Scrapbook of Faith 349
Persistent Faith 350
Leap of Faith 351
Once Blind, Now Squinting.. 352
Faith Mentor 353
Faith Believes That God Exists.. 354
Seek and Find 355
Small Faith, Big Results 356
God-Prepared Moves 357
Windows of Heaven... 358
Prayer Partners 359
The Gift of Faithful Words.. 360
Disbelief and Tears.. 361
Acting on Faith 362
Extravagant Faith 363
Restoration Time 364
Molded by the Potter... 365
Pass It On 366
Show Your Faith.. 367
Chameleon Faith Sharers 368
Blessings for the Faithful 369
Love Defined 370
The Math of Love 371
A Special Place in Someone's Heart 372
Awesome Love 373
Love's Request.. 374

Contents, continued

Socially Networked 375
Real Love... 376
Love Goes Round and Round 377
Love Is a Circle of Giving.. 378
Genuine Love.. 379
The Example of Love 380
Broken Hearts... 381
Mending Hearts.. 382
Inseparable Love 383
The Heights of Love 384
Comforting Love... 385
Love among Friends 386
Unloved by Men, Loved by God... 387
Woman with a Past.. 388
Believe in True Love.. 389
In His Loving Hands 390
Multidimensional Love 391
Lust or Love?.. 392
The Money Trap 393
Selfish Love 394
Sacrificing Dearest Love 395
Love Forgives... 396
Love at Life's End 397
Miracles Thrive with Love 398
Victorious Love... 399

Beloved, surrender wholeheartedly to Jesus Christ,
who loves you. As you drink from the deep well of
Scripture, the Lord will refresh you and cleanse you,
mold you and re-create you through His Living Word.
For the Bible is the very breath of God, giving
life eternal to those who seek Him.

—Francine Rivers

INTRODUCTION

We women treasure special memories in our hearts, and there we store our dreams, tears, unanswered questions, encouraging words, and laughter through the years. We can understand how Mary, a young woman and a new mother, treasured memories and words she didn't understand that concerned the son she loved. She pondered, reflected, wondered what it all meant, and kept these things in her heart.

Our hearts must be kept in good condition. Forgiveness cleans them and keeps them spiritually healthy. Faith in God keeps them beating steady. God's love fills us and his Holy Spirit helps us discern what to treasure and what to release—hurts and words that wound.

Pondering God's messages for us in the Bible helps us process their meaning. Treasuring the Bible keeps its words close at hand, available to recall and encourage us as we face our challenges and follow our dreams.

Mary treasured up all these things and pondered them in her heart.

Luke 2:19 NIV

Significance

God has a plan for every woman that transcends her past and even her present. We might not feel important, but we are significant to God. Whether he gives us tasks that are small or tremendous, God will use whatever we do for his glory. When we respond to him, we are significant, and what we do does make a difference. Bible passages about specific women reveal surprising impact and insights.

We are God's masterpiece. He has created us anew in Christ Jesus, so we can do the good things he planned for us long ago.

Ephesians 2:10 NLT

You Are Important

As you know, the human body is not made up of only one part, but of many parts. Suppose a foot says, "I'm not a hand, so I'm not part of the body!" Would that mean it's no longer part of the body? Or suppose an ear says, "I'm not an eye, so I'm not a part of the body!" Would that mean it's no longer part of the body? If the whole body were an eye, how could it hear? If the whole body were an ear, how could it smell? So God put each and every part of the body together as he wanted it. . . .

If one part of the body suffers, all the other parts share its suffering. If one part is praised, all the others share in its happiness.

1 Corinthians 12:14–18, 26
GOD'S WORD

We're not all in the spotlight. Your name might not be as familiar as the name of your favorite Christian author or speaker, but that doesn't make you less important.

The church at Corinth struggled with fighting among themselves. This part of the letter Paul wrote to the Corinthians emphasizes that all believers are part of Christ's body, with the same goal of living for Jesus and sharing our faith. Like these early Christians, we need to understand that the people who clean the church restrooms, feed the homeless, or care for an elderly parent are as important as those who write great Christian songs or preach to thousands.

God wants Christians to work together as Jesus' body. Each cell in the body helps the body function. We need to use our talents and gifts to fill the needs we can meet, not those someone else's abilities are needed for. We can cooperate. Express appreciation and pray for each person doing God's work, from Sunday school teachers to custodians to pastors and parents—and many more. Next time you're at church, thank some you see for their roles as part of Christ's body.

REASON FOR RESPECT

Conduct yourselves properly (honorably, righteously) among the Gentiles, so that, although they may slander you as evildoers, [yet] they may by witnessing your good deeds [come to] glorify God in the day of inspection [when God shall look upon you wanderers as a pastor or shepherd looks over his flock].

Be submissive to every human institution and authority for the sake of the Lord, whether it be to the emperor as supreme, or to governors as sent by him to bring vengeance (punishment, justice) to those who do wrong and to encourage those who do good service.

For it is God's will and intention that by doing right [your good and honest lives] should silence (muzzle, gag) the ignorant charges and ill-informed criticisms of foolish persons. . . .

Show respect for all men [treat them honorably].

1 Peter 2:12–15, 17 AMP

S he's lost my respect" is a common expression that shows judgment of others. In this passage, Peter addresses Christians who had been scattered from Rome because of persecution and continued to face challenges because of their faith. How should they act toward those who mistreated them? What's God's perspective on respect?

This passage from one of Peter's letters urges us to imitate Jesus as we relate to other people. Jesus treated people with dignity, even those who crucified him. Every individual is significant to God because he made us all, even people who hurt us or try to suppress our faith. Regardless of what a person does, he or she is still a human being created by God, and God wants everyone to believe in Jesus. Our attitudes and integrity should be above reproach, leaving no room for criticism. Then our lives will show our faith and might help someone else to believe.

When someone at work spreads rumors or criticizes you, or if neighbors complain about all the cars when you hold a home Bible study, continue to show respect. Respecting a person affirms that individual's worth as a child God loves.

GEMSTONES

You are coming to Christ, the living stone who was rejected by humans but was chosen as precious by God. You come to him as living stones, a spiritual house that is being built into a holy priesthood. So offer spiritual sacrifices that God accepts through Jesus Christ. That is why Scripture says, "I am laying a chosen and precious cornerstone in Zion, and the person who believes in him will never be ashamed." . . .

However, you are chosen people, a royal priesthood, a holy nation, people who belong to God. You were chosen to tell about the excellent qualities of God, who called you out of darkness into his marvelous light. Once you were not God's people, but now you are. Once you were not shown mercy, but now you have been shown mercy.

1 Peter 2:4–6, 9–10
GOD'S WORD

Miners search for valuable gems, sifting dirt and breaking rocks open to find them. Gems form as molten rock cools and crystallizes; they're found in a rough state and must be cut and polished to reach their full value.

Many people think they don't need Jesus and that he's of no value to them. After the Resurrection and the beginning of the church, many Jews considered Christians foolish and persecuted them. Peter wrote his letter to persecuted Christians to remind them of their value and the value of Jesus.

The imagery of the cornerstone was familiar at this time; the large stone needed to be straight and square as the first one in place. Then the building would be straight and firm. Jesus is also called precious, like a valuable gemstone that was already polished. We build on Jesus and what he did, and all our work is part of what he began.

As we build our lives on Jesus, we are viewed as living stones. When we apply God's Word or teach someone else about the Bible, we are building on what Jesus did. We become polished gemstones as we become more like Christ.

WANDERER TURNED COMMUNITY BUILDER

[Ephraim] went in to his wife, and she conceived and bore a son, and he named him Beriah, because misfortune had come upon his house. His daughter was Sheerah, who built lower and upper Beth-horon, also Uzzen-sheerah. Rephah was his son along with Resheph, Telah his son, Tahan his son, Ladan his son, Ammihud his son, Elishama his son, Non his son and Joshua his son.

Their possessions and settlements were Bethel with its towns, and to the east Naaran, and to the west Gezer with its towns, and Shechem with its towns as far as Ayyah with its towns, and along the borders of the sons of Manasseh, Beth-shean with its towns, Taanach with its towns, Megiddo with its towns, Dor with its towns. In these lived the sons of Joseph the son of Israel.

1 Chronicles 7:23–29 NASB

Sheerah is hidden among the pages of the genealogy of Ephraim, the same as her contemporary Joshua. Other women are mentioned merely because of their relationship as wife, daughter, or sister. Remarkably, Sheerah built towns. One of her towns formed a tribal boundary.

The book of Chronicles was written after God's people settled the Promised Land. It records the genealogy of God's people and provides a who's who in their history. With her people, Sheerah spent years wandering in the desert with no place to call home. She crossed the Jordan to settle in the land God promised to give them. She watched the priests and soldiers march around Jericho and saw the city walls collapse. Years of wandering gave her time to dream of a better future, a home and community. She seized the opportunity and enthusiastically built not one but three towns. She served as an architect, contractor, and community planner.

Many women continue dreaming and hoping before they have the opportunity to bring those dreams to reality. Dreams help sustain a woman during struggles. Sheerah gives women hope that we can dream big and do great things even after difficult times.

MOTHER'S GRIEF STIRS A KING

The king took the two sons of Rizpah the daughter of Aiah, whom she bore to Saul, Armoni and Mephibosheth; . . . and he gave them into the hands of the Gibeonites, and they hanged them on the mountain before the LORD, and the seven of them perished together. . . .

Then Rizpah the daughter of Aiah took sackcloth and spread it for herself on the rock, from the beginning of harvest until rain fell upon them from the heavens. And she did not allow the birds of the air to come upon them by day, or the beasts of the field by night. When David was told what Rizpah the daughter of Aiah, the concubine of Saul, had done, David went and took the bones. . . . And after that God responded to the plea for the land.

2 Samuel 21:8–12, 14 ESV

When someone dies, loved ones want closure around that person's life. It helps mothers, wives, daughters, and sisters share the significance of a loved one's life and brings a sense of peace. Rizpah is usually overlooked, yet she struggled for closure for seven months after her sons died, throughout the barley harvest season that lasted from April until October. She wasn't even a wife, just a concubine of the deposed and disgraced King Saul. She probably slept little as she stayed on the rock and kept scavengers from desecrating her sons' dead bodies.

God had instigated a drought because Saul's evil deeds against the Gibeonites, with whom Joshua had made a covenant, had not been dealt with. To appease the Gibeonites, David allowed the Gibeonites to hang and kill seven of Saul's descendants. But God cared about Rizpah and her heartache and continued to withhold rain from the land while Rizpah mourned. The drought continued until King David took the bones and had them buried.

God cares when we mourn. He understands the hearts of women who have lost someone dear and our desire to honor the persons who have died. Our pain is significant to God.

A LITTLE FLAME BURST

I would remind you to stir up (rekindle the embers of, fan the flame of, and keep burning) the [gracious] gift of God, [the inner fire] that is in you by means of the laying on of my hands [with those of the elders at your ordination].

For God did not give us a spirit of timidity (of cowardice, of craven and cringing and fawning fear), but [He has given us a spirit] of power and of love and of calm and well-balanced mind and discipline and self-control.

Do not blush or be ashamed then, to testify to and for our Lord, nor of me, a prisoner for His sake, but [with me] take your share of the suffering [to which the preaching] of the Gospel [may expose you, and do it] in the power of God.

2 Timothy 1:6–8 AMP

If you ever held your tongue or shyly kept quiet when you had an opportunity to share your faith, you can identify with Timothy, to whom Paul wrote this letter, the last letter that Paul wrote. This final message begins with urging Timothy to be bold. Timothy faced much opposition to preaching God's Word and was later imprisoned for preaching. This message is a reminder that sharing our faith is too significant to let fear limit us.

God sent the Holy Spirit to light a fire within us, to stir our hearts with passion for action, and to give us courage. The Holy Spirit will equip you to speak out and also give you self-control to wisely know when to speak and when to be silent. Start with sharing your personal experience of becoming a Christian with Christian friends. Practicing what to say can help you feel comfortable. Be authentic and talk about how God has made a difference in your life. Then share with close friends and relatives. You experience is of great importance, and your words can help change lives. The more you speak up, the easier it will become.

Words Matter

As long as you live, you, your children, and your grandchildren must fear the LORD your God. All of you must obey all his laws and commands that I'm giving you, and you will live a long time. Listen, Israel, and be careful to obey these laws. Then things will go well for you and your population will increase in a land flowing with milk and honey, as the LORD God of your ancestors promised you.

Listen, Israel: The LORD is our God. The LORD is the only God. Love the LORD your God with all your heart, with all your soul, and with all your strength. Take to heart these words that I give you today. Repeat them to your children. Talk about them when you're at home or away, when you lie down or get up.

Deuteronomy 6:2–7
GOD'S WORD

Think of your husband and how much you thought and talked about him when you were dating. Think of how you savored his words to you. God wants to occupy our minds and hearts that much. He wants to be significant to us. This passage forms the central theme of Deuteronomy as it focuses on loving God and having faith in him. Moses spoke these words from God to the new generation of Israelites, born while the people wandered in the desert, before they entered the Promised Land.

God emphasized his message by asking his people to keep his words in their hearts. He wants us to have more than head knowledge. He wants us to have a heart-to-heart loving relationship with him.

Children remember what they hear repeatedly, and words matter to God. He used words to create life. Jesus is called the Word. Jesus restated these words on loving God completely as the first and greatest commandment. For our benefit and his renown, God wants us to continually talk about him and share his love and his laws with our children.

What words did you store in your heart today?

WELCOME TO THE FAMILY

Before the world was created, God had Christ choose us to live with him and to be his holy and innocent and loving people. God was kind and decided that Christ would choose us to be God's own adopted children. God was very kind to us because of the Son he dearly loves, and so we should praise God.

Christ sacrificed his life's blood to set us free, which means that our sins are now forgiven. Christ did this because God was so kind to us. God has great wisdom and understanding. . . .

My prayer is that light will flood your hearts and that you will understand the hope that was given to you when God chose you. Then you will discover the glorious blessings that will be yours together with all of God's people.

Ephesians 1:4–8, 18 CEV

Love, memories, and time spent together unite families, and loving families enjoy welcoming new members. Some couples adopt children because they have too much love to keep it to themselves. Even though adoption takes time and can be costly, they want to expand their circle of close, loving relationships.

God adopted us. He started the adoption process before he created the world, and Jesus paid for our adoption with his life. This passage expresses our welcome into God's family.

Paul spent three years in Ephesus and wrote a letter to encourage the Christians there. The words in this passage remind us that God welcomes us with an open heart and has many blessings for his children. We are precious to God. God the Father and Jesus have so much love to give that they adopted us to create a special family. Everyone who believes that Jesus forgave our sins and died for us is welcomed into that family.

God wants us to belong and to be happy in our larger spiritual family, the church. We can welcome new people, converse with them, and extend hospitality to show we're glad to be part of God's family with them.

CALLED TO SIGNIFICANCE

Moses looked, and although the bush was on fire, it was not burning up. So he thought, "Why isn't this bush burning up? I must go over there and see this strange sight."

When the LORD saw that Moses had come over to see it, God called to him from the bush, "Moses, Moses!"

Moses answered, "Here I am!"

God said, "Don't come any closer! Take off your sandals because this place where you are standing is holy ground. I am the God of your ancestors, the God of Abraham, Isaac, and Jacob." Moses hid his face because he was afraid to look at God. . . .

God answered, "I will be with you. And this will be the proof that I sent you: When you bring the people out of Egypt, all of you will worship God on this mountain."

Exodus 3:2–6, 12 GOD'S WORD

Pharaoh's daughter adopted Moses and raised him as part of the royal family of Egypt. When he was grown, he chose to secretly defend his own people and killed an Egyptian. His deed became known and Moses fled in fear—turning his back on both his own people and his adopted family—to live in the desert. But God had other plans for Moses.

God chose Moses, an unlikely hero, to be the leader of his chosen people, to face Pharaoh, and to free the people. God allowed Moses to live as a nomadic shepherd for forty years, preparing him for wilderness life with his people later on.

Even if we've made wrong choices and hurt others, God can still use us! Follow his will now and show others the freedom and forgiveness you've experienced with Jesus.

God used fire to get the attention of Moses, and the encounter changed history. God continued to use fire to show his presence with Moses and the people as they wandered in the desert. When the church began, fire represented the presence of God's Holy Spirit. Light a candle and thank God for his presence in your life today.

TIME TO ACT SIGNIFICANTLY

Mordecai gave Hathach a copy of the orders for the murder of the Jews and told him that these had been read in Susa. He said, "Show this to Esther and explain what it means. Ask her to go to the king and beg him to have pity on her people, the Jews!"

Hathach went back to Esther and told her what Mordecai had said. She answered, ". . . It's been thirty days since he has asked for me."

When Mordecai was told what Esther had said, he sent back this reply, ". . . If you don't speak up now, we will somehow get help, but you and your family will be killed. It could be that you were made queen for a time like this!"

Esther 4:8–14 CEV

Queen Esther lived in Persia among the Jews exiled there. Esther had become queen, the wife of the Persian king Xerxes, but hid the fact that she was Jewish. Her uncle Mordecai sent her messages to ask her help to save her people.

Mordecai understood God's sovereignty. He knew that God would help his people, because he knew God's promises to restore the Jews and he trusted that the annihilation plot would fail. Esther, in the best position to help, faced a choice to act significantly or to avoid conflict by doing nothing.

Edmond Burke is credited for saying, "Evil triumphs when good people do nothing." The prime example of evil being victorious is the Holocaust, when many looked the other way and did nothing to stop the mass murders. Esther chose to help, and her bravery saved the Jews. We face a choice every day—to speak out against abortion, euthanasia, violence, and other social injustice issues or to look the other way and do nothing. We might not be in leadership positions to make a large impact, but we can choose to act significantly and make a difference.

Significant Work

You have been raised to life with Christ. Now set your heart on what is in heaven, where Christ rules at God's right side. Think about what is up there, not about what is here on earth. You died, which means that your life is hidden with Christ, who sits beside God. Christ gives meaning to your life, and when he appears, you will also appear with him in glory. . . .

You have given up your old way of life with its habits. . . .

Do your work willingly, as though you were serving the Lord himself, and not just your earthly master. . . . Christ has no favorites! He will punish evil people, just as they deserve.

Colossians 3:1–4, 9, 23, 25
CEV

Women working in the medical field partner with Christ to heal people. Women working in the service industry help others relax and enjoy what God has made. Women in the manufacturing industry help others have tools that make life easier. Think about how your work impacts lives and not just the daily grind of tasks to complete.

To avoid shallow living without real purpose, we must give up living with a non-Christian perspective. Our viewpoint is what frames our thinking. Media and non-Christians urge us to put ourselves first and get all we can. A Christian viewpoint centers on love and looks to future promises where God will give us all we need. This passage urges us to examine the emptiness of life without Jesus and to find meaning in life by choosing to live for him.

When we serve Jesus, we work to make life better. Reflect on how your work helps others. Consider the people involved in your job and how you can make them happier with a pleasant attitude and loving actions. Use your instincts as a woman to nurture people. Look to your eternal destiny and know your purpose is to live with Christ.

WALK WITH DIGNITY

Walk by the Spirit, and you will not carry out the desire of the flesh. For the flesh sets its desire against the Spirit, and the Spirit against the flesh; for these are in opposition to one another, so that you may not do the things that you please. . . .

Now the deeds of the flesh are evident, which are: immorality, impurity, sensuality, idolatry, sorcery, enmities, strife, jealousy, outbursts of anger, disputes, dissensions, factions, envying, drunkenness, carousing, and things like these, of which I forewarn you, just as I have forewarned you, that those who practice such things will not inherit the kingdom of God. But the fruit of the Spirit is love, joy, peace, patience, kindness, goodness, faithfulness, gentleness, self-control; against such things there is no law.

Galatians 5:16–17, 19–23
NASB

✳

Think of a friend who is cheerful, loving, and kind. Her life is probably full of the good fruit of the Spirit—good deeds of many kinds. Then think of someone who is grumpy, gossipy, argumentative, and mean. The two women are very different—one is living according to Christian principles; the other makes selfish choices and lives to please herself.

Choosing to be kind, generous, and a peacemaker brings unity. Choosing to continue immoral, harmful, and selfish actions causes strife. With forgiveness we have freedom from sin and our actions will produce good fruit. Paul wrote to the Galatians to explain the freedom of living as Christians, and this passage contrasts vices with Christian virtues.

We struggle to be virtuous against our natural reactions to be selfish. Patience, forgiveness, and self-control aren't easy to practice when someone spreads lies about us or steals from us. We can't win the battle alone. We need the Holy Spirit to help us change our thinking and our heart attitudes. As we change, we walk with the dignity of virtuous women, bear good fruit, and receive a significant reward of eternal life.

ACCEPT OPPORTUNITIES

Let us not become weary in doing good, for at the proper time we will reap a harvest if we do not give up. Therefore, as we have opportunity, let us do good to all people, especially to those who belong to the family of believers. . . .

May I never boast except in the cross of our Lord Jesus Christ, through which the world has been crucified to me, and I to the world. Neither circumcision nor uncircumcision means anything; what counts is a new creation. Peace and mercy to all who follow this rule, even to the Israel of God.

Finally, let no one cause me trouble, for I bear on my body the marks of Jesus.

Galatians 6:9–10, 14–17 NIV

I've seen that show before. I'm bored. There's nothing to do. Such are our thoughts when we don't see or seize the opportunities around us for doing good. At these times our thoughts reflect an attitude of seeking pleasure and self-gratification.

Paul dictated most of this letter, but he handwrote the last part to emphasize his message. Paul shared how he overcame selfishness. He so identified with Christ that he became a new person, the person God wanted him to be. He did it all with God's help and boasted that all the changes in him came from Christ.

An opportunity means the circumstances are favorable. We don't give up our other responsibilities or commitments to care for our families, rest, or work. There are seasons of life when our commitments take most of our time, but we have other seasons where we have more time to serve others outside our immediate circle. We accept opportunities when we can—cooking extra while cooking for our family to give a meal to a hurting family, visiting a lonely neighbor instead of watching television, or helping a struggling mother by watching her children when we have free time.

EXPECT PROSPERITY

Build houses, and live in them. Plant gardens, and eat what they produce. Get married, and have sons and daughters. Find wives for your sons, and let your daughters get married so that they can have sons and daughters. Grow in number there; don't decrease. . . .

I know the plans that I have for you, declares the LORD. They are plans for peace and not disaster, plans to give you a future filled with hope. Then you will call to me. You will come and pray to me, and I will hear you. When you look for me, you will find me. When you wholeheartedly seek me, I will let you find me, declares the LORD. I will bring you back from captivity. I will gather you from all the nations and places where I've scattered you, declares the LORD.

Jeremiah 29:5–6, 11–14
GOD'S WORD

A new baby, a new home, a wedding—all are exciting moments. We rejoice at new life and new love. God wanted to fill the earth with beauty, including people. He told the first man and woman to multiply, and this passage reflects that message.

Planting gardens and raising children are very similar occupations. Both require time, patience, and nurture. Both can produce great results. Both can bring new growth—plants produce seeds for future planting; children grow and continue a legacy as they marry and have children.

The growing process takes time, especially raising children. We could worry about the future, such as pestilence that hurts plants or peer pressure that hurts our children. But as we create our homes, we must trust God. His plans are for good growth and good outcomes. Ordinary days when plants are just sprouts and don't appear to be growing or a child is her usual stubborn and selfish self might not seem significant, but continuing to water the plant and pluck the weeds and continuing to show our children how to share and be kind will produce results over time. Ordinary becomes extraordinarily significant in time.

LEAVING A LEGACY

Joshua then told the two men who had served as spies, "Go into the prostitute's house, and bring her and her family out, as you promised her." So they went and brought Rahab out, along with her father and mother, her brothers, and the rest of her family. They took them all, family and slaves, to safety near the Israelite camp. Then they set fire to the city and burned it to the ground, along with everything in it, except the things made of gold, silver, bronze, and iron, which they took and put in the LORD's treasury. But Joshua spared the lives of the prostitute Rahab and all her relatives, because she had hidden the two spies that he had sent to Jericho. (Her descendants have lived in Israel to this day.)

Joshua 6:22–25 GNT

A number of women who formerly worked in abortion clinics, or owned them, now speak out against abortion. Others, like the biblical Rahab, have chosen to turn away from a sinful past of drug use or sexual addiction to start a new life.

The book of Joshua records the Israelites' conquering their enemies and settling in the Promised Land. Rahab was a prostitute in Jericho who helped the Israelites. Rahab acknowledged her faith when she met two Israeli spies. She declared that she knew God had power and had given the Israelites the land; and she asked the spies to save her. She showed faith in God and risked her own life to save the spies.

Her significant act of courage changed her life. Rahab became an ancestress of Christ when she married an Israelite. Her descendants still live among the Jews as part of her legacy. Her action was so significant that she's an example in the book of James as someone who showed faith in action. God made her relationship with him right because of her faith.

We can change, no matter what our past sins. Today's choices can make a difference for ourselves and for others.

NEVER TOO OLD

When the days for their purification according to the law of Moses were completed, they brought Him up to Jerusalem to present Him to the Lord (as it is written in the Law of the Lord, "Every firstborn male that opens the womb shall be called holy to the LORD"). . . .

And there was a prophetess, Anna the daughter of Phanuel, of the tribe of Asher. She was advanced in years and had lived with her husband seven years after her marriage, and then as a widow to the age of eighty-four. She never left the temple, serving night and day with fastings and prayers. At that very moment she came up and began giving thanks to God, and continued to speak of Him to all those who were looking for the redemption of Jerusalem.

Luke 2:22–23, 36–38 NASB

✻

Anna served God for years, but her most significant moment came late in her life when she saw baby Jesus and recognized him as the Messiah, the promised one who would save. God can use anyone, regardless of age.

Many women have found that once they have raised children they are freer to serve God in new ways and get involved in new kinds of service. Anna had been married a short time, but as a widow she gave her time to prayer and service. She is called a prophetess, meaning she spoke God's truth. Her name means "gracious" and reflected her thanks for God's grace. Anna knew the pain of losing a loved one, and in her loss she turned to serve God and pray.

How wonderful at any age to be known as someone who speaks God's truth and shares the joy of knowing Jesus! Anna's witness was a confirmation that Jesus is God. Our story of faith can help others believe in Jesus. As we gain experience in prayer and knowing the Bible, we can be even more open to teaching others about Jesus and let God choose our significant moments.

Significant Women

Jesus traveled through towns and villages, preaching the Good News about the Kingdom of God. The twelve disciples went with him, and so did some women who had been healed of evil spirits and diseases: Mary (who was called Magdalene), from whom seven demons had been driven out; Joanna, whose husband Chuza was an officer in Herod's court; and Susanna, and many other women who used their own resources to help Jesus and his disciples. . . .

Jesus' mother and brothers came to him, but were unable to join him because of the crowd. Someone said to Jesus, "Your mother and brothers are standing outside and want to see you."

Jesus said to them all, "My mother and brothers are those who hear the word of God and obey it."

Luke 8:1–3, 19–21 GNT

When we hear a great speaker or teacher, we don't always think about their finances or the people behind the scenes or how they can afford to continue the ministry.

In ancient Israel, women were not allowed to study under a rabbi but were taught homemaking skills at home and could listen to the public reading of Scripture. Jesus allowed several women to travel with him and his followers, showing that women were significant to him. Jesus had healed some of these women, and they and others used their own money to help support his traveling and teaching. These women chose to spend money on Jesus. They gave time and money to what they considered worthwhile.

Today women are free to study God's Word and many have income to spend as desired. Our checkbooks and calendars reveal where we spend time and money and reflect what we value. Consider what kinds of service you value most. Review your spending and time commitments to see if you are investing in what you say you believe. Perhaps become a financial supporter for a ministry you believe in. When our giving matches our values, we are living authentically.

STRIVING FOR POSITION

James and John, the sons of Zebedee, came to him. "Teacher," they said, "we want you to do for us whatever we ask."

"What do you want me to do for you?" he asked.

They replied, "Let one of us sit at your right and the other at your left in your glory."

"You don't know what you are asking," Jesus said. "Can you drink the cup I drink or be baptized with the baptism I am baptized with?"

"We can," they answered.

Jesus said to them, "You will drink the cup I drink and be baptized with the baptism I am baptized with, but to sit at my right or left is not for me to grant. These places belong to those for whom they have been prepared. . . . Whoever wants to be first must be slave of all."

Mark 10:35–40, 44 NIV

Have you ever struggled to sit by someone you admire? Have you paid to reserve special seats to see a performance? Have you ever been given a special place to sit as an honored guest? We often care about where we sit, the view, and who is sitting near us. Women enjoy socializing and like to choose where to sit.

James and John wanted to reserve special places in heaven. Their question attempted to manipulate Jesus. Such positions come at a price and these men, who agreed to suffer what Jesus suffered, did both die as martyrs. But Jesus doesn't sell tickets to heaven or pander to selfish desires. We cannot strive or buy our way into special positions. Jesus explained that those who will be first in heaven are those with the greatest hearts for service.

The question James and John posed appears to have displeased Jesus. He wants to answer our prayers, but he doesn't want us to try to control him or ask for special privileges, especially regarding heaven. Instead of seeking promotion or fame, serve others, and trust God to place you where he wants you to be, on earth and in heaven.

Transforming Bad Intentions

"Before our father died, he told us to ask you, 'Please forgive the crime your brothers committed when they wronged you.' Now please forgive us the wrong that we, the servants of your father's God, have done." Joseph cried when he received this message. . . .

But Joseph said to them, "Don't be afraid; I can't put myself in the place of God. You plotted evil against me, but God turned it into good, in order to preserve the lives of many people who are alive today because of what happened. You have nothing to fear. I will take care of you and your children." So he reassured them with kind words that touched their hearts. Joseph continued to live in Egypt with his father's family; he was a hundred and ten years old when he died.

Genesis 50:16–17, 19–22 GNT

Parents want to see their children get along. We trust that they will love one another after we die. However, dysfunctional families may have strained relationships because of past hurts.

The crimes of Joseph's brothers began after their father favored one child. Years later Joseph hoped for his family to be united in peace, through forgiveness. Joseph cried at his brothers' request. He'd already explained, before his brothers moved to Egypt, that God used their actions for good. The brothers' fear and guilt overshadowed Joseph's past words of forgiveness.

We might, like Joseph, need to assure an offender that we truly forgive her. The guilt of bad intentions and negative actions can cause a friend or family member to feel she did something unforgivable or to worry that we will seek revenge.

Have you been cheated, robbed, gossiped about, deceived, or hurt in another way? Like Joseph, you must ask God to show you how he is using the pain in your life for his purpose and your good. We must reassure individuals that we have forgiven them. Forgiveness can be difficult, but it is one of the most significant gifts we can give to anyone.

BIG MYSTERIES

There are three things which are too wonderful for me, four which I do not understand: the way of an eagle in the sky, the way of a serpent on a rock, the way of a ship in the middle of the sea, and the way of a man with a maid. . . .

Four things are small on the earth, but they are exceedingly wise: the ants are not a strong people, but they prepare their food in the summer; the shephanim are not mighty people, yet they make their houses in the rocks; the locusts have no king, yet all of them go out in ranks; the lizard you may grasp with the hands, yet it is in kings' palaces.

Proverbs 30:18–19, 24–28
NASB

The philosopher Agur made these wise observations about nature's intricate designs and patterns. Small creatures can astound us as we study them and their good habits. Some cooperate better than humans, without power struggles, just working for survival. Little *shephanim*, a type of timid rodent, make their homes in safe places in little nooks and crannies of rock formations. Serpent tracks can be followed on sand but not on rocks, yet it's amazing that such a slippery creature can glide upon a smooth surface. Ships at sea show us the power of waves and wind, yet leave no trail after traveling away.

Do you cringe if you see a mouse or battle against unwanted insects? We can testify to the persistence of small creatures! God can use these "unappealing" creatures to help us learn valuable lessons. They remind us to cooperate, work hard, prepare for the future, and make wise choices.

Take a nature walk or visit a zoo and rejoice in God's amazing creatures. Watch a child delight in the instinctive abilities of creatures. Learn from the abilities and instinctive habits God gave animals, reptiles, and birds.

POWERFUL WOMAN

Deborah, a prophetess, the wife of Lappidoth, was leading Israel at that time. . . . The Israelites came to her to have their disputes decided. She sent for Barak . . . and said to him, "The LORD, the God of Israel, commands you: 'Go, take with you ten thousand men of Naphtali and Zebulun and lead the way to Mount Tabor. I will lure Sisera, the commander of Jabin's army, with his chariots and his troops to the Kishon River and give him into your hands.'"

Barak said to her, "If you go with me, I will go; but if you don't go with me, I won't go."

"Very well," Deborah said, "I will go with you. But because of the way you are going about this, the honor will not be yours, for the the LORD will hand Sisera over to a woman."

Judges 4:4–9 NIV

❋

Some women seem to balance life well—family, faith, and career. These are strong, confident women. God used one such woman, Deborah, the only female judge during the time that judges ruled Israel. Deborah made decisions daily and trusted God completely while also managing her home and serving God. She played a significant role in defeating the Canaanites who still lived in Israel.

Barak, the commander of the armies, trusted Deborah, but he feared going into battle without her. She had a stronger faith and willingly followed God, even into battle against what people considered an invincible army. Barak's response resulted in a woman getting the honor he would have had. Deborah listened to God, trusted him completely, and made sure the orders were carried out. She remained faithful to God in her legal profession. We can remain faithful in any career.

The next chapter of Judges records a song Deborah sang that chronicles the battle. It refers to Deborah as "the mother of Israel," showing that she loved her people and the people loved her. When we love the people we serve in our homes, work, and country, we'll make a difference.

FULLNESS OF LIFE

My child, remember my teachings and instructions and obey them completely. They will help you live a long and prosperous life. Let love and loyalty always show like a necklace, and write them in your mind. God and people will like you and consider you a success.

With all your heart you must trust the LORD and not your own judgment. Always let him lead you, and he will clear the road for you to follow. Don't ever think that you are wise enough, but respect the LORD and stay away from evil. This will make you healthy, and you will feel strong.

Proverbs 3:1–8 CEV

We all want a full and happy life. We want to make wise decisions and see our loved ones thrive. This passage from the book of Proverbs says that if we follow God's way and let God be in control, we can prosper. Solomon wrote these words about one thousand years before Jesus' birth.

Qualities that sparkle more than jewels are love and loyalty. Loyalty is continually supporting someone or some cause. Loyalty to God is seen in how we stick to his Word daily and trust him even when we can't see the solution to a problem.

When we hear the news of breast cancer, a fatal car crash, or an unexpected job loss, we don't know what will happen next. That's when we must remain faithful to God and let him reveal the next step. We must pray about which cancer treatment to follow, how to cope with our loss, or where to seek new employment. We start by remembering that God is in control and by seeking answers in the Bible. Loyal followers are so important to God that he promises to clear away obstacles as he leads us.

DIGNITY FOR THE SICK

One Sabbath, Jesus was strolling with his disciples through a field of ripe grain. Hungry, the disciples were pulling off the heads of grain and munching on them. Some Pharisees reported them to Jesus: "Your disciples are breaking the Sabbath rules!" . . .

There was a man there with a crippled hand. They said to Jesus, "Is it legal to heal on the Sabbath?" They were baiting him.

He replied, "Is there a person here who, finding one of your lambs fallen into a ravine, wouldn't, even though it was a Sabbath, pull it out? Surely kindness to people is as legal as kindness to animals!" Then he said to the man, "Hold out your hand." He held it out and it was healed.

The Pharisees walked out furious, sputtering about how they were going to ruin Jesus.

Matthew 12:1–2, 10–14 MSG

How do you react when you pass someone in a wheelchair or see a deaf person signing? Do you show kindness and compassion? Do you open a door to help the person in the wheelchair? Are you patient with elderly people who walk slowly? How do you react when a baby spits up on you?

Jesus' great compassion for sick, powerless, and disabled individuals caused disputes with the Pharisees. These religious rulers had thirty-nine categories of actions forbidden to do on the Sabbath, each with a long list of specifically outlawed activities. Healing was one of these. The rulers never saw the need of the sick person. Jesus did not respect or bow to their little rules, which outraged these legalistic leaders and caused them to want to kill him. They cared only about their own dignity, and Jesus made them look petty and foolish.

Our actions reveal whether we have compassion. If a neighbor is hurt or sick, or an elderly neighbor is disabled, don't use your busyness or lack of money or skill as excuses from compassionate action. Take time to visit, to cook or buy a meal, or pick up groceries while you're out.

WHO IS INSIGNIFICANT?

Moses had married a Cushite woman, and Miriam and Aaron criticized him for it. They said, "Has the LORD spoken only through Moses? Hasn't he also spoken through us?" The LORD heard what they said. . . .

The LORD came down in a pillar of cloud, stood at the entrance of the Tent, and called out, "Aaron! Miriam!" The two of them stepped forward, and the LORD said, "Now hear what I have to say! When there are prophets among you, I reveal myself to them in visions and speak to them in dreams. It is different when I speak with my servant Moses; I have put him in charge of all my people Israel. So I speak to him face to face, clearly and not in riddles; he has even seen my form! How dare you speak against my servant Moses?"

Numbers 12:1–2, 5–8 GNT

※

We all can be critical, looking down on other women because of their clothes, size, or lack of faith. Catty remarks show pride and haughtiness. Miriam and her brother engaged in making critical remarks about the wife of their brother, Moses.

Cushite is another term for Egyptian. The Egyptians worshipped many idols, though there's no clue about this woman's actual faith. Miriam considered the woman insignificant and felt Moses had made a poor choice. That showed disrespect for her brother. God reprimanded Miriam and Aaron and caused them to become lepers. Moses prayed for their healing and God healed them.

It's easy to be petty and make little cutting remarks, but that doesn't please God. When we act with pride, God considers our actions insignificant, especially if we are disrespectful of God's servants. God speaks to his chosen leaders and wants us to consider his choices as worthy of good treatment. We should be careful how we speak about church leaders and their families, as well as others who give their time to serve God. When we speak against God's servants, we are also criticizing the significance of God's choices.

REAL WORTH

I was so eager that I even made trouble for the church. I did everything the Law demands in order to please God.

But Christ has shown me that what I once thought was valuable is worthless. Nothing is as wonderful as knowing Christ Jesus my Lord. I have given up everything else and count it all as garbage. All I want is Christ and to know that I belong to him. I could not make myself acceptable to God by obeying the Law of Moses. God accepted me simply because of my faith in Christ. All I want is to know Christ and the power that raised him to life. I want to suffer and die as he did, so that somehow I also may be raised to life.

Philippians 3:6–11 CEV

Have you ever tried to impress someone with your accomplishments or talents? One mother might work hard to help her child get good grades and then let everyone know when he makes the honor roll. Another woman might volunteer for an organization and try to get an award for hours of service. Someone else might work long hours and take on extra tasks for a promotion. All can be efforts to earn significance.

Paul worked hard to follow the laws of the Pharisees to be significant. Then he worked harder to crush the early Christians, thinking he was gaining God's approval. Jesus finally appeared to Paul and let him know his actions were hurting him. God turned Paul's attitude around and showed him the truth of where we find our worth.

Listen to yourself when you meet someone new—are you striving to sound important? We can't earn God's approval through deeds or achievements. We become approved when we believe in Jesus. And once we believe in Jesus, we find that our desire to look good for others doesn't matter. All that really matters is getting closer to Jesus, serving him, and knowing him better.

TRADITIONS BUILD IDENTITY

GOD said to Joshua, "Make stone knives and circumcise the People of Israel a second time." So Joshua made stone knives and circumcised the People of Israel at Foreskins Hill. . . .

GOD said to Joshua, "Today I have rolled away the reproach of Egypt." That's why the place is called The Gilgal. It's still called that.

The People of Israel continued to camp at The Gilgal.

They celebrated the Passover on the evening of the fourteenth day of the month on the plains of Jericho.

Right away, the day after the Passover, they started eating the produce of that country, unraised bread and roasted grain. And then no more manna; the manna stopped. As soon as they started eating food grown in the land, there was no more manna for the People of Israel.

Joshua 5:2–3, 9–12 MSG

Belonging to a family, a club, or a group of friends gives us a sense of acceptance and a sense of identity—we are known as someone's daughter, wife, or friend or the club secretary. Our relationships and traditions help to define us.

Just before the Israelites entered the Promise Land, God required males to be circumcised and the celebration of Passover. The people had not celebrated Passover for nearly forty years. Life would soon change, and God wanted these traditions to remind everyone of their identity as his chosen people. Circumcision signified belonging to God, and Passover celebrated and symbolized God's care in delivering his people from Egypt.

We have traditions for identity too. Baptism signifies that we belong to God. Communion symbolizes the sacrifice of Jesus, the Bread of Life, for us. A cross identifies us as people who believe in Jesus' death and resurrection. We live in the world, but our true identity is as God's daughters.

PURPOSE WITH POWER

Your faith is growing exceedingly and the love of every one of you each toward the others is increasing and abounds. . . .

With this in view we constantly pray for you, that our God may deem and count you worthy of [your] calling and [His] every gracious purpose of goodness, and with power may complete in [your] every particular work of faith (faith which is that leaning of the whole human personality on God in absolute trust and confidence in His power, wisdom, and goodness).

Thus may the name of our Lord Jesus Christ be glorified and become more glorious through and in you, and may you [also be glorified] in Him according to the grace (favor and blessing) of our God and the Lord Jesus Christ (the Messiah, the Anointed One).

2 Thessalonians 1:3, 11–12
AMP

Living with purpose gives our lives meaning. Mothers find purpose in loving and raising children. Other women might find purpose as they use talents to help people or to make the world a better place. Being loved gives us all a sense of meaning as we build relationships and make a difference in people's lives.

Paul began this letter to the Thessalonians focusing on their growing faith and love. In this passage, he moved into real worth discovered through God's purpose for each of us. God has tasks or assignments he wants each of us to do.

We seek our purpose by finding our talents and knowing our available resources. God will show us how he wants us to use our talents and resources. A generous woman might use her money and cooking talents to provide meals to people in need, and God might then provide the perfect place and volunteers needed for her to open a homeless shelter. As the shelter flourishes, her testimony reveals that God made it all happen. She can praise God for the power to fulfill her purpose. Through opportunities God gives us that use our talents, he shows us our purpose.

SIGNIFICANT ANSWER TO PRAYER

"I came today to the spring and said, 'O LORD, the God of my master Abraham, . . . behold, I am standing by the spring of water. Let the virgin who comes out to draw water, to whom I shall say, 'Please give me a little water from your jar to drink,' and who will say to me, 'Drink, and I will draw for your camels also,' let her be the woman whom the LORD has appointed for my master's son.'

"Before I had finished speaking in my heart, behold, Rebekah came out with her water jar." . . .

And they called Rebekah and said to her, "Will you go with this man?" She said, "I will go.". . .

Then Isaac brought her into the tent of Sarah his mother and took Rebekah, and she became his wife, and he loved her.

Genesis 24:42–45, 58, 67 ESV

❋

God might use us to answer someone's prayer through ordinary kindness. An elderly stranger looking for a little connection might find it when we smile as we see her. A mother worn out from a difficult day might be encouraged when we let her go in front of us in the checkout line.

As she walked to the well, Rebekah never expected to be an answer to prayer or to have the encounter change her life. Abraham had sent his servant, Eliezer, to find a wife for his son Isaac. Abraham had sent him with the confidence that God would direct Eliezer and send an angel to guide him on his journey. Eliezer acknowledged his faith in God and asked for a specific sign to help him find God's choice. This servant's prayer and its answer changed the history of a nation, as Rebekah became an ancestress of Israel.

We cannot see or understand God's long-range plans. He works as we go about our ordinary days; he often connects people as he answers prayers. Let God use you to answer the prayers of others by practicing generosity and kindness every day.

DADDY'S LITTLE GIRL

In accordance with the LORD's command to him, Joshua gave to Caleb son of Jephunneh a portion in Judah—Kiriath Arba, that is, Hebron. (Arba was the forefather of Anak.) . . .

And Caleb said, "I will give my daughter Acsah in marriage to the man who attacks and captures Kiriath Sepher." Othniel son of Kenaz, Caleb's brother, took it; so Caleb gave his daughter Acsah to him in marriage.

One day when she came to Othniel, she urged him to ask her father for a field. When she got off her donkey, Caleb asked her, "What can I do for you?"

She replied, "Do me a special favor. Since you have given me land in the Negev, give me also springs of water." So Caleb gave her the upper and lower springs.

Joshua 15:13, 16–19 NIV

When a young woman is engaged to a man her father approves of, her father likely will be willing to bless the couple in many ways. He gives his daughter whatever he can for a beautiful wedding and might bless her with a generous wedding gift. She is her daddy's little girl, and he loves her and wants the best for her.

Caleb, one of the twelve spies Moses sent into the Promised Land, found a brave husband for his daughter Acsah. This passage is also repeated in the opening chapter of Judges, showing its significance to God. Acsah's husband, Othniel, became Israel's first judge. The Negev, land in the south, was a dry area. Caleb looked at his newly married daughter and asked what she wanted. He added the gift of springs, a valuable asset to farmers, to water the land, at her request.

Getting off her donkey showed respect for her father. Acsah honored Caleb and let us glimpse a loving relationship between a father and his "little girl." Respect your father and work to build a good relationship. Also build a good relationship with God, your heavenly Father, who can respond favorably to your requests.

HEAVENLY JOY

The Pharisees and the scribes kept muttering and indignantly complaining, saying, This man accepts and receives and welcomes [preeminently wicked] sinners and eats with them. . . .

What woman, having ten [silver] drachmas [each one equal to a day's wages], if she loses one coin, does not light a lamp and sweep the house and look carefully and diligently until she finds it?

And when she has found it, she summons her [women] friends and neighbors, saying, Rejoice with me, for I have found the silver coin which I had lost.

Even so, I tell you, there is joy among and in the presence of the angels of God over one [especially] wicked person who repents (changes his mind for the better, heartily amending his ways, with abhorrence of his past sins).

Luke 15:2, 8–10 AMP

When have you searched for a misplaced item and felt relief or joy at finding it? You might have lost a necklace, your checkbook, an important paper, or the car keys. When we lose something important, we keep searching until we find it.

Jesus told this parable of the lost coin to help us understand the joy in heaven over a lost sinner whom God seeks out and saves. His listeners might have equated this special value to the ten silver coins women customarily received as a wedding gift. Such coins had sentimental as well as monetary value. We all like to celebrate, and finding something lost that we treasure is a great reason to do so—especially since sweeping the house also means we have a clean place for a party!

In heaven there is joy over every person who turns to Jesus for salvation and a new, clean heart. When you know someone who turns to God, rejoice and celebrate! Have a party on earth to reflect the party going on in heaven. Let your friend know she's so important that there's a party in heaven in her honor!

Relationships & Communication

We all began life in relationship as daughters. Sometimes our relationships are good, and sometimes they fall short of our desires. Friends, spouses, coworkers, children, and siblings are among the many relationships women enjoy. God began the world with relationship, and the Bible shows us the complex yet simple joys of interacting with other people.

All good relationships involve satisfying communication. Behind the words is the need to connect, to reach out and discover the essence of another person, to find a place of acceptance and understanding. The wisdom of the Bible on communication shows us how to get to the heart of connecting with others.

Fill me with joy by having the same attitude and the same love, living in harmony, and keeping one purpose in mind.

Philippians 2:2 GOD'S WORD

IMPRESSIONS

When you do good deeds, don't try to show off. If you do, you won't get a reward from your Father in heaven.

When you give to the poor, don't blow a loud horn. That's what show-offs do in the meeting places and on the street corners, because they are always looking for praise. I can assure you that they already have their reward.

When you give to the poor, don't let anyone know about it. Then your gift will be given in secret. Your Father knows what is done in secret, and he will reward you. . . .

When you go without eating, don't try to look gloomy as those show-offs do when they go without eating. I can assure you that they already have their reward. Instead, comb your hair and wash your face.

Matthew 6:1–4, 16–17 CEV

Jesus spoke these words to a large crowd as part of what has come to be known as the Sermon on the Mount, because the people sat on a hillside to listen. He had spoken about attitudes, relationships, love, and generosity. Now he spoke about giving and making impressions.

Showing off and giving in a way that will be noticed is not real giving. That's a staged show to get attention. It makes an impression, but not a good one. God wants us to give in secret; for example, to simply focus on addressing the need and helping the girlfriend who is hurting. When someone else needs help, that's not an opportunity to get praise or earn approval for ourselves. Jesus spoke the words in this passage at a time when rich people and religious leaders made a great performance of giving to the poor and fasting (going without food) in public. They craved attention from other people and forgot the reason for their actions and made bad impressions. When we fast, it should be to pray for a great need secretly. We can look pleasant while we plead with God and pray instead of eating.

Let's Dine Together

[Jesus] said to them, "I have earnestly desired to eat this Passover with you before I suffer. For I tell you I will not eat it until it is fulfilled in the kingdom of God." And he took a cup, and when he had given thanks he said, "Take this, and divide it among yourselves. For I tell you that from now on I will not drink of the fruit of the vine until the kingdom of God comes." And he took bread, and when he had given thanks, he broke it and gave it to them, saying, "This is my body, which is given for you. Do this in remembrance of me." And likewise the cup after they had eaten, saying, "This cup that is poured out for you is the new covenant in my blood."

Luke 22:15–20 ESV

We make holiday plans months ahead, reserving plane flights, buying gifts, and scheduling get-togethers with loved ones. We look forward to celebrating, especially holidays or special occasions. Jesus expressed how much he had looked forward to sharing the Passover celebration with his friends. The Passover commemorated God delivering his people from slavery in Egypt.

This dining together and celebrating Passover together held special significance for Jesus, because he knew he soon would be delivering everyone who would believe in him from a different slavery, a slavery to sin and death. No longer would Christians need to celebrate Passover; instead they would remember Jesus' sacrifice and celebrate unity and freedom for all believers. Jesus told his friends to follow his actions of breaking bread. Communion celebrates his sacrifice in dying for us and Jesus, the Bread of Life, as our source of life.

Passover had celebrated a special relationship with God; now Jesus would offer a new relationship with God. By offering his blood, Jesus offered his life and gave us life. We don't have to wait or celebrate only once a year. We can break bread and celebrate God's presence often.

GOD'S IDEAL RELATIONSHIPS

How can I stand up before GOD and show proper respect to the high God? Should I bring an armload of offerings topped off with yearling calves? Would GOD be impressed with thousands of rams, with buckets and barrels of olive oil? Would he be moved if I sacrificed my firstborn child, my precious baby, to cancel my sin?

But he's already made it plain how to live, what to do, what GOD is looking for in men and women. It's quite simple: Do what is fair and just to your neighbor, be compassionate and loyal in your love, and don't take yourself too seriously— take God seriously.

Attention! GOD calls out to the city! If you know what's good for you, you'll listen.

Micah 6:6–9 MSG

In the Old Testament, people offered sacrifices to worship God and petition him for help. God had established sacrifices for his people to follow; they included thank offerings, burnt animals for atonement for sin, doves for purification, other offerings for asking God for needs, and more. Each time someone offered a sacrifice to God, he hoped to please God. In this passage the prophet Micah answered a deeper question: What really pleases God? This answer is still crucial to our relationship with God today.

He wants us to live a faithful life and talk to him in prayer on a daily basis. The prophet used the phrase "to walk humbly." We must recognize that we are not God, that we have shortcomings and need God. We must be willing to learn from him. Pleasing God requires us to love kindness and mercy. This means to treat others gently, kindly, and to forgive those who hurt us. Finally, we are to do justly. We are to act fairly, respectfully, and honorably. God asks us to develop integrity and character and respect others because God made them. Pleasing God makes us better neighbors and better believers.

An Understanding Heart

He heals the brokenhearted and bandages their wounds. He counts the stars and calls them all by name. . . . The LORD supports the humble, but he brings the wicked down into the dust. . . .

He covers the heavens with clouds, provides rain for the earth, and makes the grass grow in mountain pastures. He gives food to the wild animals and feeds the young ravens when they cry. He takes no pleasure in the strength of a horse or in human might. No, the LORD's delight is in those who fear him, those who put their hope in his unfailing love.

Psalm 147:3–4, 6, 8–11 NLT

Songs like *My Favorite Things* and friends who encourage us cheer us up and remind us to think positive thoughts. God is the friend we need to turn to for help. He understands broken hearts and hurts from people we trusted. He goes beyond mere words. He has the power to heal and bind our wounds. When we focus on God's ability, we develop trust that he will support us in our struggles and bless our future.

The psalm from which this passage was taken was written when the exiles returned to Jerusalem after captivity in Babylon. As God restored the land and the hearts of the people, they sang of his greatness and his understanding.

Consider how God, your helper, made and numbered the stars that seem uncountable. He covered the heavens with clouds that are just vapors, particles in a high-energy state. He causes grass to grow by continuing the cycle of rain and sunshine and feeds wild animals to keep a balance in nature. He understands our cloudy days, our rain of tears, our sunshine moments, our need for food, and the need to be counted as people whose lives matter.

Leaven—Ingredient of Heaven

Such great crowds gathered about Him that He got into a boat and remained sitting there, while all the throng stood on the shore.

And He told them many things in parables (stories by way of illustration and comparison). . . .

He told them another parable: The kingdom of heaven is like leaven (sour dough) which a woman took and covered over in three measures of meal or flour till all of it was leavened.

These things all taken together Jesus said to the crowds in parables; indeed, without a parable He said nothing to them.

This was in fulfillment of what was spoken by the prophet: I will open My mouth in parables; I will utter things that have been hidden since the foundation of the world.

Matthew 13:2–3, 33–35 AMP

Jesus, the Bread of Life, compared the kingdom of heaven to an ingredient that women understand. Yeast, or leaven, gives the power to make bread rise. Leaven is mixed into flour so bread will rise evenly. The leaven Jesus spoke of was a type of sourdough starter. Today, women still pass on this type of leaven in what is called Amish friendship bread. In smelling the rich aroma as the bread bakes, we can reflect on the richness of heaven.

Interestingly, three measures of flour equal fifty pounds, the amount used to make the bread for the altar in the Old Testament. That bread was a flatbread prepared without yeast, a more humble form of bread that represented purity, while yeast represented the corruption of fermentation, or sin. Only at Pentecost, the Feast of the Firstfruits, did the priests offer leavened bread. The Christian church began at Pentecost, as believers first shared their faith after receiving power from the Holy Spirit.

Women often open up to one another other while sharing tea and fresh slices of bread, whether at home, in coffee shops, or online. That's a great opportunity to share faith, a true act of friendship.

LOVE THE UNLOVABLE

If someone slaps you on the right cheek, offer the other cheek also. If you are sued in court and your shirt is taken from you, give your coat, too. If a soldier demands that you carry his gear for a mile, carry it two miles. Give to those who ask, and don't turn away from those who want to borrow.

You have heard the law that says, "Love your neighbor" and hate your enemy. But I say, love your enemies! Pray for those who persecute you! In that way, you will be acting as true children of your Father in heaven. For he gives his sunlight to both the evil and the good, and he sends rain on the just and the unjust alike. If you love only those who love you, what reward is there for that?

Matthew 5:39–46 NLT

Jesus' guidelines in this passage for getting along with enemies are quite different from our normal reactions or the usual advice. The country of Israel was under Roman occupation, and Roman soldiers could force the Jewish people to serve them in various ways. Jesus urged his listeners to do what they were asked to do—twice over, to show love. Jesus wants us to love people beyond any human expectation. He wants us to be generous in loving people who are greedy, angry, and controlling. He also wants us to pray for these people.

Wrong and hurtful actions reveal people's inner hurt and inability to get along with others. Yet God treats such people fairly, sending them rain and sunshine too. He asks us to shower offensive people with sunny joy and blessings. Staying in a huddle of only loving people who love us may be nice, but it doesn't spread God's love or bring us rewards.

We can hope that enemies will change their hearts when we respond with love and kindness. We cannot control how things will turn out, but we can follow the advice and trust God will reward our efforts.

Empathy among Friends

[Job] said, "Naked I came from my mother's womb, and naked shall I return. The Lord gave, and the Lord has taken away; blessed be the name of the Lord." . . .

Now when Job's three friends heard of all this evil that had come upon him, they came each from his own place, Eliphaz the Temanite, Bildad the Shuhite, and Zophar the Naamathite. They made an appointment together to come to show him sympathy and comfort him. And when they saw him from a distance, they did not recognize him. And they raised their voices and wept, and they tore their robes and sprinkled dust on their heads toward heaven. And they sat with him on the ground seven days and seven nights, and no one spoke a word to him, for they saw that his suffering was very great.

Job 1:21; 2:11–13 ESV

Friends support one another and listen to each other's problems. Sometimes, as when we hear of a friend who lost a home in a fire or suffered another sudden loss, we feel stunned and hardly know how to respond. That is how Job's friends felt when Job lost almost everything in one day. His children died, his animals died, and enemies killed his servants. Only his wife remained. Then he was struck with a severe illness.

When Job's friends heard of the catastrophe, they went to give him sympathy. They didn't even recognize him, perhaps because great sorrow had changed his expression so much. They had no words to offer at that point. They wept and donned the garments of mourning and put ashes on their heads. Then they stayed with Job and didn't say a word for seven days and nights. Later, the poor advice they gave Job didn't help him as much as their silent comfort had.

Sometimes people just need our quiet presence. Sometimes there are no words to offer; we can only stay and pray. Girlfriends support one another, especially when tragedy strikes. Friends sit beside downcast friends with steadfast loyalty.

ENCOURAGING FRIENDSHIPS

A spoken reprimand is better than approval that's never expressed.

The wounds from a lover are worth it; kisses from an enemy do you in. . . .

Just as lotions and fragrance give sensual delight, a sweet friendship refreshes the soul. . . .

You use steel to sharpen steel, and one friend sharpens another.

If you care for your orchard, you'll enjoy its fruit; if you honor your boss, you'll be honored.

Just as water mirrors your face, so your face mirrors your heart. . . .

The purity of silver and gold is tested by putting them in the fire; the purity of human hearts is tested by giving them a little fame.

Proverbs 27:5–6, 9, 17–19, 21 MSG

Proverbs are short sayings that convey general principles or observations of life. Solomon, the wisest man who ever lived, wrote these words about friends and human hearts. The principles listed here are still true.

These verses mention that people tight with words of approval don't realize that their silence conveys rejection or indifference. Even a reprimand at least reveals truth and gives insight into our reactions to the other person's words or actions.

A sweet friendship refreshes our souls as it comes with encouragement, loyalty, and honesty. A true friend also sharpens us by making us accountable and nurturing our good qualities and virtues while showing us how to improve our weaknesses. A little hurt from a girlfriend who cares motivates us to improve. True friends bring out the best qualities in one another.

Friendship should extend into the workplace, and an honorable person will treat her boss with respect and understanding. Nurturing the relationship with your employer will be fruitful over time. Friendships can be tested. If someone becomes important and still has time for a friend, she passes the test as a girlfriend who is pure gold.

SWIFT SETTLEMENTS

I promise you that if you are angry with someone, you will have to stand trial. If you call someone a fool, you will be taken to court. And if you say that someone is worthless, you will be in danger of the fires of hell.

So if you are about to place your gift on the altar and re-member that someone is an-gry with you, leave your gift there in front of the altar. Make peace with that person, then come back and offer your gift to God.

Before you are dragged into court, make friends with the person who has accused you of doing wrong. If you don't, you will be handed over to the judge and then to the officer who will put you in jail.

Matthew 5:22–25 CEV

Anger and disputes separate families and friends. The longer a disagreement continues, the more it festers and causes damage. Defamation lawsuits and emotional damage suits are all too com-mon, even among family. Jesus spoke the words in this passage to multitudes of followers to remind them that anger at loved ones also interferes with relationship with God. Settling problems is so impor-tant that Jesus told people to make peace before going to God with an offering or gift. Before we pray or do service for God, we need to do our part in making peace with our loved ones.

Peaceful attitudes should extend to outsiders too. We are advised to negotiate and mediate settlements before a case gets to court. Swift action to make peace will lower stress, save money, and im-prove our relationships with God and others. It's a win-win situation and much better than simmering until we explode.

Jesus advised us not to just consider our own anger but also to consider whether someone has anything against us. Notice if some-one acts differently, appears angry, or says you have hurt her, and express your desire to resolve any conflicts.

Internal Divisions Ruin Relationships

Some people brought Jesus a man possessed by a demon. The demon made the man blind and unable to talk. Jesus cured him so that he could talk and see. . . .

When the Pharisees heard this, they said, "This man can force demons out of people only with the help of Beelzebul, the ruler of demons."

Since Jesus knew what they were thinking, he said to them, "Every kingdom divided against itself is ruined. And every city or household divided against itself will not last. If Satan forces Satan out, he is divided against himself. How, then, can his kingdom last? If I force demons out of people with the help of Beelzebul, who helps your followers force them out? That's why they will be your judges. But if I force demons out with the help of God's Spirit, then the kingdom of God has come to you."

Matthew 12:22, 24–28
GOD'S WORD

❊

Accusations make headlines and are usually aimed at damaging or pointing blame at someone. Candidates for office often accuse the current leadership to make themselves look better.

In this passage Jesus faced his accusers, the Jewish leaders, with logic and reasonable answers. He had cured a man of demonic possession, but the leaders complained that he used demonic powers to do it. Jesus didn't complain, voice objections, or even try to defend himself. Instead he used logic and questions to counter the accusations. His response shows how to relate to our enemies and accusers so that they will not divide us. We need to ask questions that cause people to think and seek truth.

To thrive, countries, ministries, teams, and families must have a united purpose, and the members must work together. Does your family have a mission statement, or do you need to write one? What's the purpose and mission statement of ministries you're in? Use mission statements to develop practical activities to carry out and questions that cause people to connect the results to God's love, as did curing the blind, dumb man. The works will reveal the unity of purpose.

WHAT CAUSES FIGHTS?

What causes fights and quarrels among you? Aren't they caused by the selfish desires that fight to control you? You want what you don't have, so you commit murder. You're determined to have things, but you can't get what you want. You quarrel and fight. You don't have the things you want, because you don't pray for them. When you pray for things, you don't get them because you want them for the wrong reason—for your own pleasure. . . .

But God shows us even more kindness. Scripture says, "God opposes arrogant people, but he is kind to humble people." . . .

Brothers and sisters, stop slandering each other. Those who slander and judge other believers slander and judge God's teachings. If you judge God's teachings, you are no longer following them. Instead, you are judging them.

James 4:1–3, 6, 11 GOD'S WORD

※

When little children fight, they often say "Mine," "I want it," and other phrases that reveal selfishness. Adults disguise the same selfish desires in debates and arguments.

Battles for power, wealth, or attention all come from selfish desires that cause us to put ourselves first. Even in prayer many people try to manipulate God to satisfy their desires.

The book of James shows us how to live a faithful life. That includes submitting to God's will and checking our motives. This passage urges us to look at the underlying reasons for conflicts and to compare our choices with motives that please God. Mean comments and criticism about other people flow from the same selfish desires that cause us to envy or want to hurt another woman who has what we want. We judge others when we decide whether their actions are right or wrong. Our words of slander that accuse someone show we have already judged the person. Speaking untruths against a friend or loved one is failing to love that person.

Before we act or speak we should examine our motives and check our personal reasons for our decisions.

FRIENDS DEFEND FRIENDS

The LORD our God has given you this land east of the Jordan to occupy. Now arm your fighting men and send them across the Jordan ahead of the other tribes of Israel, to help them occupy their land. Only your wives, children, and livestock—I know you have a lot of livestock—will remain behind in the towns that I have assigned to you. Help the other Israelites until they occupy the land that the LORD is giving them west of the Jordan and until the LORD lets them live there in peace, as he has already done here for you. After that, you may return to this land that I have assigned to you. . . .

Don't be afraid of them, for the LORD your God will fight for you.

Deuteronomy 3:18–20, 22
GNT

✳

As the people arrived east of the Jordan River beside the Promised Land after forty years of wandering in the desert, God didn't simply give his people the Promised Land. He had a plan to strengthen their relationships. Moses explained God's plan. This passage describes how the two tribes who had already possessed land east of the Jordan would fight for the other tribes.

Working as a team unifies us. Defending one another helps us appreciate one another. The women would remain behind while the men fought. Women would care for the livestock, and that meant plenty of work according to the comment that the tribes owned a lot of livestock. These women may have feared for the lives of the men they loved. To live peacefully while waiting, the women needed to remain focused on the promises made with the speech and the purpose of the battles.

God promised to be with them, promised a future of peace, and promised the two tribes would return. Unity among people should be a higher priority than possessing property. Focusing on God's promise of eternal life should unite Christians and give us common reasons for working together.

Praying for Family

Isaac was forty years old when he married Rebekah, the daughter of Bethuel the Aramean of Padan-aram, the sister of Laban the Aramean.

And Isaac prayed much to the Lord for his wife because she was unable to bear children; and the Lord granted his prayer, and Rebekah his wife became pregnant.

[Two] children struggled together within her; and she said, If it is so [that the Lord has heard our prayer], why am I like this? And she went to inquire of the Lord.

The Lord said to her, [The founders of] two nations are in your womb, and the separation of two peoples has begun in your body; the one people shall be stronger than the other, and the elder shall serve the younger.

When her days to be delivered were fulfilled, behold, there were twins in her womb.

Genesis 25:20–24 AMP

❊

When Rebekah suffered from infertility, her husband, Isaac, prayed for her. He persisted in prayer and God listened. Isaac's parents, Abraham and Sarah, had a difficult time having a child. Abraham even followed Sarah's advice and cultural custom to have a child with Sarah's maid when Sarah became impatient waiting on God's promise of a son. Isaac didn't try his mother's solution for becoming a dad. Instead he turned to God for help. His first response brought the solution as God granted his request.

When Rebekah felt the struggle in her womb, she asked God for insight. God revealed that her sons would be the heads of two nations and that one would serve the other. It must have been hard to hear that one son would not do as well as the other, but she didn't argue with God. We can hope that she continued praying for both sons.

This example of praying for our family reminds us that God wants to be part of family relationships. He wants us to come to him, communicate our needs, and pray for the people we love. We will gain insights as we pray and listen to God.

SUPPORTIVE FAMILY

Those from all the tribes of Israel who set their hearts on seeking the LORD . . . strengthened the kingdom of Judah and supported Rehoboam the son of Solomon for three years, for they walked in the way of David and Solomon for three years. . . .

Rehoboam loved Maacah the daughter of Absalom more than all his other wives and concubines. For he had taken eighteen wives and sixty concubines and fathered twenty-eight sons and sixty daughters. Rehoboam appointed Abijah the son of Maacah as head and leader among his brothers, for he intended to make him king. He acted wisely and distributed some of his sons through all the territories of Judah and Benjamin to all the fortified cities, and he gave them food in abundance. And he sought many wives for them.

2 Chronicles 11:16–17, 21–23 NASB

The nation of Israel split into two kingdoms because King Rehoboam made foolish decisions. He then led Judah, the southern kingdom, comprised of the two tribes of Judah and Benjamin. These tribes remained loyal to the grandson of King David, and for the first three years Rehoboam acted wisely. The people supported and strengthened his kingdom, and they all followed the way of King David, a man after God's own heart.

Rehoboam wisely kept his family close and gave them purpose, making one son, Abijah, the next king, and the others rulers of territories. He made his people happy by distributing food. During this time the kingdom prospered. However, his desire for women was just a taste of his selfishness that led him away from God. He loved his wife, Maacah, but not enough to be faithful to only her. Idolatry flourished because it was easier to give in to people's desires than to lead well.

We must be vigilant to continue to support family and follow God but not blindly support unfaithful people just because they are leaders or family. Laziness and easy choices are no excuse for leading others away from God.

CLOSE-KNIT FAMILY

All of you should be of one mind. Sympathize with each other. Love each other as brothers and sisters. Be tenderhearted, and keep a humble attitude. Don't repay evil for evil. Don't retaliate with insults when people insult you. Instead, pay them back with a blessing. . . . For the Scriptures say, "If you want to enjoy life and see many happy days, keep your tongue from speaking evil and your lips from telling lies.

Turn away from evil and do good. Search for peace, and work to maintain it. The eyes of the Lord watch over those who do right, and his ears are open to their prayers. But the Lord turns his face against those who do evil."

Now, who will want to harm you if you are eager to do good?

1 Peter 3:8–13 NLT

❋

A foreign word can help us understand an English word. We think of *sympathy* as "comforting someone over a loss." *Simpatico* is Italian for "sympathy," but we think of being *simpatico* as meaning "compatible." *Sympathy* actually means "to share the same feelings."

Girlfriends bond and become family over time, especially when we share similar feelings and enjoy harmony in the relationship. It's fun to get together when everyone gets along, blesses us with smiles and kindness, and speaks with love. Our friends become a special family.

Christians living in harmony become a close-knit family too. It starts with sympathy and compassion for others. To remain in harmony, we must control our tongues. Backstabbing and biting words divide friends. Seeking peace should be our response, even when a careless word hurts us. God listens to all our words and will bless us when we bless others. He is tenderhearted toward people who seek peace.

We need to let shared feelings become the bonds that bring us together in peace. Eagerness to please others, including helping Christians bond by using words to network and express shared feelings, will cultivate harmony and strengthen friendships.

To Love, Honor, and What?

Wives, be subject to your husbands [subordinate and adapt yourselves to them], as is right and fitting and your proper duty in the Lord.

Husbands, love your wives [be affectionate and sympathetic with them] and do not be harsh or bitter or resentful toward them.

Children, obey your parents in everything, for this is pleasing to the Lord.

Fathers, do not provoke or irritate or fret your children [do not be hard on them or harass them], lest they become discouraged and sullen and morose and feel inferior and frustrated. [Do not break their spirit.]

Servants, obey in everything those who are your earthly masters, not only when their eyes are on you as pleasers of men, but in simplicity of purpose [with all your heart] because of your reverence for the Lord.

Colossians 3:18–22 AMP

Mother Teresa wisely noted obedience in families as a key to peace on earth. She said, "If there is not that obedience and surrender of the father and mother to each other, there can be very little courage in the parents to ask that obedience of their children. And if today we are having all the troubles with family life, I think it begins there."

This passage shows God's concern for families that starts with the woman's role. Without respect for authority, we have anarchy and division. Without gentle obedience in relationships, there's little peace. As a woman respects a man, it opens his heart, and he responds with love.

When parents have a godly relationship, an example is set for children to obey. Every relationship is two-way, and that includes how the father responds to his children. Fathers should not be too harsh or provoke their children. A mother's gentle touch motivates children to obey and respect their father.

We are all servants of God, and many of us are employees. Those relationships also require obedience to keep order and peace. Respectfully honoring others is one way to show reverence to God, and that pleases him.

STRONG MARRIAGES

Here is another thing you do. You cover the LORD's altar with tears, weeping and groaning because he pays no attention to your offerings and doesn't accept them with pleasure. You cry out, "Why doesn't the LORD accept my worship?" I'll tell you why! Because the LORD witnessed the vows you and your wife made when you were young. But you have been unfaithful to her, though she remained your faithful partner, the wife of your marriage vows.

Didn't the LORD make you one with your wife? In body and spirit you are his. And what does he want? Godly children from your union. So guard your heart; remain loyal to the wife of your youth. "For I hate divorce!" says the LORD, the God of Israel. "To divorce your wife is to overwhelm her with cruelty."

Malachi 2:13–16 NLT

God desires us to be faithful to our spouses. God hates divorce but loves his people. There's a connection between faith to God and commitment to a spouse. God rewards faithful spouses in answering their prayers.

The prophet Malachi's words follow two harsh critiques of bad behavior. He warned the priests for not glorifying God and not studying and living God's Word. Then Malachi gave the people the message that unfaithfulness to God and idolatry would lead to their downfall. They believed they could serve God once a week and do whatever they desired the rest of the time, but that didn't work well. God didn't answer them when they prayed because they failed to live faithfully all week.

When we are unfaithful to God, it's easy to be unfaithful to one another. Where we find men and women committed to God, we also find men and women committed to faithfulness in marriage.

Divorce is viewed here not just as sin but as cruelty. Rejecting a spouse causes pain and suffering. Broken promises harm families and society. Faith to God is a key to building strong families.

Don't Be the Bad Woman

Stay away from a bad woman! Don't even go near the door of her house. . . .

You should be faithful to your wife, just as you take water from your own well. And don't be like a stream from which just any woman may take a drink. Save yourself for your wife and don't have sex with other women. Be happy with the wife you married when you were young.

She is beautiful and graceful, just like a deer; you should be attracted to her and stay deeply in love.

Don't go crazy over a woman who is unfaithful to her own husband! The LORD sees everything, and he watches us closely.

Proverbs 5:8, 15–21 CEV

We all know women who use sensuality and flirting as weapons for attracting men. They've started down a bad path in life. From there it is easy to slip into adultery and break up families because they want to be the center of attention. Look at this passage and consider your own behavior as a woman. Don't become the other woman, the one who entices a man away from his wife.

When a man stares at a woman, that can lead to the sin of lust. Then he may move to unfaithfulness. The passage notes the move from unfaithfulness with one woman to multiple women. It also suggests that a woman who has been unfaithful in marriage, who can't stay happy with her own man, is not likely to be a good choice. A woman should work on being attractive and beautiful for her own man and not seek flattery and pleasure elsewhere.

In desert lands of the Bible, people considered water a precious commodity. They protected their wells. Sex and love are not cheap commodities to use for temporary pleasure. Choose to be a refreshing drink of pure water for one man.

ALWAYS A DAUGHTER

Children, you belong to the Lord, and you do the right thing when you obey your parents. The first commandment with a promise says, "Obey your father and your mother, and you will have a long and happy life."

Parents, don't be hard on your children. Raise them properly. Teach them and instruct them about the Lord.

Slaves, you must obey your earthly masters. Show them great respect and be as loyal to them as you are to Christ. Try to please them at all times, and not just when you think they are watching. . . . Gladly serve your masters, as though they were the Lord himself, and not simply people. You know that you will be rewarded for any good things you do, whether you are slaves or free.

Ephesians 6:1–8 CEV

Every woman is a daughter and will remain a daughter forever, even if her earthly father dies. These words from the apostle Paul about how believers should conduct relationships include helpful instruction for us as daughters.

When a daughter honors her father, God blesses her with good days and a long life. Honoring isn't the same as obeying. To honor means to respect and love. Little children need to be obedient, while grown daughters need to continue honoring their fathers. This should extend to unseen times, such as speaking respectfully about parents to friends. This is one of the Ten Commandments and not just advice for daughters who have godly fathers.

These words from Paul command parents not to be harsh with their children. Fathers are encouraged to teach their daughters about their faith and discipline them.

This passage also advises slaves. Children can feel like slaves and want their own way. Obeying their parents can be difficult, but it leads to good life skills. Workers should view performing their jobs as a way to serve God. Pleasing God as a loving daughter makes work easier. Honoring parents leads to respecting employers and good work skills.

IN-LAW RELATIONS

Ruth said, "Do not urge me to leave you or turn back from following you; for where you go, I will go, and where you lodge, I will lodge. Your people shall be my people, and your God, my God. Where you die, I will die, and there I will be buried. Thus may the LORD do to me, and worse, if anything but death parts you and me.". . .

Then the women said to Naomi, "Blessed is the LORD who has not left you without a redeemer today, and may his name become famous in Israel. May he also be to you a restorer of life and a sustainer of your old age; for your daughter-in-law, who loves you and is better to you than seven sons, has given birth to him."

Ruth 1:16–17; 4:14–15 NASB

⁂

Television shows and jokes are full of bad-mother-in-law examples, but that doesn't mean mothers-in-law are evil. In Ruth's life, the connection begun by the man who brought Ruth and Naomi together remained after he died. Ruth's pledge to her mother-in-law stands out as a tribute to Naomi. Totally committed to their relationship, Ruth followed Naomi to a strange land, left behind her country's idols, and chose to follow God. Ruth's persistence in caring for Naomi brought praise from the women who knew them.

Ruth remarried, and by Jewish law the baby belonged to Naomi's late son. This little one gave Naomi a legacy and filled her life again. Ruth completely trusted her mother-in-law to rear her son. But neither woman really understood the larger picture of God's plan. The child, named Obed, became the grandfather of King David and ancestor of Jesus.

These women show us how people with different backgrounds can bond with love and faith. They bridged the legal tie to become a united and loving family. Look for and find the good qualities in the mother of your husband, the woman who helped shape the man you love.

In-Law Advice

When Moses' father-in-law saw everything Moses was doing for the people, he asked, "Why are you doing this for the people? Why do you sit here alone, while all the people stand around you from morning until evening? . . . You and your people will wear yourselves out. This is too much work for you. You can't do it alone! Now listen to me, and I'll give you some advice. May God be with you! You must be the people's representative to God and bring their disagreements to him. . . .

"But choose capable men from all the people, men who fear God, men you can trust, men who hate corruption. Put them in charge of groups of 1,000, or 100, or 50, or 10 people." . . .

Moses listened to his father-in-law and did everything he said.

Exodus 18:14, 18–19, 21, 24
GOD'S WORD

✳

Whom do you call for advice? Whom do you trust has your best interest at heart? Most of us don't usually seek advice from our in-laws, although it is often given. Moses didn't ask Jethro, his father-in-law, for advice, but he got some anyway.

On a visit when he brought Moses' wife and sons to him, Jethro observed how hard Moses worked and what little time he had for family. Many leaders get so caught up in work that they neglect their children and spouses. As a father Jethro knew the importance of strong family relationships.

Jethro had already established a relationship with Moses. Moses met Jethro with honor, kissed him, and told him all that God had done for the Israelites. Jethro rejoiced at the news and worshipped God. Establishing a relationship brings trust that allows people to give advice.

Jethro saw the strain Moses worked under to solve everyone's problems. Jethro wanted the best for his daughter and grandsons. He advised Moses to delegate the work to men faithful to God. Delegating tasks relieves burdens. Moses followed the advice. In-laws *can* be the best ones to give insightful advice.

GREAT LEADERSHIP

Hezekiah became king when he was twenty-five years old; and he reigned twenty-nine years in Jerusalem. . . . He did right in the sight of the LORD, according to all that his father David had done.

In the first year of his reign, in the first month, he opened the doors of the house of the LORD and repaired them. . . . [Then he said,] "Now it is in my heart to make a covenant with the LORD God of Israel, that His burning anger may turn away from us." . . .

There were also many burnt offerings with the fat of the peace offerings and with the libations for the burnt offerings. Thus the service of the house of the LORD was established again. Then Hezekiah and all the people rejoiced over what God had prepared for the people.

2 Chronicles 29:1–3, 10, 35–36 NASB

Young leaders often have energy, dreams, and goals. Hezekiah, the fifteenth king of Judah, ascended the throne at twenty-five years old. He started his rule by repairing and opening the temple. Hezekiah became one of the best kings and reformers of Judah. He reestablished the nation's relationship with God by renewing the covenant, the agreement between God and his people. That relationship remained strong throughout his life. Hezekiah showed his humility when he rejoiced over what God did and understood that God was the one in charge. Hezekiah's name means "Yahweh [the Hebrew name for God] strengthens," and he drew his strength from God.

Dreams and goals need God's power to thrive. When we make plans, we should first turn to God and renew our commitment to him. Hezekiah restored the doors that symbolized restoring the open door of communication with God. We open communication with God by opening the Bible, studying it, and talking to God. Hezekiah knew his people followed the king's example of relating to God. He took his role seriously. As Christians we are role models for others, both new believers and unbelievers seeking God. Our relationship with God will influence them.

FOLLOW YOUR LEADER

The LORD is my shepherd, I shall not want. He makes me lie down in green pastures; He leads me beside quiet waters. He restores my soul; He guides me in the paths of righteousness for His name's sake.

Even though I walk through the valley of the shadow of death, I fear no evil, for You are with me; Your rod and Your staff, they comfort me. You prepare a table before me in the presence of my enemies; You have anointed my head with oil; my cup overflows. Surely goodness and lovingkindness will follow me all the days of my life, and I will dwell in the house of the LORD forever.

Psalm 23 NASB

Sheep are vulnerable, dumb, and slow-footed. It's wonderful for little lambs to receive tender care from a good shepherd.

Jesus is our Shepherd who cares lovingly for us. The comparison in this famous passage shows us how he wants to relate to us—as closely as a shepherd. Shepherds lead their sheep to rest and the refreshment of cool flowing streams of water and fresh grass. God wants to lead us to peace and a safe place to rest and live. Shepherds know sheep wander and get into trouble, getting caught in holes or streams or brambles and falling off cliffs. The shepherd's staff pulls the sheep back, out of danger. Using it might look harsh, but this is the fastest way to keep the animal safe. The trust developed between the sheep and the shepherd is strong enough that the lambs don't panic. God might use people or circumstances to pull us back, out of danger.

The psalm progresses from shepherd to host. In the Israelite culture, a good host protected his guests and offered visitors the best food, oil, and drink. God offers us eternal protection and supplies all our needs.

It's Your Choice

"If you are not willing to serve him, decide today whom you will serve, the gods your ancestors worshiped in Mesopotamia or the gods of the Amorites, in whose land you are now living. As for my family and me, we will serve the LORD."

The people replied, "We would never leave the LORD to serve other gods!" . . .

Joshua told them, "You are your own witnesses to the fact that you have chosen to serve the LORD."

"Yes," they said, "we are witnesses."

"Then get rid of those foreign gods that you have," he demanded, "and pledge your loyalty to the LORD, the God of Israel."

The people then said to Joshua, "We will serve the LORD our God. We will obey his commands."

So Joshua made a covenant for the people that day.

Joshua 24:15–16, 22–25 GNT

God gave us free will to make our own choices. Our most important choice is whether to accept God and serve him only or serve our own desires or idols. Idols are anything or anyone we worship besides God. To choose God, we must eliminate idols and make a firm commitment of loyalty to God. It doesn't matter where we live or what the people around us choose to do. If we choose God, we must look at our Lord for how to live.

Joshua spoke these words shortly before he died. He had spent his life serving and obeying God, through forty years in the desert with Moses and the Israelites and then leading the people into the Promised Land and through many battles. He understood commitment and the choice he gave the people. He also knew many clung to idols instead of staying loyal to God.

God asks us to enter into a relationship with him where we enter into a promised life of blessings and eternal life with him. Our commitment means we agree to obey God and not put anything or anyone else first. Following God means we will evaluate our choices to keep him first.

CHOOSE GOD FIRST

The LORD is for me, so I will have no fear. What can mere people do to me? . . .

It is better to take refuge in the LORD than to trust in princes.

Though hostile nations surrounded me, I destroyed them all with the authority of the LORD. Yes, they surrounded and attacked me, but I destroyed them all with the authority of the LORD. . . .

The LORD is my strength and my song; he has given me victory. Songs of joy and victory are sung in the camp of the godly. The strong right arm of the LORD has done glorious things!

Psalm 118:6, 9–11, 14–15 NLT

※

Little children cling to their parents, especially when they feel afraid. We learn early to turn to someone we trust for help. But human beings, no matter how powerful, cannot match God's ability to help us. We need to understand that if the Lord is with us, we have no reason to fear. He always keeps our best interests in mind and will use every situation to help us.

An anonymous psalmist wrote the words in this passage. Surrounded by nations, greatly outnumbered in men's eyes, he had only God as his ally. With God's help he cut off his enemies. His testimony gives hope and courage to generations of people. When we hear testimonies of the great things God has done for people, we listen. The mighty works of God still inspire us to trust in him and know that the power of the one true God outnumbers nations of people.

Others' testimonies should help us trust in God. Girlfriends are good, but God is still our best friend. Start a journal describing what God has done in your life and record how he brings victory to situations. Then share God's work in your life.

FOREVER TOGETHER

Jesus [said], "You've come looking for me not because you saw God in my actions but because I fed you, filled your stomachs—and for free. . . .

"The real significance of that Scripture ['He gave them bread from heaven to eat'] is not that Moses gave you bread from heaven but that my Father is right now offering you bread from heaven, the *real* bread." . . .

They jumped at that: "Master, give us this bread, now and forever!"

Jesus said, "I am the Bread of Life. The person who aligns with me hungers no more and thirsts no more, ever. I have told you this explicitly because even though you have seen me in action, you don't really believe me. Every person the Father gives me eventually comes running to me. And once that person is with me, I hold on and don't let go."

John 6:26, 32, 34–37 MSG

❋

When televangelists interview people with miraculous testimonies, viewers tune in. But Jesus doesn't want us to seek him simply because he has power to restore health or provide our needs. He wants us to see and believe that he is God.

God doesn't want us stuck in the past, marveling only at what God did through Moses and in the Old Testament. He wants us to understand what he is doing now and to know how much he cares for us.

Jesus fed more than five thousand people from just a tiny lunch of bread and fish. That was amazing, but the continual miracle that Jesus is the Bread of Life and gives us the *real* bread of heaven should grab our attention even more. That he fills the emptiness not in our stomachs, but in our hearts, should inspire us to follow him. When we turn to him, he won't let go or ever give up on us.

Jesus offers us a relationship that includes his loyalty forever. We can trust that if we run to him, he will open his arms and surround us with his love. Believe in him, and he will respond.

ANGELS AMONG US

Keep on loving each other as brothers and sisters. Don't forget to show hospitality to strangers, for some who have done this have entertained angels without realizing it! Remember those in prison, as if you were there yourself. Remember also those being mistreated, as if you felt their pain in your own bodies. . . .

I urge you, dear brothers and sisters, to pay attention to what I have written in this brief exhortation.

I want you to know that our brother Timothy has been released from jail. If he comes here soon, I will bring him with me to see you.

Greet all your leaders and all the believers there. The believers from Italy send you their greetings.

May God's grace be with you all.

Hebrews 13:1–3, 22–25 NLT

For Paul, a Roman prison was just another bump in his life's journey, and he wanted to be in Rome to share the good news of Jesus. Paul, a Roman citizen, had requested a trial in Rome after Jews brought charges against him. Paul and his friends, including Timothy, continued sharing their faith in and out of jail. Paul noted that circumstances can change at any time. We can be fine one day and suffer hardship the next. To Paul a roller-coaster life was part of being a Christian.

Paul considered the reality of angels as natural as any other aspect of his life. We should live as though we are entertaining angels every time we entertain strangers. When we treat someone as though she is an angel, opening our home to extend hospitality or simply greeting a salesclerk or other stranger we encounter as we would an angel, we are practicing our faith well. Love for fellow believers should be a habit, a practice we develop.

The spiritual realm and the earthly realm overlap more than we realize. Smile and encourage everyone you see, for you might be glimpsing sight of an angel.

LITTLE CHILDREN, BIG ANGELS

Jesus called a child over and had the child stand near him. Then he said: "I promise you this. If you don't change and become like a child, you will never get into the kingdom of heaven. But if you are as humble as this child, you are the greatest in the kingdom of heaven. And when you welcome one of these children because of me, you welcome me.

"It will be terrible for people who cause even one of my little followers to sin. Those people would be better off thrown into the deepest part of the ocean with a heavy stone tied around their neck! . . .

"Don't be cruel to any of these little ones! I promise you that their angels are always with my Father in heaven."

Matthew 18:2–6, 11 CEV

Little babies and children are helpless and in need of protection. God gives them special protection by assigning angels to each child. Those angels see the face of God. They are powerful beings with access to the Father and the throne of heaven.

Christ's words remind us that children are precious to God, and he wants us to keep that inner child within us. The childlike wonder and awe of God, and the humility of a child who understands the need of someone more powerful than herself, help us understand God as our protector.

Smile at a child and you give God a smile. He made these delightful little ones with their energy and curiosity and wants us to welcome them into our hearts and lives. He also warns us not to let children sin. We must not ask children to lie for us or encourage any bad habits. We need to discipline children and carefully show them how to follow God by the way we live.

Spend time around children and look at the world through the eyes of a child. Let a child's curiosity inspire you to rediscover joy in God and his creation.

COVENANT RELATIONSHIP

If you will indeed obey my voice and keep my covenant, you shall be my treasured possession among all peoples. . . .

You shall have no other gods before me.

You shall not make for yourself a carved image. . . . You shall not bow down to them. . . .

You shall not take the name of the LORD your God in vain. . . .

Remember the Sabbath day, to keep it holy. . . .

Honor your father and your mother. . . .

You shall not murder.

You shall not commit adultery.

You shall not steal.

You shall not bear false witness. . . .

You shall not covet.

Exodus 19:5; 20:3–5, 7–8, 12–17 ESV

When God first began relating to the nation of Israel as their God, he gave them this set of rules that we call the Ten Commandments. The first few help define relationship with God, and the rest define relationships among people. God wants us to put him first, treasure him, speak reverently about him, and he promises to treasure those who obey his commands. He asked his people to keep one day holy and committed to rest and to praising him. The Sabbath is the seventh day of the week. Christians worship and keep the principles of rest on Sunday because Jesus rose on a Sunday, the first day of the week.

The commandments seem like a list of don'ts, except for the one about honoring parents. "Don't steal, lie, or covet" helps us treat others well.

When Jesus came, he restated the ten as two positive commands—love God and love others. The bigger picture here is the relationship God desires. He wants a relationship built on trust and faith with commitment; this is called a covenant. God desires to be connected to us with a mutual agreement to be faithful and loving to one another.

The Gift of Words

We are part of the same body. Stop lying and start telling each other the truth. Don't get so angry that you sin. Don't go to bed angry and don't give the devil a chance.

If you are a thief, quit stealing. Be honest and work hard, so you will have something to give to people in need.

Stop all your dirty talk. Say the right thing at the right time and help others by what you say.

Don't make God's Spirit sad. The Spirit makes you sure that someday you will be free from your sins.

Stop being bitter and angry and mad at others. Don't yell at one another or curse each other or ever be rude. Instead, be kind and merciful, and forgive others, just as God forgave you because of Christ.

Ephesians 4:25–32 CEV

Do you prefer insults or compliments? How about kindness or anger? The questions sound silly because of course we naturally prefer positive words. Words should be used to help others and not as weapons to wound.

Our human response when we are hurt is anger, but following Christ means following his example. Christ forgave those who crucified him and forgave us for all our sins. He can help us forgive and replace anger with kindness.

When a store clerk is rude, we can be pleasant. When someone criticizes our hair or clothes, we can thank her for sharing ways to improve. When a spouse complains about the meal we cooked, we can offer to fix something else next time that might satisfy him better.

Mercy reaches out with love to forgive when someone has wronged us. Kindness offers gentle words and actions to show love. Kindness in our hearts helps us say the right things at the appropriate time to help someone feel better, feel respected, and feel loved. Kindness is the response to develop when others are rude, to soften the speaker's heart and root out bitterness with love.

POWERFUL WORDS

I, Paul, make my appeal to you with the gentleness and kindness of Christ. I'm the one who is humble when I'm with you but forceful toward you when I'm not with you. I beg you that when I am with you I won't have to deal forcefully with you. I expect I will have to because some people think that we are only guided by human motives. Of course we are human, but we don't fight like humans. The weapons we use in our fight are not made by humans. Rather, they are powerful weapons from God. With them we destroy people's defenses, that is, their arguments and all their intellectual arrogance that oppose the knowledge of God. We take every thought captive so that it is obedient to Christ.

2 Corinthians 10:1–5
GOD'S WORD

Words can be used for good rather than destruction. When we use words to change minds and make holes in arguments that oppose God, we defend our faith and our God. But in this passage Paul states his dependence on weapons *other* than words.

Paul defended his authority against false teachers who tried to sway people to accept immorality. He used prayer, faith, and love with kindness. He also used the Old Testament Scriptures to refute false arguments.

Capturing our thoughts before we form them into words gives us an opportunity to reform or reframe them to Jesus' standards. Pause and think, *What would Jesus think, say, or do?* That helps us examine our motives to be sure we're not guided by pride, anger, or intimidation.

As we pray for people, God works in their hearts. As we love others, we communicate God's truth and break down barriers and defenses. Giving someone a compliment or cooking her a meal communicates love that opens hearts; then we might have an opportunity to speak truth. Calm but powerful words help others see truth when they hold fast to intellectual pride or poor arguments.

GOSSIP OR INFORMATION?

I always give thanks to my God for you because of the grace he has given you through Christ Jesus. For in union with Christ you have become rich in all things, including all speech and all knowledge. . . .

By the authority of our Lord Jesus Christ I appeal to all of you, my friends, to agree in what you say, so that there will be no divisions among you. Be completely united, with only one thought and one purpose.

For some people from Chloe's family have told me quite plainly, my friends, that there are quarrels among you. Let me put it this way: each one of you says something different. One says, "I follow Paul"; another, "I follow Apollos"; another, "I follow Peter"; and another, "I follow Christ." Christ has been divided into groups!

1 Corinthians 1:4–5, 10–13
GNT

God created women to value relationships. We love to share news about the people in our lives. But be careful about your motives! This passage mentions Chloe, who told Paul about quarrels in her church. Chloe's family looked to him for guidance when they feared divisions might split the community of believers.

Can you distinguish between gossip and communication that seeks to help, that wants good for others? It helps to know what gossip looks like: idle chatter about other people, passing on rumors, and divulging confidences. Our focus when we gossip is on ourselves and not on what's best for the people we're talking about.

When someone asks you to pray for her addiction or concern that her husband might be unfaithful, pray, but don't give details if you ask others to pray. Talking about the friend's husband to make your marriage look better would be gossip. Simply ask others to pray for a special intention.

Disagreements about which leader to follow had split the people in the Corinthian church. Paul pointed out that we're not to follow men, but Christ, who doesn't cause division. Like Paul, our words should be guided by desiring harmony.

Seasoned Conversation

Pray for us also, that God may open a door to us for the Word (the Gospel), to proclaim the mystery concerning Christ (the Messiah) on account of which I am in prison; that I may proclaim it fully and make it clear [speak boldly and unfold that mystery], as is my duty.

Behave yourselves wisely [living prudently and with discretion] in your relations with those of the outside world (the non-Christians), making the very most of the time and seizing (buying up) the opportunity.

Let your speech at all times be gracious (pleasant and winsome), seasoned [as it were] with salt, [so that you may never be at a loss] to know how you ought to answer anyone [who puts a question to you].

Colossians 4:3–6 AMP

We season food and use salt to bring out the natural flavor or to spice up the taste. Seasoning our speech with salt is an interesting analogy. Too much salt on food makes us gag. Sharing our faith should be done graciously and moderately.

As Paul preached about Christ to Jews and to Gentiles, he experienced persecution. He understood how sharing Christ could rub people the wrong way! He waited for the right moments and God's chosen audience to speak up.

Speak in response to questions about your life or how to cope with problems. Opportunities can come after we survive something such as breast cancer or a miscarriage with trust in God; then we can offer hope to others facing a similar difficulty. Waiting for God to provide an opening takes prayer and good communication skills. It requires listening and observing opportunities.

In Bible times salt was used with the grain offering as a symbol of friendship and communion with God. Seasoning conversation with salt should help us connect others with God. As a symbol of friendship, let salt remind you to speak conversationally as a friend instead of preaching.

CONVERSATION PEACE

Through Him then, let us continually offer up a sacrifice of praise to God, that is, the fruit of lips that give thanks to His name. And do not neglect doing good and sharing, for with such sacrifices God is pleased.

Obey your leaders and submit to them, for they keep watch over your souls as those who will give an account. Let them do this with joy and not with grief, for this would be unprofitable for you.

Pray for us, for we are sure that we have a good conscience, desiring to conduct ourselves honorably in all things. . . .

Now the God of peace, who brought up from the dead the great Shepherd of the sheep through the blood of the eternal covenant, even Jesus our Lord, equip you in every good thing to do His will.

Hebrews 13:15–18, 20–21
NASB

A basket or silver bowl of fruit makes a beautiful centerpiece. Sweet, juicy fruit pleases the eye and the palette. Wholesome fruit is a healthy offering to family and friends. The writer of this passage says that because of what Jesus accomplished for us, God wants us to offer him fruit too—our obedience, our acts of service, and especially our prayers of thanks, praise, and requests for the well-being of others.

When we praise God, we look beyond ourselves and discover his unlimited love and power. As we converse with God, we develop a relationship with him. When we pray for others, we focus on their needs. That someone else is sick, in need of a job, or has a dispute to resolve helps us sympathize with other people.

Peace is possible when we care for others. Our prayer for God's will to be done for others releases God's power to help them. Praise shapes our consciences, helping us to see life through God's heart. Our obedient actions and praises are pleasing offerings to God. He wants our actions—and our words—to spread true peace.

Deep, Living Words

What God has said isn't only alive and active! It is sharper than any double-edged sword. His word can cut through our spirits and souls and through our joints and marrow, until it discovers the desires and thoughts of our hearts. Nothing is hidden from God! He sees through everything, and we will have to tell him the truth.

We have a great high priest, who has gone into heaven, and he is Jesus the Son of God. That is why we must hold on to what we have said about him. Jesus understands every weakness of ours, because he was tempted in every way that we are. But he did not sin! So whenever we are in need, we should come bravely before the throne of our merciful God. There we will be treated with undeserved kindness.

Hebrews 4:12–16 CEV

All people need deep friendships, and women especially long to have deep, intimate, reciprocal relationships. Closeness like that requires openness and honesty on the part of both people. God wants to have a deep, meaningful relationship with each of us, and the Bible is where he shares openly and speaks to us honestly. His words go deep and invite us to open up and share what we hide even from ourselves, such as a belief that we are worthless or better than other people. We might hide sins of adultery or greed, criticism or coveting what others have.

As you let the words of the Bible penetrate your heart, you can be more transparent and speak more truthfully to God. Jesus understands our sinful human nature because when he lived in the confines of a human body, he was tempted just as we are. Because of his sinless life and subsequent death and resurrection, we can talk to God about anything. He will treat us with mercy and kindness no matter what secrets are exposed.

It can hurt, but like a surgeon's scalpel or laser, the cutting edge heals us and makes us stronger.

SLOW TO SPEAK

My dear friends, you should be quick to listen and slow to speak or to get angry. If you are angry, you cannot do any of the good things that God wants done. You must stop doing anything immoral or evil. Instead be humble and accept the message that is planted in you to save you.

Obey God's message! Don't fool yourselves by just listening to it. If you hear the message and don't obey it, you are like people who stare at themselves in a mirror and forget what they look like as soon as they leave. . . . God will bless you in everything you do, if you listen and obey, and don't just hear and forget.

If you think you are being religious, but can't control your tongue, you are fooling yourself, and everything you do is useless.

James 1:19–26 CEV

Controlling what we say can be one of the most important and difficult things for women to accomplish. We like talking and can get caught up in chatter. But if we believe the Bible is true, its words should be our standard for behavior and for speech. We are fooling ourselves if we think we can ignore what God says and still believe we are living a Christian life.

When we live according to biblical principles, God will bless us in all that we do, in every facet of our lives. Disobedience puts up barriers and blocks God from blessing us the way he wants to. Inability to control our tongues reveals that God's love is not controlling our emotions. When we yell at our children and launch into calling them stupid or lazy, we are letting anger control our tongues. When we make a sarcastic comment to a friend about her clothes or hair, we are probably letting jealousy control our tongues. Emotional reactions are natural, but letting them control us is a choice. We must stop, check our emotions, and choose to love so that love will control our tongues.

COMMUNICATING WITH INTEGRITY

Think of farmers who wait patiently for the spring and summer rains to make their valuable crops grow. Be patient like those farmers and don't give up. The Lord will soon be here! Don't grumble about each other or you will be judged, and the judge is right outside the door.

My friends, follow the example of the prophets who spoke for the Lord. They were patient, even when they had to suffer. In fact, we praise the ones who endured the most. You remember how patient Job was and how the Lord finally helped him. The Lord did this because he is so merciful and kind.

My friends, above all else, don't take an oath. You must not swear by heaven or by earth or by anything else. "Yes" or "No" is all you need to say.

James 5:7–12 CEV

When we plant seeds, we must wait for the flowers or fruit or vegetables to grow. Waiting requires patience that is learned through times of waiting and being rewarded for the wait. The seasons teach patience to a farmer or gardener. We can't speed the growing process or cause rain to fall. Reaping the crop of flowers or produce rewards our patience and makes it easier to patiently persevere during the next season of scorching sun or cold winds.

We cannot rush our days or rush the Lord's timing in coming to earth again. He wants us to patiently persevere and trust his timing. While we wait, we need to mind our manners and our speech, respecting him. Actions of integrity should follow our words, proving that every yes and no was honored.

Listening fosters integrity and patience. When we listen to a friend's request to help with the church picnic, we understand what's needed. If we decline, by listening we have shown respect and concern. If we commit to help, we understand our responsibility. Integrity indicates wholeness and is seen when we remain constant through the seasons, in our lives and in our speech.

A BIT OF CONTROL

By putting a bit into the mouth of a horse, we can turn the horse in different directions. It takes strong winds to move a large sailing ship, but the captain uses only a small rudder to make it go in any direction. Our tongues are small too, and yet they brag about big things.

It takes only a spark to start a forest fire! The tongue is like a spark. It is an evil power that dirties the rest of the body and sets a person's entire life on fire with flames that come from hell itself. . . . Our tongues get out of control. They are restless and evil, and always spreading deadly poison.

My dear friends, with our tongues we speak both praises and curses. . . . Can clean water and dirty water both flow from the same spring?

James 3:3–6, 8–11 CEV

※

A bit in the mouth of a horse, attached to reins, allows the rider to control her horse. Pulling the reins pulls on the mouth and turns the horse in the direction you want it to turn. Although the bit is small, it allows even a small rider to control a large, powerful animal. Our speech proves much harder to direct and keep on the right trail.

James wrote this passage in a letter to help Christians live their faith daily. Our words reveal how we live our faith. Have you thanked someone for her gift and then complained about it? Have you spoken kindly on the phone and pressed the mute button to yell at your children? Do you yell driving to or from church but sing praises to God when you get there? Do you compliment someone and then talk about her behind her back? All of these are examples of letting your mouth speak good and evil at the same time.

We need to let the Holy Spirit guide our words so we will use our tongues for good. Each morning ask the Holy Spirit to direct your thoughts and words.

Voice Recognition

All who came before Me are thieves and robbers, but the sheep did not hear them. I am the door; if anyone enters through Me, he will be saved, and will go in and out and find pasture. The thief comes only to steal and kill and destroy; I came that they may have life, and have it abundantly.

I am the good shepherd; the good shepherd lays down His life for the sheep. . . .

I am the good shepherd, and I know My own and My own know Me, even as the Father knows Me and I know the Father; and I lay down My life for the sheep. I have other sheep, which are not of this fold; I must bring them also, and they will hear My voice; and they will become one flock with one shepherd.

John 10:8–11, 14–16 NASB

With voice recognition software, our computers can type what we say aloud. Our phones can dial the numbers or names that we say. Each of us has a unique, identifiable pattern of speech. If you raise animals or live with pets, you know that an animal soon learns to recognize its owner's voice. We are Jesus' sheep, and as such we know his voice. We hear him speak to us in the Bible and in our hearts. Following his voice leads to life—a full life here on earth and eternal life as well.

Other voices also call to us. We have an enemy who seeks to steal and destroy our lives. These voices tell us all religions are the same, horoscopes can predict the future, and truth is relative. Those voices disagree with the Bible.

When sheep hear a voice they don't recognize, they scatter and run away. When you hear something that seems contrary to Scripture, stop listening and examine Scripture to find the truth.

This passage tells us that following the right voice leads to abundant life, while following the wrong voice leads to death. Pray and listen for your Shepherd's voice, and follow him.

A FARMER'S TALE

When a very great throng was gathering together and people from town after town kept coming to Jesus, He said in a parable:

A sower went out to sow seed; and as he sowed, some fell along the traveled path and was trodden underfoot, and the birds of the air ate it up.

And some [seed] fell on the rock, and as soon as it sprouted, it withered away because it had no moisture.

And other [seed] fell in the midst of the thorns, and the thorns grew up with it and choked it [off].

And some seed fell into good soil, and grew up and yielded a crop a hundred times [as great]. As He said these things, He called out, He who has ears to hear, let him be listening and let him consider and understand by hearing!

Luke 8:4–8 AMP

❋

Jesus often spoke in parables—little stories with a teaching point. Stories have power and imagery that we recall easily. Jesus' stories contain truth and meaning for us to dig out as we reflect. He used familiar objects and settings in his stories, such as farming.

Women love stories and buy much more fiction than men. We like to share stories about our romances, children, prayer answers, and trips. We tell stories to help children learn a lesson and use analogies to illustrate points. Jesus cushioned a point in his stories and used good storytelling techniques to highlight the point and enhance the listener's pleasure.

In this story, Jesus used the power of repetition with the phrase "And some seed fell." Repetition is a technique that builds suspense and keeps the listener focused. In the parable, a chain of cause and effect occurred as Jesus told what resulted at each place the seed fell. People listened for the next cause and effect. Jesus didn't give an explanation, as he believed listeners who pondered the story could draw the conclusion for themselves. Apply good storytelling techniques whenever you share your faith.

THE REAL MEANING

The seed is the word of God. The ones along the path are those who have heard. Then the devil comes and takes away the word from their hearts, so that they may not believe and be saved. And the ones on the rock are those who, when they hear the word, receive it with joy. But these have no root; they believe for a while, and in time of testing fall away. And as for what fell among the thorns, they are those who hear, but as they go on their way they are choked by the cares and riches and pleasures of life, and their fruit does not mature. As for that in the good soil, they are those who, hearing the word, hold it fast in an honest and good heart, and bear fruit with patience.

Luke 8:11–15 ESV

In private, Jesus shared the message behind the parable of the soils. The seed is God's message, and the soils represent how people receive the message. The parable contains important truths for women who want their faith to count.

Hearing God's message is more than an intellectual pursuit of gathering and analyzing information. We are not computers, storing data. We respond from our hearts to the messages we hear. If the ground of our hearts is plowed up and ready, the seed of God's words can fall there and find a good environment to take root, sprout, grow, and produce change.

In the Bible, *good* means "acceptable." We need to accept God's words and let our actions grow from them. If we accept forgiveness and God's command to forgive others, we will be kind when someone hurts us, willing to forgive. We must weed out careless words, complaints, sarcastic comments, and other destructive habits that keep God's words from growing in our hearts.

If we accept that God loves everyone, we will have love in our hearts and more easily accept other people and bear fruits of kindness and respect toward other people.

WORDS FROM THE HEART

Either make the tree sound (healthy and good), and its fruit sound (healthy and good), or make the tree rotten (diseased and bad), and its fruit rotten (diseased and bad); for the tree is known and recognized and judged by its fruit.

You offspring of vipers! How can you speak good things when you are evil (wicked)? For out of the fullness (the overflow, the superabundance) of the heart the mouth speaks.

The good man from his inner good treasure flings forth good things, and the evil man out of his inner evil storehouse flings forth evil things. . . .

On the day of judgment men will have to give account for every idle (inoperative, non-working) word they speak.

For by your words you will be justified and acquitted, and by your words you will be condemned and sentenced.

Matthew 12:33–37 AMP

It sounds too obvious to state that good fruit depends on the soundness, or goodness, of the tree that grows the fruit. This fact has many implications.

Fruit depends on the tree for water and nutrients. If the tree isn't soundly rooted and watered, the fruit won't develop. The fruit of the lips depends on the heart's condition. If it isn't watered with the love of God and God's Word, then words of love for God and other people cannot grow. Words blossom and spring from the heart.

Jesus gave this analogy to the Pharisees after they revealed their unbelief when they accused him of using Satan's power to perform miracles. Jesus wants our faith to be sound. When we hear repeated anger, criticism, and complaints from someone, that's a signal that hurt, anger, and evil are growing and festering in that person's heart.

A sound heart produces wholesome words. We'll be held accountable for the damage caused by our words, so listen to your words. Your words cause others to smile, frown, or cry. Do you need to weed out evil by asking for forgiveness? Do you need to express love more?

DOGGED CONVERSATION

A Canaanite woman from that territory came to him and began to shout, "Have mercy on me, Lord, Son of David! My daughter is tormented by a demon."

But he did not answer her at all. Then his disciples came to him and urged him, "Send her away. She keeps shouting behind us."

Jesus responded, "I was sent only to the lost sheep of the nation of Israel."

She came to him, bowed down, and said, "Lord, help me!"

Jesus replied, "It's not right to take the children's food and throw it to the dogs."

She said, "You're right, Lord. But even the dogs eat scraps that fall from their masters' tables."

Then Jesus answered her, "Woman, you have strong faith! What you wanted will be done for you." At that moment her daughter was cured.

Matthew 15:22–28
GOD'S WORD

A talkative woman never gives up, especially when in great need. Jesus ignored her, but she pleaded louder. The disciples couldn't take her chatter anymore and asked Jesus to stop her. She overheard Jesus answer the disciples and realized he knew she was not an Israelite, not one of God's chosen people. She became bolder. She knelt and worshipped Jesus. She changed from just pleading for a miracle, as if Jesus were a magician, to recognizing his deity.

Jesus explained he had a mission to the Israelites. He couldn't give her bread. He called her a dog, a term Jews used to refer to Gentiles. But this woman had a quick mind and a fast answer. She responded that masters gave dogs scraps from the table; a scrap would be enough for her. Her reply expressed her acceptance of Jesus as her master, her God. Then he granted her request and commended her faith.

How wonderful to know that we can engage in discussion with God! He may change the conversation to refine our thinking. Keep talking and pleading, but also listen.

EFFECTIVE PRAYER

When you pray, you must not be like the hypocrites. For they love to stand and pray in the synagogues and at the street corners, that they may be seen by others. . . . But when you pray, go into your room and shut the door and pray to your Father who is in secret. . . .

And when you pray, do not heap up empty phrases as the Gentiles do. . . . Do not be like them, for your Father knows what you need before you ask him. Pray then like this:

"Our Father in heaven, hallowed be your name. Your kingdom come, your will be done, on earth as it is in heaven. Give us this day our daily bread, and forgive us our debts, as we also have forgiven our debtors. And lead us not into temptation, but deliver us from evil."

Matthew 6:5–13 ESV

Some women like to arrive late to make a grand entrance. They communicate that they want to be noticed and need attention. That's what Jesus said about hypocrites whose motive for praying is to be seen by other people. Prayer goes best in a quiet place where we can focus on God and listen attentively to his response. God doesn't want empty chatter or distracted pray-ers. He wants us to really talk to him from our hearts.

The prayer Jesus gave his disciples is a model for effective prayer. In the Gospel of Matthew, this passage is with Jesus' Sermon on the Mount. In the Gospel of Luke, Jesus gives this model when the disciples ask him to teach them how to pray. He probably taught it more than once.

Read the prayer and reflect on how Jesus prayed. He praised God the Father, trusted that God is in control, and asked for God's help. Whatever our needs, we can tell God. We must also stop and listen. He might remind us of a verse in the Bible, give us peace in our hearts, put a plan in our minds, or even speak to us directly.

A LITTLE WHISPER

[Elijah] was told, "Go, stand on the mountain at attention before GOD. GOD will pass by."

A hurricane wind ripped through the mountains and shattered the rocks before GOD, but GOD wasn't to be found in the wind; after the wind an earthquake, but GOD wasn't in the earthquake; and after the earthquake fire, but GOD wasn't in the fire; and after the fire a gentle and quiet whisper.

When Elijah heard the quiet voice, he muffled his face with his great cloak, went to the mouth of the cave, and stood there. A quiet voice asked, "So Elijah, now tell me, what are you doing here?" Elijah said it again, "I've been working my heart out for GOD, . . . because the people of Israel have abandoned your covenant, destroyed your places of worship, and murdered your prophets."

1 Kings 19:11–14 MSG

❋

Elijah, one of God's most famous prophets, hid in a cave, afraid that the Israelites had all turned to idolatry and killed all the other prophets. He felt discouraged, alone, and isolated. God spoke in a gentle whisper and asked one question.

Our response to a question reveals how well we listen. Elijah never answered God's question. Elijah's words tumbled out as he gave himself credit for working for God and recounted recent events that revealed his fears. But God already knew all Elijah had done. After Elijah finished releasing his fears, God sent him back where he belonged, with tasks to perform.

Are you letting circumstances get the best of you and causing you to hide your faith and do nothing? Do you feel defeated or afraid? God knows your situation and that you're not alone.

God's little whisper, his quiet, gentle voice, calmed Elijah. Stop running around with busyness and the noise of activity. Take time, sit, and quietly listen for God to speak. Listen for God's calming voice and his reminder that he has work for you to do. Tell him your fears. Then, like Elijah, do what God wants you to do.

GREAT DISCOVERY

Shaphan delivered the king's order to Hilkiah, and Hilkiah told him that he had found the book of the Law in the Temple. Hilkiah gave him the book, and Shaphan read it. . . .

When the king heard the book being read, he tore his clothes in dismay. . . .

"This is what I, the LORD God of Israel, say: You listened to what is written in the book, and you repented and humbled yourself before me, tearing your clothes and weeping, when you heard how I threatened to punish Jerusalem and its people. I will make it a terrifying sight, a place whose name people will use as a curse. But I have heard your prayer, and the punishment which I am going to bring on Jerusalem will not come until after your death. I will let you die in peace."

2 Kings 22:8, 11, 18–20 GNT

Written words are a mainstay of communication, especially in social networks and business dealings. In the time of King Josiah, few books or written documents existed, yet the most important one had been lost and forgotten. When Hilkiah found it and King Josiah heard God's law, his reaction was exactly what ours should be when we realize that we have not been obeying God—Josiah repented and spent the rest of his life following God and reforming himself and his people. God said he would punish the people who had turned away from the law, but out of compassion for Josiah, he would delay punishment until Josiah died. There are consequences to not following God.

In so many areas of life, we need instruction to succeed. Recipes turn out best when we follow the directions completely. Nurses follow procedures to be certain that nothing is missed. The plants and flowers in our gardens grow beautifully when we give them the right environment in which to grow. The principle is the same with faith. Don't let your Bible gather dust on a shelf. Read it and let it change your life.

ECHOES OF NATURE

"Rain and snow come down from the sky. They do not go back again until they water the earth. They make it sprout and grow so that it produces seed for farmers and food for people to eat. My word, which comes from my mouth, is like the rain and snow. It will not come back to me without results. It will accomplish whatever I want and achieve whatever I send it to do."

You will go out with joy and be led out in peace. The mountains and the hills will break into songs of joy in your presence, and all the trees will clap their hands.

Isaiah 55:10–12 GOD'S WORD

What sounds of nature do you most enjoy? Birds chirping, little creatures scampering, leaves rustling? The patter of a soft rain or snowfall? Creation echoes messages from God to us today and will one day break out in joyful singing and applause when God's kingdom is fully established. Creation does God's bidding now and helps us glimpse his majesty.

Women often bring nature into their homes through paintings, decorations, or vases or flowers and potted plants. Nature speaks to us, reminding us of the beauty God created. It is also a reminder of cycles of growth and productivity God designed in nature. Water can change a parched land of thornbushes into a thriving garden.

So too God's Word causes growth in people and softens a dry, bitter heart to help it grow again. Take a walk in your neighborhood or park and notice the sounds, sights, and smells of God's creation. Look at signs of growth. Then reflect on how God has caused growth in you. God's Word, the Bible, waters our lives and accomplishes God's will. When we thrive and produce fruit, we also echo God's message of love to people around us.

BURNING LIPS

I saw the Lord sitting on a high and lofty throne. The bottom of his robe filled the temple. Angels were standing above him. Each had six wings. . . .

So I said, "Oh, no! I'm doomed. Every word that passes through my lips is sinful. I live among people with sinful lips. I have seen the king, the LORD of Armies!"

Then one of the angels flew to me. In his hand was a burning coal that he had taken from the altar with tongs. He touched my mouth with it and said, "This has touched your lips. Your guilt has been taken away, and your sin has been forgiven."

Then I heard the voice of the Lord, saying, "Whom will I send? Who will go for us?"

I said, "Here I am. Send me!"

Isaiah 6:1–2, 5–8 GOD'S WORD

※

In a powerful vision, Isaiah saw the holiness and majesty of God and his own sinful nature. Then Isaiah responded enthusiastically to God's call. He didn't even know the task when he expressed his willingness to go for God. God is not limited to speech or written words. He can communicate with us through a vision, a dream, an angel, or any way he chooses. Isaiah's vision made clear what we all need to understand—God's greatness and our sin.

The burning coal in Isaiah's vision symbolized that God had removed Isaiah's sin. God will cleanse us when we recognize our sins, and he will prepare us for the tasks he gives us. He transformed Isaiah's speech so God could use him to share his message.

God wants to give us dreams and send us to speak for him. Women love talking and sharing news, but we must be ready to speak for God. We must have our mouths cleansed from negative language and practice using our lips to speak with kindness; then God will ask us to speak. All he wants is to have us respond with a willing heart, no matter what the task.

Enlightening Words

He was the source of life, and that life was the light for humanity.

The light shines in the dark, and the dark has never extinguished it.

God sent a man named John to be his messenger. John came to declare the truth about the light so that everyone would become believers through his message. John was not the light, but he came to declare the truth about the light.

The real light, which shines on everyone, was coming into the world. He was in the world, and the world came into existence through him. Yet, the world didn't recognize him. . . .

The Word became human and lived among us. We saw his glory. It was the glory that the Father shares with his only Son, a glory full of kindness and truth.

John 1:4–10, 14 GOD'S WORD

Have you ever testified in court? A witness answers questions and states facts about an event or a person. The words of a witness ultimately can condemn or free the one on trial.

John the Baptist, a cousin of Jesus, used words to introduce Jesus to the world and to testify about who Jesus was. The Gospel of the apostle John begins as a testimony to both John the Baptist and Jesus. John calls Jesus the *life*, the *light*, and the *word*. These are more than descriptions or similes; they are truths about Christ.

Jesus, the Word, was present at Creation. This passage states that everything was made through Jesus. At last a time came when God sent Jesus himself to communicate in the flesh so people could see him and experience his love up close and personal.

In the Bible we can experience Jesus through our senses in what he did and how he interacted with people. Much of our communicating is through expression, body language, and touch. Our smiles transform our faces and let our love shine forth. We understand God better because Jesus came and showed his love through his actions.

ANGELIC VOICES

The angel said, "Don't be afraid. I'm here to announce a great and joyful event that is meant for everybody, worldwide: A Savior has just been born in David's town, a Savior who is Messiah and Master. This is what you're to look for: a baby wrapped in a blanket and lying in a manger." At once the angel was joined by a huge angelic choir singing God's praises. . . .

As the angel choir withdrew into heaven, the sheepherders talked it over. "Let's get over to Bethlehem as fast as we can and see for ourselves what God has revealed to us." They left, running, and found Mary and Joseph, and the baby lying in the manger. Seeing was believing. They told everyone they met what the angels had said about this child. All who heard the sheepherders were impressed.

Luke 2:10–18 MSG

Think of a soft, soothing voice, a melodic song that calms your spirit. Music can help us relax. Or it can help us rejoice! On the first Christmas, joy filled heaven and overflowed into the sky as a choir of angels gave praise to God because Jesus, the Savior, had been born.

The angel's message and the heavenly singing moved the shepherds. They ran to Bethlehem, found the baby, and believed the angelic message. Amazingly, the rapture of an angelic concert hadn't totally convinced them, but the sight of the tiny infant did. The shepherds told everyone they met about Jesus.

Word of mouth is still the most powerful way to spread news. Your personal testimony can change lives. Your excitement and wonder at what you have experienced God doing in your life inspires other people. The angels could not contain their joy to heaven as it overflowed to the sky. Our joy at God's working in us should overflow.

People love the stories of good that happens in people's lives, especially if it helps them believe something similar can happen to them. God's power through us is impressive, and that's what we should share.

SKYWRITING

The heavens declare the glory of God, and the sky above proclaims his handiwork. Day to day pours out speech, and night to night reveals knowledge. There is no speech, nor are there words, whose voice is not heard. Their voice goes out through all the earth, and their words to the end of the world. . . .

The fear of the LORD is clean, enduring forever; the rules of the LORD are true, and righteous altogether. More to be desired are they than gold, even much fine gold; sweeter also than honey and drippings of the honeycomb. . . .

Let the words of my mouth and the meditation of my heart be acceptable in your sight, O LORD, my rock and my redeemer.

Psalm 19:1–4, 9–10, 14 ESV

A plane zips through the sky in loops and engraves a white message across a clear blue canopy. People look up and follow the flow of letters to grasp the meaning. God uses a different type of skywriting to reveal himself. The stars and other heavenly bodies display his handiwork and communicate his power. As astronomers continue to study the sky, they've discovered that there are countless more lights hanging above us than we can see with our eyes.

All of creation whispers truths about God that echo and agree with what the Bible says about him. God's commands are brighter than the sun and other lights he created, for they light our hearts and minds. Nature confirms God's power.

Sometimes we feel hopeless, whether it's because of our inability to fix our hair on a bad hair day or not knowing what to do in a crisis. We can look up at the testimony in the sky and see God's power and feel hope. We can realize, like David when he wrote this psalm, that such a creative God has the wisdom we need. We can find that wisdom in the Bible, in the words God gave us.

FEAR OF SPEAKING

Moses objected, "They won't trust me. They won't listen to a word I say. They're going to say, 'GOD? Appear to him? Hardly!'" . . .

Moses raised another objection to GOD: "Master, please, I don't talk well. I've never been good with words, neither before nor after you spoke to me. I stutter and stammer."

GOD said, "And who do you think made the human mouth? And who makes some mute, some deaf, some sighted, some blind? Isn't it I, GOD? So, get going. I'll be right there with you—with your mouth! I'll be right there to teach you what to say."

He said, "Oh, Master, please! Send somebody else!"

GOD got angry with Moses: "Don't you have a brother, Aaron the Levite? He's good with words. . . . In fact, . . . he's on his way to meet you."

Exodus 4:1, 10–14 MSG

※

Does the thought of public speaking make you tremble or feel queasy? Most people rate speaking in public as their number one fear. Moses felt it when God called him to speak to the Israelites and the pharaoh of Egypt. We easily relate to Moses' excuses, especially given the size of the task—*I'm not good enough. I'm not capable. Someone else will do a better job!* God offered, as the Creator of mouths and words, to coach Moses.

God wants us to accept his calling without complaint and trust that he will equip us and make us good communicators. Our first thought might be, *How can I teach Sunday school since I'm not good with speaking or making lesson plans?* or *I couldn't pray to open the event because I can't speak in front of a group of women.*

Let your second thought be, *God must have plans to help me love children more or to give me courage.* Trust that he will equip you if he is the one who called you. Think about how this opportunity lets you serve God and share his love.

SHINING SPEAKERS

It is God who produces in you the desires and actions that please him.

Do everything without complaining or arguing. Then you will be blameless and innocent. You will be God's children without any faults among people who are crooked and corrupt. You will shine like stars among them in the world as you hold firmly to the word of life. Then I can brag on the day of Christ that my effort was not wasted and that my work produced results. My life is being poured out as a part of the sacrifice and service I offer to God for your faith. Yet, I am filled with joy, and I share that joy with all of you. For this same reason you also should be filled with joy and share that joy with me.

Philippians 2:13–18
GOD'S WORD

When actresses or singers perform, spotlights shine to enhance their costumes and performances—to make them dazzle. If you are a child of God, you are a shining star as you hold on to his Word and obey him. God is the producer who brings out the best in us, and we please him more than the dazzle of any Hollywood special effects. People notice our lives without any stage or spotlight as we make our decisions based on God's forgiveness and love.

When we grumble, complain, or argue, we are not shining for God. We're probably expressing dissatisfaction that our selfish desires have not been met.

When you wake and thank God for the day, read Scripture, and feel joy, you are turning on the light within you. You will then shine through pleasant words, encouragements, and service. When you share with enthusiasm answers to prayer or how God has changed your heart, you shine and you let God shine through you.

Like Paul, we want to know that our efforts are not wasted, that our lives matter. Our lives matter to God and will matter to others if we live as shining lights for God.

Pleasant Words

It's much better to be wise and sensible than to be rich. . . . If you know what you're doing, you will prosper. God blesses everyone who trusts him. Good judgment proves that you are wise, and if you speak kindly, you can teach others. Good sense is a fountain that gives life, but fools are punished by their foolishness. You can persuade others if you are wise and speak sensibly.

Kind words are like honey— they cheer you up and make you feel strong. . . . Worthless people plan trouble. Even their words burn like a flaming fire. Gossip is no good! It causes hard feelings and comes between friends.

Proverbs 16:16, 20–24, 27–28 CEV

Do you check the caller ID before you answer a call? We smile when the caller has a voice we want to hear, someone who lifts our spirits and adds joy to our days. We cringe and might not even pick up the call if it's from someone who tears us down or usually offers only negative messages. The contrast between someone who causes strife and someone who speaks from a wise heart is noticeable. Insults, profanity, lies, and evil thoughts cause grief and hurt. Pleasant words, sweet speech, and truth reveal a heart of understanding.

Two people might speak about the same topic, but the words used— positive or negative, wise or foolish—bring different outcomes.

Thanking people on a committee, suggesting small changes, and praising their work fosters group unity and inspires people to do more. Criticizing workers, spreading rumors about their ineptness, and forgetting to thank them causes division and workers to quit, no matter how worthy the cause.

If we want to be honey to others, and not set scorching fires, we need to seek wisdom and think before we speak. Wisdom and understanding begin with trusting the Lord.

Bringing Out the Best

Build up hope so you'll all be together in this, no one left out, no one left behind. I know you're already doing this; just keep on doing it.

And now, friends, we ask you to honor those leaders who work so hard for you, who have been given the responsibility of urging and guiding you along in your obedience. Overwhelm them with appreciation and love! . . .

Our counsel is that you warn the freeloaders to get a move on. Gently encourage the stragglers, and reach out for the exhausted, pulling them to their feet. Be patient with each person, attentive to individual needs. And be careful that when you get on each other's nerves you don't snap at each other. Look for the best in each other, and always do your best to bring it out.

1 Thessalonians 5:11–15 MSG

Being left out or forgotten, or not receiving an invitation we hoped for, leaves us feeling alone and isolated. When others take time to include us, they build hope and show they appreciate our company. In this passage, Paul advised the Christians in Thessalonica to encourage the church's leaders by showing them attention and appreciation.

Who in your circle of friends needs to receive attention and appreciation from you? Does your pastor's wife need a friend to take her to lunch and express thanks for how hard she and her husband work? Or can you call a ministry leader after an event and let her know how much the event and her work meant? Can you offer to bake a meal for a leader's family on the day of an event they are directing or send her flowers? Can you get a gift for your Bible study leader or send a note to a family member who is leading her family alone while her husband is deployed in a war zone?

God asks us to overwhelm leaders with love and expressions of gratitude as they work hard to prepare, guide us, and impart wisdom.

STRANGE PROPOSAL

[Boaz] went to the pile of barley and lay down to sleep. Ruth slipped over quietly, lifted the covers and lay down at his feet. During the night he woke up suddenly, turned over, and was surprised to find a woman lying at his feet. "Who are you?" he asked.

"It's Ruth, sir," she answered. "Because you are a close relative, you are responsible for taking care of me. So please marry me."

"The LORD bless you," he said. "You are showing even greater family loyalty in what you are doing now than in what you did for your mother-in-law. You might have gone looking for a young man, either rich or poor, but you haven't. Now don't worry, Ruth. I will do everything you ask; as everyone in town knows, you are a fine woman."

Ruth 3:7–11 GNT

Ruth, a young widow, supported herself and her mother-in-law, Naomi, by gleaning wheat behind the harvesters who worked for Boaz. Celebrating the harvest provided an opportunity for seduction, but that was never Ruth's intent. Instead she followed the Jewish custom of asking for the protection of marriage from Boaz, a relative of Naomi. Covering a woman meant marriage. Ruth gave her request simply and directly. When you need something, don't play games or give hints. Use direct and honest communication.

Boaz had already expressed his respect for Ruth and her devotion to taking care of Naomi when he said, "May you have a full reward from the LORD God of Israel, to whom you have come for protection!" (Ruth 2:12). The actual words asked God to spread his wings over Ruth and showed his intention to marry her.

Asking God to protect people communicates concern. Pray with a student about to leave for college, a soldier before her deployment, before a friend's surgery, or when a young woman gets engaged. Ask God to protect them from harm, to give them wisdom, and to bless them. Commit to continue praying for the person.

VOICING CONCERN

After Passover his parents left, but they did not know that Jesus had stayed on in the city. They thought he was traveling with some other people, and they went a whole day before they started looking for him. When they could not find him with their relatives and friends, they went back to Jerusalem and started looking for him there.

Three days later they found Jesus sitting in the temple, listening to the teachers and asking them questions. . . .

When his parents found him, they were amazed. His mother said, "Son, why have you done this to us? Your father and I have been very worried, and we have been searching for you!"

Jesus answered, "Why did you have to look for me? Didn't you know that I would be in my Father's house?"

Luke 2:43–46, 48–49 CEV

Getting separated from someone in a crowd causes anxiety. Worry can lead to angry outbursts and trigger miscommunication where we miss the mark of expressing true concerns or don't hear the fear in the voice of the other person. But Mary voiced her concern with a simple question and an "I statement" about her own feelings rather than an accusing "you statement" about what Jesus had done. Jesus gave a simple answer: Didn't they know he'd be in his favorite place, the house of his heavenly Father?

Mary's remarkably gifted son could converse at age twelve with the city's spiritual leaders, but he didn't overreact to Mary's worry. The exchange reminds us to be calm, in spite of anxieties, and communicate our feelings truthfully to others.

When an employee doesn't come to work, say, "I'm worried that you're sick or something happened, and I'm worried about the status of the project." If a spouse is late, say, "I was worried you might have had an accident. I'd feel better if you called when you're delayed." Allay worries if you're delayed, sick, or forgot a meeting by calling and apologizing. Good communication eases people's minds.

THE WRONG LIST TO BE ON

Worthless liars go around winking and giving signals to deceive others. They are always thinking up something cruel and evil, and they stir up trouble. But they will be struck by sudden disaster and left without a hope.

There are six or seven kinds of people the LORD doesn't like: Those who are too proud or tell lies or murder, those who make evil plans or are quick to do wrong, those who tell lies in court or stir up trouble in a family.

Obey the teaching of your parents—always keep it in mind and never forget it.

Proverbs 6:12–21 CEV

Most of us have been hurt by rumors or lies at some point. Lies place doubt in our minds and cause us to look at others through false lenses. Lies cause fighting, rivalry, and contention and can divide girlfriends and sisters, cause pain, and sever relationships. Often, the heart of someone who gossips or uses words to hurt is full of anger, evil, bitterness, and jealousy. Sometimes we try to inflict pain to ease our own pain.

God hates all forms of hurtful communication. Every individual is God's creation, made in his image, and valuable to him. If you see a girlfriend having lunch with a man, don't jump to conclusions and spread rumors. If you're tempted to tell others what you saw, ask yourself why. Are you jealous of the woman? Do you want to appear important and show you know more than your friends? Let the temptation lead you to correct your heart.

The antidote to hurtful words is to dwell on God's words to keep you focused on truth and love. When you hear a rumor about yourself, forgive those involved and replay God's words of love in your mind.

CONSEQUENCES

No one is respected unless he is humble; arrogant people are on the way to ruin.

Listen before you answer. If you don't, you are being stupid and insulting. . . .

Do you want to meet an important person? Take a gift and it will be easy.

The first person to speak in court always seems right until his opponent begins to question him.

If two powerful people are opposing each other in court, casting lots can settle the issue.

Help your relatives and they will protect you like a strong city wall, but if you quarrel with them, they will close their doors to you.

You will have to live with the consequences of everything you say. What you say can preserve life or destroy it; so you must accept the consequences of your words.

Proverbs 18:12–13, 16–21 GNT

Did you ever receive a strange answer to a question, as though the other person didn't listen to your query? You felt insulted and disrespected, and the other person appeared foolish. All of our communication, whether with words or by actions, has consequences that we must live with. The book of Proverbs, and this passage especially, emphasizes the results of what we say and do.

Replay a recent conversation in your mind and decide if you responded appropriately to any questions or comments. Reflect on your last family disagreement and think about why you wanted your way and what the other person wanted. Did you revert to thoughts about a favored sister or envision a younger brother as still being a troublemaker? Respect the people your siblings have become and stop letting past problems cloud current conversations. Show support for a family member starting a new venture or making a change in her life. Families can provide strength throughout your life.

Show respect when you converse by focusing on the other person while you listen. If you're unsure of what is meant, ask questions or repeat what you think you heard. Listening helps us understand the speaker.

Be Still and Know God

We will not fear though the earth gives way, . . . though its waters roar and foam. . . . There is a river whose streams make glad the city of God, the holy habitation of the Most High. . . . The nations rage, the kingdoms totter; he utters his voice, the earth melts. . . .

Come, behold the works of the Lord, how he has brought desolations on the earth. He makes wars cease to the end of the earth; he breaks the bow and shatters the spear; he burns the chariots with fire. "Be still, and know that I am God. I will be exalted among the nations, I will be exalted in the earth!"

Psalm 46:2–4, 6, 8–10 ESV

Gurgling brooks and crashing waves emit sounds we recognize. Earthquakes cause the ground and buildings to rumble and shake. The roars and rumbles make us fearful or fill us with awe. We understand God's power through his works in nature and through people. He is the one who will bring peace and make war cease.

This psalm is a victory song celebrating the Israelites' victory over their enemies that also prophesies future and final victory. God speaks through his mighty works as a reminder to his people that God will prevail over their enemies.

God speaks of his future city. We will one day see and hear that heavenly river. Meanwhile, we know God by being quiet and observing his work. Look around and see all he made to know he is creative and loves us, and praise him. It's hard for women who love talking to be still and observant, but that's when we experience God. We will hear him in nature and we can hear him speak in our hearts when we're quiet. We will know he is God because we will recognize the authority and love in his voice.

Understanding Men

Peter wept outside, alone. A man committed the first murder in a rage of jealousy, but yet a man obeyed God and saved humankind. God commands women to respect their husbands. Each glimpse of a man in the Bible can leave us wondering, despairing, or hoping as we work at understanding men. By finding delight in a man's actions, women come to understand what makes a man unique.

> The girl followed Paul and the rest of us and kept yelling, "These men are servants of the Most High God! They are telling you how to be saved."

Acts 16:17 CEV

Competing Boys at Heart

She ran at once to Simon Peter and the other disciple, the one Jesus loved, breathlessly panting, "They took the Master from the tomb. We don't know where they've put him."

Peter and the other disciple left immediately for the tomb. They ran, neck and neck. The other disciple got to the tomb first, outrunning Peter. Stooping to look in, he saw the pieces of linen cloth lying there, but he didn't go in. Simon Peter arrived after him, entered the tomb, observed the linen cloths lying there, and the kerchief used to cover his head not lying with the linen cloths but separate, neatly folded by itself. Then the other disciple, the one who had gotten there first, went into the tomb, took one look at the evidence, and believed. . . .

The disciples then went back home.

John 20:2–8, 10 MSG

Acting like rivals and not fellow mourners, Peter and John ran to investigate after receiving the news that Christ's body was missing. (Historians believe "the other disciple, the one Jesus loved" mentioned in this passage refers to John, the author.) John arrived at the tomb first and peered in but didn't enter. Peter impulsively rushed past John into the tomb. It seems he needed to win in some way. Both men observed the interior of the tomb in detective fashion. John tells us that he saw and then he believed. Did he understand the reality of the Resurrection at this point? Did Peter? They might have believed only that the body was really gone. We don't know because it's not reported whether the two talked or shared reactions. They stopped investigating, seemed to forget Mary's fears, and returned to their own homes.

From childhood to manhood, men compete. In retelling adventures they emphasize heroism: "I believed when I saw." We cannot rush a man into discussing a problem or expect him to notice our emotions. Men want to make up their own minds. In reality, most men, usually single-focused, prefer to think and ponder facts alone.

DID HE REALLY LISTEN?

"Yes, Master, you know I love you."

Jesus said, "Shepherd my sheep."

Then he said it a third time: "Simon, son of John, do you love me?"

Peter was upset that he asked for the third time, "Do you love me?" so he answered, "Master, you know everything there is to know. You've got to know that I love you."

Jesus said, "Feed my sheep. I'm telling you the very truth now: When you were young you dressed yourself and went wherever you wished, but when you get old you'll have to stretch out your hands while someone else dresses you and takes you where you don't want to go." He said this to hint at the kind of death by which Peter would glorify God. And then he commanded, "Follow me."

John 21:16–19 MSG

Most women talk much more than most men. We often re-peat things to make sure our man actually listened and "got it." We might push to see if he will give a more passionate answer that shows real engagement in the conversation. Getting a man's atten-tion isn't easy. If this has been your experience, know that it's not an isolated or new experience. Jesus asked Peter the same question three times and repeated a request for Peter to care for his sheep (those who would believe). Jesus likely repeated his question and request to counter Peter's three denials of Jesus on the night before the Crucifixion.

Jesus used different words for *love* in his questioning. The first two times he used the word *agape*, meaning to love God with a sacrificial love. The third time Jesus used the word *phileo*, meaning affectionate love between friends. All three times Peter responded with the word *phileo*—I love you as a friend. The third time Peter emphasized his love and gave a much more passionate answer to wipe out all doubt. Purposeful repetition might annoy men, but it also gets attention.

GOD, IS THAT YOU? REALLY?

"I am putting some wool on the ground where we thresh the wheat. If in the morning there is dew only on the wool but not on the ground, then I will know that you are going to use me to rescue Israel." That is exactly what happened. When Gideon got up early the next morning, he squeezed the wool and wrung enough dew out of it to fill a bowl with water.

Then Gideon said to God, "Don't be angry with me; let me speak just once more. Please let me make one more test with the wool. This time let the wool be dry, and the ground be wet." That night God did that very thing. The next morning the wool was dry, but the ground was wet with dew.

Judges 6:37–40 GNT

Some men are door checkers. They lock the door and then test it to see if it's really locked. They tug and twist to ensure the mechanism engaged and works properly. Men might do this nightly, a continual test for quality control of objects in their lives. They start these habits as boys who break toys to investigate how things work. They don't take things at face value. Gideon was no exception.

The events in this passage happened during the time of the judges, before Israel had kings. Gideon tested God a few times. He used a fleece as a reality check and quality-control test. He tried not to anger God, but he just couldn't keep himself from checking to confirm that God really wanted him to be the new leader to battle the Midianites.

Gideon could hardly believe God had called him, a little nobody from the least important tribe of Israel. God sought out the most unlikely hero to show the world his own power. God patiently responded, as he knew once he passed Gideon's test he would earn Gideon's loyalty and complete faith. Rejoice in men who care enough to perform safety checks!

Gone Fishin'

Simon Peter said, "I'm going fishing!" The others said, "We will go with you." . . .

Early the next morning Jesus stood on the shore, but the disciples did not realize who he was. Jesus shouted, "Friends, have you caught anything?"

"No!" they answered.

So he told them, "Let your net down on the right side of your boat. . . ."

They did, and the net was so full of fish that they could not drag it up into the boat.

When Simon heard that it was the Lord, he put on the clothes that he had taken off while he was working. Then he jumped into the water. . . .

Jesus took the bread in his hands and gave some of it to his disciples. He did the same with the fish. This was the third time that Jesus appeared.

John 21:3–7, 13–14 CEV

❋

Instead of sharing the news of the Resurrection, the disciples went fishing. They didn't pass the news on to their social networks or stick close to Jesus to learn what he wanted them to do next. Nope. They went to sea and sat in their boat, casting their nets but catching no fish. In the morning Jesus appeared on the shore and directed them to a catch of more fish than they could lift into the boat. The scene replayed an earlier big catch when Jesus first called his disciples. Now Peter reacted by plunging into the water and swimming to Jesus; then all the disciples joined Jesus for breakfast.

Where guys connect to God and one another become places they want to revisit and experiences they want to repeat. When facing problems, men often return to what's familiar and fun, like fishing, camping, or hobbies. They find comfort in the familiar surroundings of a boat, their garage, or a tent. Jesus patiently met his friends where they felt comfortable before giving them a new mission in life.

When our men face challenges, we can comfort them with familiar foods and encourage favorite pastimes.

Loyalty among Guys

After David had finished talking with Saul, Jonathan became one in spirit with David, and he loved him as himself. . . .

And Jonathan made a covenant with David because he loved him as himself. . . .

Saul told his son Jonathan and all the attendants to kill David. But Jonathan was very fond of David and warned him, "My father Saul is looking for a chance to kill you. Be on your guard tomorrow morning; go into hiding and stay there. I will go out and stand with my father in the field where you are. I'll speak to him about you and will tell you what I find out." . . .

Jonathan said to David, "Go in peace, for we have sworn friendship with each other in the name of the LORD, saying, 'The LORD is witness between you and me.'"

1 Samuel 18:1, 3; 19:1–3; 20:42 NIV

※

Jonathan and David became fast friends, but King Saul's jealousy of David arose as David outdid Saul's victories. Jonathan felt no jealousy—even though he realized that David, and not he himself—would be the next king. Jonathan tried to convince his father that David's deeds benefited Saul and the people, but eventually he realized that Saul did indeed plan to kill David. This passage describes the courageous plan Jonathan set up to help David escape. David, anointed to succeed Saul as king of Israel, ran for his life. He would be a fugitive for years.

Men don't usually have as many friends as women do, but they tend to develop strong bonds that last through the years. A man of integrity won't harm a friend no matter who tries to influence him to evil action. Jonathan used archery practice and where he shot his arrows to send a message to David. He sent an arrow far off to let David know to flee for his life, far from Saul—an early form of text messaging!

Women can learn to be better friends by observing men with strong friendships who don't let pettiness part them.

MEN AND COURAGE

The Lord said to him, "Get up and go to the house of Judas on Straight Street. When you get there, you will find a man named Saul from the city of Tarsus. Saul is praying, and he has seen a vision. He saw a man named Ananias coming to him and putting his hands on him, so that he could see again."

Ananias replied, "Lord, a lot of people have told me about the terrible things this man has done to your followers in Jerusalem." . . .

The Lord said to Ananias, "Go! I have chosen him to tell foreigners, kings, and the people of Israel about me." . . .

Ananias left and went into the house where Saul was staying. Ananias placed his hands on him and said, "Saul, the Lord Jesus has sent me."

Acts 9:11–17 CEV

Saul of Tarsus, a Jew, zealously persecuted Christians until God intervened and Jesus appeared to Saul on the road to Damascus. Then God gave a believer named Ananias a mission to minister to Saul, but Ananias complained that Saul had authority to imprison Christians. God didn't respond to the complaint but commanded Ananias to go because he had chosen Saul to serve him. Ananias didn't question God a second time but went quickly and placed his hands on Saul. His courage grew as he entered the room, and he did more than God asked as he remained with Saul for several days.

Women think of men as courageous, not shrinking from mice or men. But Ananias's first reaction was not trust in God's strength but fear of a man. However, men take orders well, and when God commanded, Ananias braced up like a good soldier and followed orders. Mark Twain said that courage is not the absence of fear but acting in spite of it. Men act when needed, and the action increases adrenaline and courage. Once adrenaline flows, men bravely do more than expected. Trust that men who believe in God will be courageous when needed.

A Guy Party

He looked up and saw three men standing there. As soon as he saw them, he ran out to meet them. Bowing down with his face touching the ground, he said, "Sirs, please do not pass by my home without stopping; I am here to serve you. Let me bring some water for you to wash your feet; you can rest here beneath this tree. I will also bring a bit of food; it will give you strength to continue your journey. You have honored me by coming to my home, so let me serve you."

They replied, "Thank you; we accept." Abraham hurried into the tent and said to Sarah, "Quick, take a sack of your best flour, and bake some bread.". . .

Then they asked him, "Where is your wife Sarah?"

"She is there in the tent," he answered.

Genesis 18:2–6, 9 GNT

God had promised Abraham would father a nation, but for years nothing happened. Ishmael, Abraham's son by Sarah's servant, was thirteen when the men in this passage appeared. Old Abraham treated them as special guests and offered them a feast. He wanted to make this a treat and asked Sarah to whip up one of his favorites, with the finest ingredients. Abraham then prepared a calf and started grilling. He cooked the beef and served his guests. A guy party is a great way for men to bond and then open up in conversation.

Only after eating did the men ask about Abraham's wife. Abraham didn't invite her to join the group, perhaps because of the customs of the time, but he pointed out that she was nearby. Then the Lord prophesied about Sarah's pregnancy that would birth the nation of Israel. And out of Sarah's hearing, he told Abraham the bad news about plans of destruction.

Food followed by directness characterizes many men, as does shielding women from hearing bad news. Women like to share news quickly, before feasting, but men prefer eating first. So before launching an important discussion, try filling your man's stomach.

Mourning Lost Friendship

As Samuel turned to go, Saul grabbed the edge of Samuel's robe. It tore! Samuel said, "The LORD has torn the kingdom of Israel away from you today, and he will give it to someone who is better than you. Besides, the eternal God of Israel isn't a human being. He doesn't tell lies or change his mind." . . .

Even though Samuel felt sad about Saul, Samuel never saw him again.

The LORD was sorry he had made Saul the king of Israel.

One day he said, "Samuel, I've rejected Saul, and I refuse to let him be king any longer. Stop feeling sad about him. Put some olive oil in a small container and go visit a man named Jesse, who lives in Bethlehem. I've chosen one of his sons to be my king."

1 Samuel 15:27–29, 35; 16:1
CEV

When someone we love fails us, that's hard. When we see a loved one fail God, that can tear us apart and force us to make difficult choices. Samuel had anointed Saul as Israel's first king. Now he had to remove the kingdom from Saul because Saul had disobeyed God. He had not waited for Samuel to offer a sacrifice to God and had offered it himself, and he hadn't followed God's orders to kill all the Amalekites and take no plunder. God expects complete obedience, especially from leaders. Caught between love for God and Saul, Samuel grieved.

Samuel made his choice to follow God, severed the relationship with Saul, and killed Agag, but that didn't stop his emotional response. Men don't show emotions a lot, but despite this their emotions are often deep and lasting. Then God sent Samuel to anoint a new king, David. This action gave Samuel a new focus and reenergized his own mission as priest, judge, and prophet of Israel. With a new mission and purpose, Samuel stopped mourning.

When facing difficult problems, men need to look to God for strength and purpose. Men work best when they have objectives and goals, especially from God.

AUTHORITATIVE TONE

When he entered Capernaum, a centurion came forward to him, appealing to him, "Lord, my servant is lying paralyzed at home, suffering terribly."

And he said to him, "I will come and heal him."

But the centurion replied, "Lord, I am not worthy to have you come under my roof, but only say the word, and my servant will be healed. For I too am a man under authority, with soldiers under me. And I say to one, 'Go,' and he goes, and to another, 'Come,' and he comes, and to my servant, 'Do this,' and he does it."

When Jesus heard this, he marveled and said to those who followed him, "Truly, I tell you, with no one in Israel have I found such faith." . . .

And the servant was healed at that very moment.

Matthew 8:5–10, 13 ESV

❋

Mothers are amazed when a child ignores their commands but immediately follow the same directions from a man. There seems to be something in a man's deep voice that inspires obedience more than the higher-pitched voice of a woman.

Capernaum was a thriving village on the Sea of Galilee, a few miles from the Jordan River. Caravans stopped there to resupply, and a main Roman road ran through the northern part of the town. Jesus set up his headquarters at Capernaum. His return to the village caught the attention of a centurion, a Roman soldier who led one hundred soldiers.

Men size up other men quickly and respect the authority they perceive in a man. Jesus' authority impressed the centurion. Because the centurion used his authority to accomplish work, he understood the authority of Jesus and expressed faith in the power of Christ's commands.

Jesus marveled and praised this man's faith and healed his servant from a distance—for distance and space never limit God.

Soldiers understand authority and the chain of command and know the power of commands and words. The authority of Jesus can capture a man's attention.

Not Man Enough

Elkanah had two wives, Hannah and Peninnah. Peninnah had children, but Hannah did not. . . .

Each time Elkanah offered his sacrifice, he would give one share of the meat to Peninnah and one share to each of her children. And even though he loved Hannah very much he would give her only one share, because the Lord had kept her from having children. Peninnah, her rival, would torment and humiliate her, because the Lord had kept her childless. This went on year after year; whenever they went to the house of the Lord, Peninnah would upset Hannah so much that she would cry and refuse to eat anything. Her husband Elkanah would ask her, "Hannah, why are you crying? Why won't you eat? Why are you always so sad? Don't I mean more to you than ten sons?"

1 Samuel 1:2, 4–8 GNT

A man wants to meet his wife's needs and reacts with frustration when his actions don't make her happy. Elkanah's frustration showed when he asked Hannah if he wasn't as good as ten sons. He wanted to know if he was man enough for her, man enough to satisfy her longings. Elkanah loved Hannah very much and gave to her generously, but he also pitied her because God had kept her from bearing children. Obviously he did not satisfy her needs completely, for she could not eat or smile. Elkanah was not God and could not fulfill all Hannah's desires.

Women need to understand that no one man—no one person—can meet all our needs. We have to trust God with our desires. God doesn't want us to look to a man, especially a husband, as God. God wants us to know his capabilities are greater than human abilities.

After Elkanah's questions described in this passage, Hannah left the meal and poured out her heart to God in a prayer. God answered and fulfilled her longing for a child with a son who became a great judge of Israel.

LOUD REJECTION, PRIVATE WEEPING

A female servant saw him as he sat facing the glow of the fire. She stared at him and said, "This man was with Jesus."

But Peter denied it by saying, "I don't know him, woman."

A little later someone else saw Peter and said, "You are one of them."

But Peter said, "Not me!"

About an hour later another person insisted, "It's obvious that this man was with him. He's a Galilean!"

But Peter said, "I don't know what you're talking about!" Just then, while he was still speaking, a rooster crowed. Then the Lord turned and looked directly at Peter. Peter remembered what the Lord had said: "Before a rooster crows today, you will say three times that you don't know me."

Then Peter went outside and cried bitterly.

Luke 22:56–62 GOD'S WORD

❋

Three times Peter loudly protested that he had no connection to Jesus. This occurred after soldiers arrested Jesus the evening before his crucifixion. Only when Jesus looked at Peter and Peter heard a rooster crow did Peter face the truth of his denials. Jesus had warned Peter only hours earlier that Peter would deny him three times before the rooster crowed.

Peter left everyone and hid his tears. Men might protest and complain loudly, but the deeper emotions of sorrow and regret are usually hidden. Tears shed by men are seldom seen. That causes women to think men don't care and don't own up to their mistakes. That's not a good assumption.

Jesus understood Peter and also understood the remorse Peter would feel. Before the denial even took place, Jesus had informed Peter that Satan had demanded permission to shake him up. Jesus also stated that he had already prayed for Peter, and that once Peter turned back to God, he could strengthen other people. As Peter mulled this over, the memory of Jesus' words would bring hope. Jesus knows that hope encourages men to overcome failure.

The Way to a Man's Heart

[Abigail] was discerning and beautiful, but [Nabal] was harsh and badly behaved; he was a Calebite. . . .

One of the young men told Abigail, Nabal's wife, "Behold, David sent messengers out of the wilderness to greet our master, and he railed at them." . . .

Then Abigail made haste and took two hundred loaves and two skins of wine and five sheep already prepared and five seahs of parched grain and a hundred clusters of raisins and two hundred cakes of figs, and laid them on donkeys. . . .

When Abigail saw David, she hurried and got down from the donkey and fell before David on her face and bowed to the ground. . . .

And David said to Abigail, "Blessed be the LORD, the God of Israel, who sent you this day to meet me!"

1 Samuel 25:3, 14, 18, 23, 32 ESV

❋

David had protected Nabal's property, but when he asked Nabal to supply some food to his army, Nabal refused. This happened when Nabal held a feast for his workers celebrating the sheepshearing. David expected him to be generous on this occasion. Nabal's name meant "fool," and he responded to David foolishly.

Appeasing an angry man takes discernment and action. Abigail, Nabal's wife, worked to appease David. She loaded up plenty of food, including fig cakes, lamb, and wine, to present a feast for David and his men. She understood the way to a man's heart is through appetizing food. When she met David, already anointed as the next king of Israel, she asked that all blame be on her and that David not take vengeance himself for Nabal's response. Her words revealed her faith.

Abigail spoke to David, a man deeply devoted to God, and acknowledged David fought for God. She really knew how to relate to men. She connected to David's need and faith. David responded and blessed God, noted that God had sent her, and let God deal with Nabal. Nabal soon died, and David then married Abigail.

PURSUIT

"Why are you so helpful? Why are you paying attention to me? I'm only a foreigner."

Boaz answered her, "People have told me about everything you have done for your mother-in-law after your husband died. They told me how you left your father and mother and the country where you were born. They also told me how you came to people that you didn't know before." . . .

Ruth replied, "Sir, may your kindness to me continue. You have comforted me and reassured me, and I'm not even one of your own servants."

When it was time to eat, Boaz told her, "Come here. Have some bread, and dip it into the sour wine." So she sat beside the reapers, and he handed her some roasted grain. She ate all she wanted and had some left over.

Ruth 2:10–11, 13–14
GOD'S WORD

Ruth questioned Boaz's generosity. She underestimated both her inward and outward beauty. But Boaz had noticed her the first time he saw her gleaning in his field, before he knew her name. Ruth, a widow, had left her native land to remain with her widowed mother-in-law. The book of Ruth, written during the time judges ruled Israel, is a beautiful story of love and redemption.

Impoverished, Ruth picked up scraps of grain the harvesters left behind. Boaz had just told her not to glean in anyone else's field and had told his men not to harm her. He respected her actions and service to her mother-in-law, Naomi, who was actually related to Boaz.

After this, Boaz pursued Ruth a little more. He invited her to eat with his workers and handed her roasted grain. On this lunch "date," they dipped bread together, and she ate all she wanted. Dipping bread together showed Boaz's acceptance of her, even knowing her Moabite heritage.

Men feel protective as they develop an interest in a woman and then notice her character. Their actions reveal love and interest more than their words.

BELOVED MOTHER AND WIFE

She is not afraid of snow for her household, for all her household are clothed in scarlet. She makes bed coverings for herself; her clothing is fine linen and purple. Her husband is known in the gates when he sits among the elders of the land. . . . Strength and dignity are her clothing, and she laughs at the time to come. She opens her mouth with wisdom, and the teaching of kindness is on her tongue. She looks well to the ways of her household and does not eat the bread of idleness. Her children rise up and call her blessed; her husband also, and he praises her.

Proverbs 31:21–23, 25–28 ESV

In Bible days a man of importance sat among the elders at the city gate, a place of respect and honor. His wife could help him attain this position if she ran their household well. But a man is first his mother's little boy, and that relationship influences his choice of a bride.

Any bride might feel pressured to live up to a mother-in-law who cooks well, has a good career, and is considered by her son to have a beautiful character, like the famous, accomplished woman this passage describes. A boy trusts his mother and knows her laughter, her kindness, her strength, and he trusts her ability to care for him. He expects his wife will be like his mother and might forget that a younger woman is less experienced.

Tension and rivalry can enter the relationship between a mother and her daughter-in-law when a man praises his mother to his potential wife. The man might be clueless that he started a problem! A wise man praises both women without comparing their talents. He appreciates his wife's efforts while understanding that she is just starting down the path of an accomplished woman.

PICTURING MARRIAGE

Be courteously reverent to one another.

Wives, understand and support your husbands in ways that show your support for Christ. The husband provides leadership to his wife the way Christ does to his church, not by domineering but by cherishing. So just as the church submits to Christ as he exercises such leadership, wives should likewise submit to their husbands. . . .

No one abuses his own body, does he? No, he feeds and pampers it. That's how Christ treats us, the church, since we are part of his body. And this is why a man leaves father and mother and cherishes his wife. No longer two, they become "one flesh." . . . And this provides a good picture of how each husband is to treat his wife, loving himself in loving her, and how each wife is to honor her husband.

Ephesians 5:21–24, 29–31, 33 MSG

Photographers capture wedding memories so we can hang up beautiful pictures of the day a man and a woman become husband and wife. But the real picture God wants us to see is how a marriage should work in his eyes. This passage focuses on believers' responsibilities within marriage.

To understand Christ, we listen to his words in the Bible and talk with him in prayer. Likewise, we need to listen to our husbands and communicate well. These words remind us to submit to our husbands, and they tell men to pamper, lead, cherish, and cling to their wives to join the two as one. Women often hate the idea of submission, but that's part of supporting a man.

If a man loves a woman, he will guide his wife and family in making good choices. If both spouses are courteous and honor one another, the two will seek the best for each other.

These verses remind us that men need respect and women need to feel cherished. Meeting the needs of one another develops a happy union.

WANDERING EYES

In the spring of the year, the time when kings go out to battle, David sent Joab, and his servants with him, and all Israel. And they ravaged the Ammonites and besieged Rabbah. But David remained at Jerusalem.

It happened, late one afternoon, when David arose from his couch and was walking on the roof of the king's house, that he saw from the roof a woman bathing; and the woman was very beautiful. . . .

And one said, "Is not this Bathsheba, the daughter of Eliam, the wife of Uriah the Hittite?" So David sent messengers and took her, and she came to him, and he lay with her. (Now she had been purifying herself from her uncleanness.)

Then she returned to her house. And the woman conceived, and she sent and told David, "I am pregnant."

2 Samuel 11:1–5 ESV

In King David's time, kings fought yearly battles, but for some reason this passage doesn't tell us, David chose to remain behind this time and not accompany his men. That left him idle, and his lazy days gave way to wandering eyes. He observed a woman bathing on her rooftop and kept looking, noticing her beauty. He couldn't get the beautiful image out of his mind.

David didn't resist temptation or head to battle. He investigated, discovered the woman's identity, and found out she was married. He pressed on in spite of her marital status and God's laws and sent for her—"took her" implies coercion. A woman who has a husband fighting for a powerful leader is not likely to ignore such a summons. She went, and David slept with her.

David's sin changed the course of history, splitting his kingdom and triggering sexual sins within his own family. His country no longer prospered as it had when David followed God completely.

Idleness opens the door to temptation, and men's reactions bring consequences for women. Knowing how much our bodies can tempt men should help us choose modesty in dress and movement.

COVER-UPS

Uriah answered, "The sacred chest and the armies of Israel and Judah are camping out somewhere in the fields with our commander Joab and his officers and troops. Do you really think I would go home to eat and drink and sleep with my wife? I swear by your life that I would not!" . . .

David invited him for dinner. Uriah ate with David and drank so much that he got drunk, but he still did not go home. He went out and slept on his mat near the palace guards. Early the next morning, David wrote a letter and told Uriah to deliver it to Joab. The letter said: "Put Uriah on the front line where the fighting is the worst. Then pull the troops back from him, so that he will be wounded and die."

2 Samuel 11:11, 13–15 CEV

※

Uriah, the husband David wronged by sleeping with his wife, Bathsheba, proved to be a man of honor. David hoped to cover up his sin and Bathsheba's subsequent pregnancy by bringing Uriah off the battlefield to his wife, but Uriah refused to go home and indulge in sex while his troops were in the field. Uriah's integrity didn't sway David's cover-up efforts. Instead of confessing to Uriah and admitting his sin, David plotted Uriah's death. He sent orders to place Uriah in harm's way, where the enemy killed Uriah in battle.

Joab followed the orders that led to Uriah's death, but later he betrayed David by killing David's son Absalom and then plotting against both David and Solomon. Men hold less respect for another man when they have seen him acting sinfully.

It's amazing what schemes men conjure up to cover sin, especially sexual sins. Because David later admitted his sin and sorrowed over it, God called David a man after his own heart. David's love for God was strong. But no matter how much men are committed to God, they are still human and can fail to make godly choices. They need our prayers.

BOOMERANG

[Nathan said,] "The poor man had only one lamb, which he had bought. He took care of it, and it grew up in his home with his children. He would feed it some of his own food, let it drink from his cup, and hold it in his lap. The lamb was like a daughter to him. One day a visitor arrived at the rich man's home. The rich man didn't want to kill one of his own animals to fix a meal for him; instead, he took the poor man's lamb and prepared a meal for his guest." David became very angry at the rich man. . . .

"You are that man," Nathan said to David. . . .

"I have sinned against the LORD," David said.

Nathan replied, "The LORD forgives you; you will not die. . . . Your child will die."

2 Samuel 12:3–5, 7, 13–14
GNT

The prophet Nathan used a story to get David to admit that he had sinned. David had committed adultery with Bathsheba, had her husband killed when Bathsheba became pregnant, and married her. David might have felt everything in the palace was fine again. But God sent Nathan to confront David. His powerful story enraged David, and he declared that the man who would take someone else's beloved sheep deserved to die. Nathan spoke four little words that struck David to the core. Yes, he was the man.

David had many wives, while Uriah had only one wife, whom he cherished. David confessed and repented of his sin. God forgave David, but he suffered the consequences with the death of Bathsheba's child.

Consequences of sin have a way of boomeranging to expose sin and give people another chance to repent. Confronting a man, especially one who deviously covers up his sin or even a mistake, is difficult. The power of a story can reach a man and reveal the truth about his actions, as can this story concerning David. Knowing God already and the hope of forgiveness help a man repent.

DID I DO THAT?

(She [Tamar] did this because she realized that Shelah was grown up now, and she hadn't been given to him in marriage.)

When Judah saw her, he thought she was a prostitute because she had covered her face. Since he didn't know she was his daughter-in-law, he approached her by the roadside and said, "Come on, let's sleep together!"

She asked, "What will you pay to sleep with me?"

"I'll send you a young goat from the flock," he answered.

She said, "First give me something as a deposit until you send it."

"What should I give you as a deposit?" he asked.

"Your signet ring, its cord, and the shepherd's staff that's in your hand," she answered.

So he gave them to her. Then he slept with her, and she became pregnant.

Genesis 38:14–18 GOD'S WORD

✳

Judah, the leader of the ancestral tribe of Jesus, was a widower at the time of the events in this passage. His two older sons, who had been married to Tamar one after the other, had died childless. Judah had an obligation to let his remaining son marry Tamar, but Judah withheld him in fear that this son would die also and leave Judah with no descendants.

So Tamar used prostitution to seduce Judah. She stood near a heathen temple masquerading as a temple prostitute, a woman engaging in sex as part of her idolatry. Tamar coerced Judah to leave his signet ring and staff with her, which would later prove his identity. Judah assumed she wanted the customary payment of a goat to sacrifice. Judah fell right into her trap.

Tamar, a Canaanite and not a worshipper of the one true God, didn't ask for God's help, nor did she appeal to her father to seek justice for her. She lacked trust in men. Instead of plotting, we should enlist God's help for justice. Judah showed little trust in God to provide descendants. A poor relationship with God can lead men to make bad choices.

FAIRNESS

"The men of the place said, 'No cult prostitute has been here.'"

And Judah replied, "Let her keep the things as her own, or we shall be laughed at. You see, I sent this young goat, and you did not find her."

About three months later Judah was told, "Tamar your daughter-in-law has been immoral. Moreover, she is pregnant by immorality."

And Judah said, "Bring her out, and let her be burned."

As she was being brought out, she sent word to her father-in-law, "By the man to whom these belong, I am pregnant." And she said, "Please identify whose these are, the signet and the cord and the staff."

Then Judah identified them and said, "She is more righteous than I, since I did not give her to my son Shelah."

Genesis 38:22–26 ESV

※

Judah didn't always make good choices, but this passage shows that when confronted, he accepted the blame and made amends. When confronted by the truth that Tamar carried his child, he admitted his fault. He married Tamar and she gave birth to twins, although he never slept with her again. One of the twins, Perez, became an ancestor of Christ.

Judah is an example of someone who became a better man over time. He learned from his mistakes. Earlier in life, Judah had convinced his brothers not to kill Joseph, but he also suggested that they sell Joseph into Egyptian slavery. Here we see Judah trying to fulfill his pledge to pay the unknown prostitute with a goat. Later in Egypt, before Joseph had revealed his identity to his brothers, Judah offered to take his brother Benjamin's place in prison.

Tamar didn't confront Judah personally but sent him the proof of their connection. She let the evidence speak for her. Men can improve and make more godly choices if they are willing to admit their faults and mistakes. Evidence that points to a man's responsibility can be key to inspiring honorable and responsible behavior.

Perspectives on Flowers

The LORD God took the man and put him into the garden of Eden to cultivate it and keep it. . . .

Then the LORD God said, "It is not good for the man to be alone; I will make him a helper suitable for him." . . . But for Adam there was not found a helper suitable for him. So the LORD God caused a deep sleep to fall upon the man, and he slept; then He took one of his ribs and closed up the flesh at that place. The LORD God fashioned into a woman the rib which He had taken from the man, and brought her to the man. The man said, "This is now bone of my bones, and flesh of my flesh; she shall be called Woman, because she was taken out of Man."

Genesis 2:15, 18, 20–23 NASB

Life for man began in a garden, with a purpose. Adam had jobs to do for God, to tend the Garden and name the animals. As he named the animals, not one met his need for a suitable partner. Man felt alone without a woman. God fashioned a woman from Adam's rib, and she started life in the Garden as his companion.

For many men, a yard and garden is work and has purpose. For women, a garden is home, beauty, and linked to the joy of receiving flowers from a man. A woman still enjoys the beauty of fragrant flowers and other expressions that say her man considers her so needed in life that he views her as an integral part of his existence.

Adam immediately reacted to Eve. He felt a connection to her and knew her as an extension of himself. Adam immediately felt unity with Eve and considered her a gift from God. Minus one rib, one that might have guarded his heart, he realized she delighted him and filled his heart. Men want women to complete them, partner with them, and appreciate their work. Thank men in your life for working hard.

MISPLACED FAITH

Samuel was displeased with their request for a king; so he prayed to the LORD, and the LORD said, "Listen to everything the people say to you. You are not the one they have rejected; I am the one they have rejected as their king. Ever since I brought them out of Egypt, they have turned away from me and worshiped other gods; and now they are doing to you what they have always done to me. So then, listen to them, but give them strict warnings and explain how their kings will treat them.". . .

[Samuel explained,] "He will take a tenth of your flocks. And you yourselves will become his slaves. When that time comes, you will complain bitterly because of your king, whom you yourselves chose, but the LORD will not listen to your complaints."

1 Samuel 8:6–9, 17–18 GNT

Samuel served as judge, priest, and prophet of Israel. The people's request for a king like the leaders of other nations had upset Samuel. They had rejected God as their leader. They ignored their history—God prospered them when they remained faithful and allowed suffering when they turned away. Samuel's explanation of taxes and kings' enslaving their children didn't deter the people's desire for an earthly king. God gave them free choice and they chose to turn away from his guidance.

People still complain about taxes and government-imposed rules. Samuel failed to convince people to keep their focus on God. Yet many men still listen more to humanistic arguments and put more trust in political leaders than in God, as seen in where they spend their time. Although men profess belief in God, they attend church much less frequently than women. Jesus started the church with a group of Spirit-filled men. We need to pray for men to be spirit-filled, encourage churches to invest in men's ministries and leadership, preach on tough male issues, and use men's skills to help people so they will feel they belong and find value in attending church.

A MAN OF INTEGRITY

"He [Job] hasn't changed, even though you persuaded me to destroy him for no reason."

Satan answered, "There's no pain like your own. People will do anything to stay alive." . . .

"All right!" the LORD replied. "Make Job suffer as much as you want, but just don't kill him." Satan left and caused painful sores to break out all over Job's body—from head to toe.

Then Job sat on the ash-heap to show his sorrow. And while he was scraping his sores with a broken piece of pottery, his wife asked, "Why do you still trust God? Why don't you curse him and die?"

Job replied, "Don't talk like a fool! If we accept blessings from God, we must accept trouble as well." In all that happened, Job never once said anything against God.

Job 2:3–4, 6–10 CEV

Job and his wife lost all their children and every possession they owned in one day. Then God let Satan attack Job's body with sores, leaving him an aching mess from head to toe. A man who had lost everything didn't need his wife to nag him. She was all Job had left, but she didn't comfort him. She only complained.

Job gave one of the best responses to suffering found in the Bible when he told his wife that we must be willing to accept trouble from God if we accept blessings from him. Job didn't complain or speak against God. Job had integrity—an undivided heart. He patiently endured his suffering, his wife, and later on even the bad advice of his friends. Job later stated that he would still trust God even if God killed him, but he would argue his case to find out why God let him suffer. Job's trust and faith in God remained and still inspire people facing hardships.

Men of integrity understand that life's not always perfect and trouble comes to every home. Such men persevere and endure the hard times while patiently waiting for better days.

THE ROMANTIC LOVER

Behold, you are beautiful, my love, behold, you are beautiful! Your eyes are doves behind your veil. Your hair is like a flock of goats leaping down the slopes of Gilead. Your teeth are like a flock of shorn ewes that have come up from the washing, all of which bear twins, and not one among them has lost its young. Your lips are like a scarlet thread, and your mouth is lovely. Your cheeks are like halves of a pomegranate behind your veil. Your neck is like the tower of David, built in rows of stone; on it hang a thousand shields, all of them shields of warriors. . . . You are altogether beautiful, my love; there is no flaw in you.

Song of Solomon 4:1–4, 7
ESV

Men want to be romantic and please a woman with words of love. But what men perceive as beautiful might not match a woman's idea. Hair "like a flock of goats" says "scraggly and uncombed" to a woman but "rich and pricey" to a man who raises goats. Lips "like a scarlet thread" imply a thin, tight mouth, but men see costly red thread woven into soft fabric and identify the color and richness with lovely lips. Cheeks like a pomegranate might sound garishly bright and blotchy to a woman but to a man can depict the sweetness of a blushing bride. To a man, jewels on the neck resemble symbols of victory and shields of protection.

This passage on beauty reflects a man's imagery. What a man enjoys blends with his values. A man who likes fishing might think about his wife in terms of calm water, jumping fish, and a fine lure! God made women's and men's minds to think differently, but the bottom line is that the man finds the woman a beautiful and flawless creation of God. Rejoice when your man tries to state what he finds attractive.

FINDING A CONGENIAL WIFE

A parent is worn to a frazzle by a stupid child; a nagging spouse is a leaky faucet.

House and land are handed down from parents, but a congenial spouse comes straight from GOD.

Life collapses on loafers; lazybones go hungry.

Keep the rules and keep your life; careless living kills.

Mercy to the needy is a loan to GOD, and GOD pays back those loans in full.

Discipline your children while you still have the chance; indulging them destroys them.

Let angry people endure the backlash of their own anger; if you try to make it better, you'll only make it worse.

Take good counsel and accept correction—that's the way to live wisely and well.

Proverbs 19:13–20 MSG

The book of Proverbs often sounds like a list of tips for practical living strung together like individual pearls on a beautiful necklace. The proverbs in this passage address humility and give advice regarding children and a good wife.

Men first look at outward beauty and often must live with the consequences of a poor choice. Women who are mothers realize that they can pass on wealth to their sons and discipline them, but they cannot create the perfect wife. The soul of a person comes from God; thus we need to pray for the future spouses of our children.

Parents are role models. Good role models are not lazy, careless, or angry. We can use our time to help the needy and show our sons the importance of seeking character over looks. Reactions to angry people and acceptance of criticism model godly virtues. If we don't focus too much on our outward looks and fashion but develop inner qualities, we show boys the importance of looking deeper when seeking a wife.

Raising boys to become responsible husbands means guiding them in living well and disciplining them in doing chores, working hard, and keeping commitments.

WHY DON'T THEY LISTEN?

To Adam He said, "Because you have listened to the voice of your wife, and have eaten from the tree about which I commanded you, saying, 'You shall not eat from it'; cursed is the ground because of you; in toil you will eat of it all the days of your life. Both thorns and thistles it shall grow for you; and you will eat the plants of the field; by the sweat of your face you will eat bread, till you return to the ground, because from it you were taken; for you are dust, and to dust you shall return."

Now the man called his wife's name Eve, because she was the mother of all the living.

Genesis 3:17–20 NASB

This account is one of the most familiar passages in the Bible. Adam didn't listen to God but he did listen to his wife, and that landed him in grave trouble. God had words for Eve and also for Adam—serious consequences would result. Childbirth would be painful, but women would desire their husbands. (He didn't need to say this to Adam, for Adam hardly took his mind or eyes off Eve from the moment he saw her.) Adam's only response was to name Eve. It's easy to wonder if he might have stopped listening when God told Eve that women would give birth with pain, although he did catch that women would be mothers. Adam had never toiled, sweated, or seen a thistle, so he might not have understood all that God was telling him. He didn't ask for advice but looked at his wife. Adam appears to have looked more than he listened and to have heard only what interested him at the time.

Men tend to be single focused. Stopping at the first intriguing thought reveals that one main focus at a time is probably best when communicating with a man.

PRIDE OR INTEGRITY?

Daniel so distinguished himself among the administrators and the satraps by his exceptional qualities that the king planned to set him over the whole kingdom. At this, the administrators and the satraps tried to find grounds for charges against Daniel in his conduct of government affairs, but they were unable to do so. . . .

Then they said to the king, "Daniel, who is one of the exiles from Judah, pays no attention to you, O king, or to the decree you put in writing. He still prays three times a day." . . .

So the king gave the order, and they brought Daniel and threw him into the lions' den. . . .

"My God sent his angel, and he shut the mouths of the lions. They have not hurt me, because I was found innocent in his sight."

Daniel 6:3–4, 13, 16, 22 NIV

❋

Daniel's integrity impressed the king so much that he selected Daniel to be his top leader during Israel's captivity in Babylon. Daniel didn't check popularity polls or worry about rivalry but focused on his faith and work. Jealous men plotted to cause trouble for Daniel. They flattered the king and appealed to his weakness—his pride. They suggested a rule that people could bow only to the king, and this pleased the king. They used this rule to attack Daniel's faith and eliminate their competition.

The king prayed for God to spare Daniel's life since he liked and trusted Daniel. After God shut the lions' mouths and spared Daniel, the king had the devious men and their families thrown into the lions' den. God's unlimited ability is above the power of kings and evil people. This passage inspires courage and faith in God's power to prevail over evil plans.

Faithful people should willingly serve God above political laws and fear of punishment. Women should seek faithful men of integrity, men who completely trust God's ability to prosper them and keep them safe from harmful plots. Men who trust God wholeheartedly are steadfast and courageously face the future.

DIPLOMATIC ARGUMENTS

One member, a Pharisee named Gamaliel, who was an expert in religious law and respected by all the people, stood up and ordered that the men be sent outside the council chamber for a while. Then he said to his colleagues, "Men of Israel, take care what you are planning to do to these men! . . .

"After [Theudas], at the time of the census, there was Judas of Galilee. He got people to follow him, but he was killed, too, and all his followers were scattered.

"So my advice is, leave these men alone. Let them go. If they are planning and doing these things merely on their own, it will soon be overthrown. But if it is from God, you will not be able to overthrow them. You may even find yourselves fighting against God!"

Acts 5:34, 37–39 NLT

Gamaliel used a clever argument to divert a council of men from making a rash decision. As a good diplomat, Gamaliel looked at issues from various perspectives and took a middle road to reason with the council. He didn't accuse anyone or stir up the current situation. Instead, he viewed the situation with a historical perspective. He looked to past religious movements and the results. He pointed out facts and truths of what happened with a man called Judas of Galilee. He led everyone to look in a new direction and view a similar situation to bring hope that the current situation would be resolved as easily. People respect a peacemaker and someone who helps them see more objectively. They also trust someone who gives them hope.

However, Gamaliel also stated an eternal truth—God's plans are sovereign. First he calmed the people and then he reminded them God was in control. He remained open to the possibility that the new religious movement might be God's plan. A tactful man uses reason while remaining open to all possibilities. A diplomatic man is humble enough to know God triumphs over man's plans.

MOVED BY HOSPITALITY

One day Elisha was traveling through Shunem, where a rich woman lived. She had invited him to eat with her. So whenever he was in the area, he stopped in to eat. She told her husband, "I know he's a holy man of God. . . . Let's make a small room on the roof and put a bed, table, chair, and lamp stand there for him. He can stay there whenever he comes to visit us."

One day he came to their house, went into the upstairs room, and rested there. . . .

Elisha said, "At this time next spring, you will hold a baby boy in your arms."

She answered, "Don't say that, sir. Don't lie to me. You're a man of God."

But the woman became pregnant and had a son at that time next year, as Elisha had told her.

2 Kings 4:8–11, 16–17
GOD'S WORD

The woman in this passage enjoyed company and opening her home to strangers. She recognized and supported Elisha's work. She made a room, furnished it, decorated it, and offered it to Elisha, one of God's prophets, whenever he traveled to her town. Elisha listened to God and not people. Her hospitality touched him, and he wanted to do something kind for her. He discovered through his servant that she desired a child. Elisha trusted that God would grant her a son and prophesied that she would become a mother in a year.

The woman, older and childless, resisted hoping in what seemed impossible. A false prophecy would hurt her too much after years of yearning for a baby, and she protested to Elisha not to lie. Elisha didn't say another word but let time speak for him, and his words came true.

Men are moved by the kindness of hospitality. Elisha believed God could do anything for this woman who had shown him such consideration. The passage reveals that God responds to women who care for the needs of his workers. Men appreciate kindness and hospitality. They show appreciation through action more than words.

PLEASING YOUR MAN

Three days later Esther dressed in her royal robes and took up a position in the inner court of the palace in front of the king's throne room. The king was on his throne facing the entrance. When he noticed Queen Esther standing in the court, he was pleased to see her; the king extended the gold scepter in his hand. Esther approached and touched the tip of the scepter. The king asked, "And what's your desire, Queen Esther? What do you want? Ask and it's yours—even if it's half my kingdom!"

"If it please the king," said Esther, "let the king come with Haman to a dinner I've prepared for him."

"Get Haman at once," said the king. . . .

"Now, what is it you want? Half of my kingdom isn't too much to ask! Just ask."

Esther 5:1–6 MSG

Esther was a Jewish woman married to a Persian king. They didn't share the same faith. Three days had passed, spent in fasting with her people. Dressed beautifully, Esther stood silently.

Esther was queen but had no power. She couldn't even approach the king or enter the court unless he summoned her. By walking into the court, she risked her life, for the penalty of displeasing the king was death. The king stopped all proceedings to ask Esther what she wanted and offered to give her anything. A woman can get the attention of a man who loves her without a word.

Esther didn't plunge into her need. She asked him to dinner along with Haman, his assistant. The king didn't hesitate. He ordered his men to get Haman at once, revealing his desire to be with Esther.

Esther prevailed when she asked the king to spare the lives of her people Haman had plotted to destroy. The account is the basis of the celebration of Purim. Appealing to a man with beauty and good food softens him up for a favorable response, especially when your actions are accompanied and motivated by faith.

SECRET MISSIONS

"Go get Isaac, your only son, the one you dearly love! Take him to the land of Moriah, and I will show you a mountain where you must sacrifice him to me on the fires of an altar." So Abraham got up early the next morning and chopped wood for the fire. He put a saddle on his donkey and left with Isaac and two servants for the place where God had told him to go.

Three days later Abraham looked off in the distance and saw the place. . . .

Abraham put the wood on Isaac's shoulder, but he carried the hot coals and the knife. As the two of them walked along. Isaac said, "Father, we have the coals and the wood, but where is the lamb for the sacrifice?"

"My son," Abraham answered, "God will provide the lamb."

Génesis 22:2–4, 6–8 CEV

Abraham left on a dangerous mission with his son Isaac. There's no indication that Abraham shared the plan with his wife, Sarah. It would have been hard to tell her that God had asked Abraham to offer their only son as a sacrifice.

Abraham didn't reveal the plan to Isaac either. He packed for a campout and sacrifice and took his son with him. Isaac was familiar with sacrificing to God, and he questioned his dad about the lamb that was needed. Abraham left his men behind as he and Isaac climbed the mountain and told his son, in a short sentence, that God would provide the lamb. Men often tell others only what they need to know.

A mission for God is one a man can trust and follow. Sharing it too soon could bring arguments and division or fear. Abraham knew the mission for four days but kept it to himself. This famous passage reveals Abraham's complete faith in God.

God responded to Abraham's willingness to carry out the mission by stopping the sacrifice and providing a ram in place of Isaac. That must have been a joyful sacrifice!

CHOICES

Career, motherhood, missions, and other life choices women face today were also choices in front of women in the Bible. How they chose among their options and made decisions reveals their strength of character and provides insight for women today.

This day I call heaven and earth as witnesses against you that I have set before you life and death, blessings and curses. Now choose life, so that you and your children may live.

Deuteronomy 30:19 NIV

UNPREDICTABILITY OF LIFE

The fastest runner doesn't always win the race, and the strongest warrior doesn't always win the battle. The wise sometimes go hungry, and the skillful are not necessarily wealthy. And those who are educated don't always lead successful lives. It is all decided by chance, by being in the right place at the right time. . . .

I have watched the way our world works. There was a small town with only a few people, and a great king came with his army and besieged it. A poor, wise man knew how to save the town, and so it was rescued. But afterward no one thought to thank him. So even though wisdom is better than strength, those who are wise will be despised if they are poor. What they say will not be appreciated for long.

Ecclesiastes 9:11, 13–16 NLT

Most people know someone with a good education who has nothing to show for it. Sometimes sports teams win that are not as trained or skilled as the losing team. These situations surprise us and show us that life is unpredictable.

King Solomon, the wisest man who ever lived, observed life and people and summed up his reflections on life in the book of Ecclesiastes. He noted that strength, education, and wisdom are not the only deciding factors for success. Opportunity and being in the right place at the right time also impact outcomes. Wise people keep a lookout for opportunities and seize the moment.

Solomon also observed how people respond to wealth and prestige, choosing to listen to rich leaders in positions of authority over someone wiser, but poor. Too often we judge others by financial status. Consider how you respond to advice and where you turn for help. Do you ask richer friends or someone who has proven wise in the past?

Apply wisdom to your own situations and appreciate any source of real wisdom. Work at becoming wiser through studying your past experiences and seeking God in the Bible.

THE PRICE OF CURIOSITY

When morning came, the angels urged Lot to hurry, saying, Arise, take your wife and two daughters who are here [and be off], lest you [too] be consumed and swept away in the iniquity and punishment of the city.

But while he lingered, the men seized him and his wife and his two daughters by the hand, for the Lord was merciful to him; and they brought him forth and set him outside the city and left him there.

And when they had brought them forth, they said, Escape for your life! Do not look behind you or stop anywhere in the whole valley; escape to the mountains [of Moab], lest you be consumed.

And Lot said to them, Oh, not that, my lords! . . .

But [Lot's] wife looked back from behind him, and she became a pillar of salt.

Genesis 19:15–18, 26 AMP

※

It's hard not to peek. We touch to verify the truth of a wet-paint sign and look when someone tells us not to look. Lot's wife discovered how unwise such self-willed activity can be.

God decided to destroy Sodom, where Abraham's nephew Lot lived, and Gomorrah, two extremely immoral towns. God sent angels to rescue Lot and his family before he consumed the cities with fire. The angels warned them not to look back but to stay focused on escaping to the mountains of Moab. Lot talked them into letting him stop at the small village of Zoar first. Lot's wife let her curiosity— or perhaps her longing for her home and her former life—get the best of her, and it cost her everything. *Zap!* She turned into a pillar of salt. In one instant she lost her family and her life.

Lot and his daughters kept moving forward without looking back, arrived in Zoar, and later went into the mountains. He didn't seek Abraham or find suitable husbands for his daughters, and his daughters made sinful choices. When God calls us, he wants us to focus on the future and seek his direction.

BENEFICIAL LIVING

"Everything is permissible"—but not everything is beneficial. "Everything is permissible"—but not everything is constructive. Nobody should seek his own good, but the good of others.

Eat anything sold in the meat market without raising questions of conscience, for, "The earth is the Lord's, and everything in it."

If some unbeliever invites you to a meal and you want to go, eat whatever is put before you without raising questions of conscience. . . .

So whether you eat or drink or whatever you do, do it all for the glory of God. Do not cause anyone to stumble, whether Jews, Greeks or the church of God—even as I try to please everybody in every way. For I am not seeking my own good but the good of many, so that they may be saved.

1 Corinthians 10:23–27, 31–33 NIV

God gives us free will, so we have choices, but not every choice is beneficial or good. Paul gave the advice in this passage to help new Christians living in a city where idol worshippers made sacrifices to their idols and then sold the sacrificed meat in the marketplace. His words encourage us today to consider how our decisions will impact other people.

Some foods or diets can be harmful, especially if indulged in excessively. Drugs, alcohol, and tobacco products can have serious consequences. People observe our habits, so we need to set good examples. If we abuse alcohol, overindulge in food, or never exercise, we might lead others to copy us and fail at living healthy lives.

Paul balanced his advice with the wise reminder that pleasing God should always drive and guide our decisions. As we thank God for our food, enjoy the natural, healthy foods he created, and use meals as times to build relationships, we honor God. Sharing meals with friends who don't yet know him also provides opportunities to share our faith without judging their lifestyle.

MORNING ATTITUDES

You have bereaved my soul and cast it off far from peace; I have forgotten what good and happiness are. And I say, Perished is my strength and my expectation from the Lord.

[O Lord] remember [earnestly] my affliction and my misery, my wandering and my outcast state, the wormwood and the gall. My soul has them continually in remembrance and is bowed down within me.

But this I recall and therefore have I hope and expectation:

It is because of the Lord's mercy and loving-kindness that we are not consumed, because His [tender] compassions fail not.

They are new every morning; great and abundant is Your stability and faithfulness.

The Lord is my portion or share, says my living being (my inner self); therefore will I hope in Him and wait expectantly for Him.

Lamentations 3:17–24 AMP

Happiness and peace can be elusive. Worry causes sleeplessness that makes it hard to face a new day. Getting out of bed, preparing for work, getting children up, or peering in a mirror and knowing we have to fix our hair and faces can seem daunting. Dwelling on the stresses in our lives leads to a downcast soul, and that makes for unhappiness.

Jeremiah wrote this sorrowful lament after the Babylonians had conquered Jerusalem in the southern kingdom after a long siege. Israel's enemies had destroyed the temple, killed many people, and made slaves of the rest. This passage flows into a pep talk on hoping and waiting for God with reminders that he responds and is good.

Instead of dwelling on our troubles, we can remember that God's compassions never fail and his mercies are new every day. We can wake to every new day determined to seek God's blessings. We can think of three reasons to be grateful. We can look for blessings all day long, even small simple smiles or acts of kindness. Praying gives us hope for a better future as we wait for the God who answers.

MAXIMIZING POTENTIAL

The servant who had been given 5,000 coins brought them in with the 5,000 that he had earned. . . .

"Wonderful!" his master replied. "You are a good and faithful servant. I left you in charge of only a little, but now I will put you in charge of much more. Come and share in my happiness!" . . .

The servant who had been given 1,000 coins then came in and said, ". . . I was frightened and went out and hid your money in the ground. Here is every single coin!"

The master of the servant told him, ". . . You could have at least put my money in the bank, so that I could have earned interest on it."

Then the master said, "Now your money will be taken away and given to the servant with 10,000 coins!"

Matthew 25:20–21, 24–28
CEV

❋

Opportunities allow us to take risks and show our talents, but fear can hold us back. In this parable, or story, Jesus spoke about three servants, or employees, and how they applied their talents with the resources given them. Two did well and doubled their money, but one dug a whole, buried the coins, and did nothing but worry. Fear, and perhaps laziness, paralyzed this servant, and he wasted his gifts.

The story has a larger lesson, because Jesus compares it to preparing for heaven until he comes to earth again. He wants us to be ready to give an account of what we do with the gifts of talent, resources, and time he gives us here. He wants us to consider that we really work for God and all we have really belongs to God—down to the last dollar. We need to think of what we can do for God to multiply our resources and make life better for others.

We are caretakers in God's kingdom. Invest your talent in ministry or work that helps people, willingly serve with trust in God, and make the most of every day.

Mary's Response

The angel said to her, "Do not be afraid, Mary, for you have found favor with God. And behold, you will conceive in your womb and bear a son, and you shall call his name Jesus." . . .

And Mary said to the angel, "How will this be, since I am a virgin?"

And the angel answered her, "The Holy Spirit will come upon you, and the power of the Most High will overshadow you; therefore the child to be born will be called holy—the Son of God. And behold, your relative Elizabeth in her old age has also conceived a son, and this is the sixth month with her who was called barren. For nothing will be impossible with God."

And Mary said, "Behold, I am the servant of the Lord; let it be."

Luke 1:30–31, 34–38 ESV

The angel Gabriel's first words to Mary, a young virgin, were "Do not be afraid." Angels are powerful beings; in the Bible their appearance overwhelms people. Though all Jewish girls knew the prophecy that someday a virgin would give birth, at this moment the news must have seemed surreal. But despite the angel's awesome presence, Mary stayed focused on his message.

Women understand conception, pregnancy, and birth. Mary listened to the angel and then questioned how God would cause her to be pregnant. She asked the obvious question and the angel answered. It sounded so amazing that Gabriel also gave her more miraculous information: Mary's relative Elizabeth, an older woman, was pregnant. Verifying this news would confirm the angel's message, but Mary doesn't seem to have needed confirmation.

Most women choose their baby's name, but Mary didn't get that choice. She knew her purpose and remained steadfast in spite of the threat that Joseph, her fiancé, might end their engagement. She agreed to be God's servant without knowing everything about her future or her son's future. We don't need to know the details about our future when we trust our days to God.

COSTLY CHOICES

Is there anyone here who, planning to build a new house, doesn't first sit down and figure the cost so you'll know if you can complete it? If you only get the foundation laid and then run out of money, you're going to look pretty foolish. Everyone passing by will poke fun at you: "He started something he couldn't finish."

Or can you imagine a king going into battle against another king without first deciding whether it is possible with his ten thousand troops to face the twenty thousand troops of the other? And if he decides he can't, won't he send an emissary and work out a truce?

Simply put, if you're not willing to take what is dearest to you, whether plans or people, and kiss it good-bye, you can't be my disciple.

Luke 14:28–33 MSG

We would look foolish if we started dressing and putting on makeup but ran out of time and left the house with only one eye done or without our shoes. Foreclosures and bankruptcies happen too often as people buy homes without solid financial plans. We want something unaffordable to start with and don't count the cost to keep it up. Poor planning leads to serious consequences.

Before beginning a task, we need to know how long it will take and what work or money is involved.

In the middle of talking about what it takes to be his follower, Jesus warned us that those who can't finish what they start look foolish. When we commit our lives to loving God, we need to consider our commitment to Christ of more value than favorite pastimes or even our loved ones. If we begin a ministry or say we will pray for someone's need, we must understand what is involved, stick with it, and complete the task. Understand your talents and God's vision for your life and evaluate what proposed tasks and projects require before you agree to take on a new commitment.

PRAYER RELEASES POWER

Jesus went to a mountain to pray. He spent the whole night in prayer to God. When it was day, he called his disciples. He chose twelve of them and called them apostles. They were Simon (whom Jesus named Peter) and Simon's brother Andrew, James, John, Philip, Bartholomew, Matthew, Thomas, James (son of Alphaeus), Simon (who was called the Zealot), Judas (son of James), and Judas Iscariot (who became a traitor). . . .

A large crowd of his disciples and many other people were there. They had come from all over Judea, Jerusalem, and the seacoast of Tyre and Sidon. They wanted to hear him and be cured of their diseases. Those who were tormented by evil spirits were cured. The entire crowd was trying to touch him because power was coming from him and curing all of them.

Luke 6:12–19 GOD'S WORD

Wherever you find a thriving church or Christian family, you will probably find prayer warriors behind the scenes. Prayer releases power and energy but is often underestimated.

Jesus spent a night praying. The next day he decisively chose his disciples. Jesus had healed many people in Capernaum some time earlier. News of the healings spread, and a crowd pressed in to get near and be healed. The following day many people came to hear Jesus and received healing. His prayer released great power and discernment. Jesus prayed often, talking to God the Father and asking him for strength. The people saw a difference in him and wanted to touch him because his power healed many diseases.

Now news travels by "word of mouse" through social networks as well as by word of mouth. Before you praise someone's preaching or healing, find out how much prayer is behind the minister, for that's what releases God's power. Miracles happen, especially when people pray. When we wake during the night, it might be God nudging us to pray more. We should pray for our ministers, leaders, husbands, children, grandchildren, and any projects we want to see succeed.

Choose to Love

Love your enemies, and be good to everyone who hates you. . . .

If someone slaps you on one cheek, don't stop that person from slapping you on the other cheek. If someone wants to take your coat, don't try to keep back your shirt. Give to everyone who asks and don't ask people to return what they have taken from you. Treat others just as you want to be treated. . . .

If you are kind only to someone who is kind to you, will God be pleased with you for that? Even sinners are kind to people who are kind to them. . . .

But love your enemies and be good to them. Lend without expecting to be paid back. Then you will get a great reward, and you will be the true children of God in heaven.

Luke 6:27, 29–31, 33, 35 CEV

❋

Even people who don't know God are kind to people who are kind to them. A woman stands out if she is kind to people who hurt her, cheat her, or take advantage of her. Jesus' words in this passage from the Sermon on the Mount remind us that those who practice unconditional love are called God's children and will be rewarded in heaven. Life and love should not be measured by what we get or by fair exchanges but by what we give. We can choose to act with love rather than react with our first emotional response—usually something negative.

When someone hurts you, close your eyes and think about how you wish she had behaved and act that way toward this person. When someone asks to borrow something, lend it with the thought that God is asking you to consider it a gift the person may never return. Don't keep a record of what you do for others but continue to love and be kind. God will watch and keep track of your deeds. We might not always be thanked, but our love and kindness have potential to soften hearts.

TIMELY CHOICES

The kingdom of heaven will be like ten virgins who took their lamps and went to meet the bridegroom. . . .

For when the foolish took their lamps, they took no oil with them, but the wise took flasks of oil with their lamps. . . .

But at midnight there was a cry, "Here is the bridegroom! Come out to meet him."

Then all those virgins rose and trimmed their lamps. And the foolish said to the wise,

"Give us some of your oil, for our lamps are going out."

But the wise answered, saying, "Since there will not be enough for us and for you, go rather to the dealers and buy for yourselves." And while they were going to buy, the bridegroom came, and those who were ready went in with him to the marriage feast, and the door was shut.

Matthew 25:1, 3–4, 6–10 ESV

Have you ever run out of gas and missed an appointment? Forget to bring directions or recharge your cell phones, then raced off to a party without being prepared? Needed to cook for unexpected guests but not had on hand all the ingredients? Consequences follow when we run out of gas or get lost, and we miss out. Wise women develop habits of readiness—they check the gas gauge, recharge their phones regularly, and stock their pantries well.

Jesus told this parable after he had been teaching about the end of time. No one knows when the end will come, he said, so we should always be ready, like the wise women who had extra oil for their lamps. Jesus used the story to teach us about heaven. He compared heaven to a great wedding feast and the preparations to having lamp fuel and being present when the bridegroom arrived.

Light is often used to represent the light of Christ, and Christians are called the lights of the world. Our lamps remain lit and ready for Christ's return when we spend time daily with God and fill our hearts with God's love.

Precious Knitting

You formed my inward parts; you knitted me together in my mother's womb. I praise you, for I am fearfully and wonderfully made. Wonderful are your works; my soul knows it very well. My frame was not hidden from you, when I was being made in secret, intricately woven in the depths of the earth. Your eyes saw my unformed substance; in your book were written, every one of them, the days that were formed for me, when as yet there were none of them. . . .

Search me, O God, and know my heart! Try me and know my thoughts! And see if there be any grievous way in me, and lead me in the way everlasting!

Psalm 139:13–16, 23–24 ESV

The debate about when life begins rages on as people debate whether an embryo is a baby or a blob of tissue. The Bible makes it clear that within the womb is human life and that God is knitting together every cell and planning a future for each person he creates. For God, life begins at conception, and so does his interaction with us.

King David wrote this psalm. He lost a baby and valued life. He sought God with his whole heart, wanting to know God better. God knows us the best and can search our hearts and minds because he formed them. God can lead us in how we should live and what choices we should make. He made time and days for us and designed a pattern for our lives when he fashioned our bodies. He saw each of us in our least form, as an embryo, and never considered us a worthless blob.

God wants us to trust that we are exactly the way he wanted us to be, down to our little toenails. Ask God to show you any faults or sin and to reveal his plans for you. Listen for his response.

CHILDREN ARE GIFTS

Without the help of the LORD it is useless to build a home or to guard a city. It is useless to get up early and stay up late in order to earn a living. God takes care of his own, even while they sleep.

Children are a blessing and a gift from the LORD. Having a lot of children to take care of you in your old age is like a warrior with a lot of arrows. The more you have, the better off you will be, because they will protect you when your enemies attack with arguments.

Psalm 127 CEV

Countries that rely on farming usually have citizens with large families, especially undeveloped countries. Many hands help with the work, and each child is viewed as another blessing, another member of the team. Children transform a house into a home and a couple into a family.

This passage is a well-known psalm that children are often taught to help them understand how precious they are to God. Children are gifts from God, blessings to bring joy.

Modern medicine and contraceptives allow women to plan for children and to limit how many we have. It's complex to think about whether women should choose when and how many children to have or to let God choose and bless us with the children he wants to give us. The psalm indicates that the more children families raise, the better off they'll be. More children will provide more protection and a larger nuclear community.

In more-industrialized societies, many people view children as inconvenient and can hardly wait for a child to start school and be occupied to free up their own time. But we should view children and choices regarding life from God's perspective and value each individual.

CHOOSE FULLNESS OF LIFE

An excellent wife who can find? She is far more precious than jewels. The heart of her husband trusts in her, and he will have no lack of gain. . . . She rises while it is yet night and provides food for her household and portions for her maidens. She considers a field and buys it; with the fruit of her hands she plants a vineyard. She dresses herself with strength and makes her arms strong. She perceives that her merchandise is profitable. Her lamp does not go out at night. . . .

She opens her hand to the poor and reaches out her hands to the needy.

Proverbs 31:10–11, 15–18, 20 ESV

Women want to do it all: raise a family, build a career, and enjoy friends, shopping, and fun. Solomon, the wisest man ever, observed and wrote about a woman with a full life. This woman balanced and maximized her time. She raised a family, dabbled in real estate, helped the poor, ran a business, gardened, and fed and clothed her family—and people praised her. She appears to have worked from home but interacted with merchants and others. One word, *willing*, describes her attitude. She chose her activities and wanted to complete projects. She thrived. She also hired help and gave them good portions, or pay, to retain them. She worked hard, rising early and staying up late when she needed to—not much TV time for her!

Her husband trusted her completely, indicating a happy marriage. She had strength, so she must have followed a healthy diet and exercised. She made good choices in her marriage partner and career.

This woman shows we can live a full life. It's probably not done overnight and relies on making wise decisions, such as when to hire help. Like growing a garden, balance takes time and continual commitment.

STAY ON TRACK

You won't cry anymore. The LORD will certainly have pity on you when you cry for help. As soon as he hears you, he will answer you. The Lord may give you troubles and hardships. But your teacher will no longer be hidden from you. You will see your teacher with your own eyes.

You will hear a voice behind you saying, "This is the way. Follow it, whether it turns to the right or to the left."

Then you will dishonor your silver-plated idols and your gold-covered statues. You will throw them away like clothing ruined by stains. You will say to them, "Get out!"

The Lord will give you rain for the seed that you plant in the ground, and the food that the ground provides will be rich and nourishing.

Isaiah 30:19–23 GOD'S WORD

✳

Do you cry easily? Tears can be cathartic. Tears flow from the heart, and our tears touch God's heart. He has pity on us when we are hurting, and he responds as soon as we cry. When we have had a good cry, we are more ready to listen.

This chapter of Isaiah's prophecies addresses problems the Israelites encountered when they turned to Egypt for help against their Assyrian enemies, who had attacked them. God warned his people not to seek help from Egypt, a country that worshipped idols. He wanted to be their help, but they ignored God's advice. Isaiah prophesied for many years and continually tried to turn people's hearts and loyalty back to God.

When we really listen and hear God's voice, nothing else will match it. However, we often cry out for help to the wrong people and seek solace in the wrong places. God's direction will make us realize that our idols are worthless. God continually shows us he's in charge as he waters the earth with rain and causes food to grow. His faithful care of the earth is a reminder that he will always provide for us.

A GREAT DISH

In a large house some dishes are made of gold or silver, while others are made of wood or clay. Some of these are special, and others are not. That's also how it is with people. The ones who stop doing evil and make themselves pure will become special. Their lives will be holy and pleasing to their Master, and they will be able to do all kinds of good deeds.

Run from temptations that capture young people. Always do the right thing. Be faithful, loving, and easy to get along with. Worship with people whose hearts are pure. Stay away from stupid and senseless arguments. These only lead to trouble, and God's servants must not be troublemakers. They must be kind to everyone, and they must be good teachers and very patient.

2 Timothy 2:20–24 CEV

This passage of Paul's letter to Timothy compares believers to the containers within a large house. All are made of different materials and all have different uses. The house is our community or church family, and the material our "container" is made of, Paul says, is up to us—determined by how we act, by what we think and do.

God calls women to be golden or sterling silver containers, polished and given places of honor in the house. In contrast, evil people don't serve honorable purposes. We want to be, instead, women God chooses to be used for ministry.

These words to Timothy also remind us how treasured people act. Desire a pure heart, not silver- or gold-plated but pure from the inside out. Make choices that reflect this desire. Start doing what pleases God. Women with pure hearts are kind, patient, and not argumentative.

Just as leaving gold and silver exposed to the air causes them to tarnish, being tempted exposes women to bad choices. Purity and kindness are choices. Not arguing when we disagree is also a choice. We make ourselves pure daily through God's forgiveness and obeying God.

DOUBLE SHIFTS

He stayed with them and worked, for they were tentmakers by trade. And he reasoned in the synagogue every Sabbath, and tried to persuade Jews and Greeks. . . .

And when they opposed and reviled him, he shook out his garments and said to them, "Your blood be on your own heads! I am innocent. From now on I will go to the Gentiles."

And he left there and went to the house of a man named Titius Justus, a worshiper of God. His house was next door to the synagogue. . . .

And the Lord said to Paul one night in a vision, "Do not be afraid, but go on speaking and do not be silent, for I am with you, and no one will attack you to harm you, for I have many in this city who are my people."

Acts 18:3–4, 6–7, 9–10 ESV

Women today lead busy lives, with careers, families, and ministries. Do you rush from daytime to evening activities? Double shifts and full lives are not new, as we can see in this passage.

Paul, a tentmaker by trade, preached and evangelized by day and made tents in his spare time in order to support himself. Paul had a physical affliction too, so he had to cope with that. When people opposed him, Paul changed his focus from reaching Jews to reaching Gentiles. God gave Paul a vision to encourage him and promised to protect him.

When our lives are busy, we need to continually evaluate our choices. We may need to adjust or make changes in response to God or circumstances. Paul's real ministry became reaching the Gentiles. God allowed opposition to redirect Paul.

When problems plague our busy days, it might be God's way of asking us to rethink our choices and our lives' direction. Like Paul, as long as we are following God, we need not fear harm, for God will be with us. God will also reveal other Christians with whom we can network to share the work and our needs.

Choosing Life

The king of Egypt said to the Hebrew midwives, one of whom was named Shiphrah and the other Puah, "When you serve as midwife to the Hebrew women and see them on the birthstool, if it is a son, you shall kill him, but if it is a daughter, she shall live."

But the midwives feared God and did not do as the king of Egypt commanded them, but let the male children live.

So the king of Egypt called the midwives and said to them, "Why have you done this, and let the male children live?"

The midwives said to Pharaoh, "Because the Hebrew women are not like the Egyptian women, for they are vigorous and give birth before the midwife comes to them.". . .

And because the midwives feared God, he gave them families.

Exodus 1:15–19, 21 ESV

※

Before you were born, people made choices. Someone chose to give you birth and someone chose to raise you. It might have been the same people. The Egyptian midwives in this passage faced a choice regarding life.

The family of Jacob had arrived in Egypt during a famine, when God reconnected them with Joseph, Jacob's son, whom they had sold into slavery many years before. Joseph now ruled Egypt under the pharaoh and had stored grain to save lives during the famine.

Life changed after Joseph died and other rulers took over. The Egyptians feared the Israelites would become powerful and take over their country. For nearly four hundred years, the Israelites multiplied and prospered despite their slavery. Then Pharaoh tried to kill the male Hebrew babies and oppressed the people even more.

The midwives feared God more than the wrath of Pharaoh. They couldn't bring themselves to destroy life that God created. They chose to deceive Pharaoh with lies rather than turn from God. God blessed the women for preserving life and gave them families. God values life and supports people who choose life.

CREATIVE, RESPONSIBLE LIVING

Live creatively, friends. If someone falls into sin, forgivingly restore him, saving your critical comments for yourself. You might be needing forgiveness before the day's out. Stoop down and reach out to those who are oppressed. Share their burdens, and so complete Christ's law. If you think you are too good for that, you are badly deceived.

Make a careful exploration of who you are and the work you have been given, and then sink yourself into that. Don't be impressed with yourself. Don't compare yourself with others. Each of you must take responsibility for doing the creative best you can with your own life.

Be very sure now, you who have been trained to a self-sufficient maturity, that you enter into a generous common life with those who have trained you, sharing all the good things

Galatians 6:1–6 MSG

꽃

Our God is a creative God, and he made us to be creative as well. In our world are many options for creativity. God wants us to be creative and to apply creativity first to our relationships.

Paul wrote a letter to the church in Galatia to emphasize grace—undeserved kindness from God. In this passage, Paul urges passing on God's grace as we relate to people. God forgives us and we should forgive others. It's not a matter of whether someone deserves forgiveness; it's that we should think more creatively, like God the Creator, show others that forgiveness is possible, and trust we'll be forgiven when needed.

God wants us to think like him about our work as well. When he made the world, he paused and enjoyed it. We too should enjoy our creativity. Joy in work is good if it doesn't turn into competition or pride. Looking at work from fresh perspectives helps us think of new ideas to improve our work or develop new methods. Putting design and personality into work gives it our brand, our touch. Living creatively is confidently applying our talents to all we do.

THE ANSWER IS BLOWIN' IN THE WIND

There was a man named Nicodemus, a Jewish religious leader who was a Pharisee. . . .

Jesus [said], "I tell you the truth, unless you are born again, you cannot see the Kingdom of God."

"What do you mean?" exclaimed Nicodemus. "How can an old man go back into his mother's womb and be born again?"

Jesus replied, "I assure you, no one can enter the Kingdom of God without being born of water and the Spirit. . . . So don't be surprised when I say, 'You must be born again.' The wind blows wherever it wants. Just as you can hear the wind but can't tell where it comes from or where it is going, so you can't explain how people are born of the Spirit."

"How are these things possible?" Nicodemus asked.

John 3:1, 3–5, 7–9 NLT

Gentle breezes rustle trees while hurricane-force winds topple houses and tall buildings. Scientists who study wind explain that wind doesn't have a specific start or end point because it's a dynamic system. Whenever there's a pressure difference between two places, air moves to equalize the pressure. Moving air creates wind.

Jesus spoke to a Jewish leader one night and compared some attributes of the Holy Spirit to the wind. We can't see the wind or explain how people are born of the Spirit. That caused Nicodemus to question spiritual rebirth. This educated leader who studied the Scriptures tried to analyze thoughts that sounded difficult to understand. Jesus wanted him to move from trying to comprehend mysteries of God to believing.

The unseen wind helps us understand other unseen forces, such as the Holy Spirit. How we are reborn of the Spirit is not as important as knowing that we *are* and that God changes us on the inside and provides a special Helper to remain with us. We need not puzzle over how such things are possible—we can simply be thankful that God brings change and thank God for his constant presence.

NEW 'TUDES

I order you to stop living like stupid, godless people. Their minds are in the dark, and they are stubborn and ignorant and have missed out on the life that comes from God. They no longer have any feelings about what is right, and they are so greedy that they do all kinds of indecent things.

But that isn't what you were taught about Jesus Christ. He is the truth, and you heard about him and learned about him. You were told that your foolish desires will destroy you and that you must give up your old way of life with all its bad habits. Let the Spirit change your way of thinking and make you into a new person. You were created to be like God, and so you must please him and be truly holy.

Ephesians 4:17–24 CEV

At a buffet we're tempted to load our plates with food. We could take a little at a time and return for a little more, eating moderately. But greed often wins out as we pile up tasty dishes. Greed is just one symptom of caring more about satisfying our pleasures than behaving in a godly, and healthy, manner. Greed for food can lead to weight gain and poor health. Greed for things can lead to overspending and other bad habits. God calls us to make better choices.

Paul wrote this letter to encourage Christians to grow spiritually and become more like Christ. We need to examine our habits and take an inventory of what we do with our money and time to discover what habits we need to change. We must give up ways that hurt us. The first step isn't a diet or a budget but turning to the Holy Spirit and studying how Christ wants us to live.

The Spirit can change our desires and our thinking to view life from God's perspective. With the Spirit's help we can release bad habits, unhealthy spending, and the need to have everything we see.

PATTERNS AND REPETITIONS

We must keep going in the direction that we are now headed.

My friends, I want you to follow my example and learn from others who closely follow the example we set for you.

I often warned you that many people are living as enemies of the cross of Christ. And now with tears in my eyes, I warn you again that they are headed for hell! They worship their stomachs and brag about the disgusting things they do. All they can think about are the things of this world.

But we are citizens of heaven and are eagerly waiting for our Savior to come from there. Our Lord Jesus Christ has power over everything, and he will make these poor bodies of ours like his own glorious body.

Philippians 3:16–21 CEV

Some people wake up, exercise, shower, and read the Bible. Others grab coffee, prepare for the day, and go without a prayer. We are creatures of habit with patterns that fill our days. God desires that we build good habits and patterns that reflect our faith in a future with him.

In this passage, Paul helps us understand the value of choosing Christ as the central focus of our lives. Paul shed tears for unbelievers, especially those who are proud of the wrong that they do. He had no envy of people rich in worldly possessions, because he looked toward heaven and not earthly pleasure or security. Have you let go of chasing after trends and accumulating possessions? Do you love your neighbors, family, and others who don't know Christ enough to weep for their souls?

In contrast to the sorrow we feel for the lost, we also have joy and eagerness for our future with Christ in our resurrection bodies. Do you feel eagerness and joy when you think of eternal life with God? Heaven is the direction we are headed, and our life choices should be made based upon our citizenship there.

LAZINESS INVITES CALAMITY

You lazy fool, look at an ant. Watch it closely; let it teach you a thing or two. Nobody has to tell it what to do. All summer it stores up food; at harvest it stockpiles provisions. So how long are you going to laze around doing nothing? How long before you get out of bed? A nap here, a nap there, a day off here, a day off there, sit back, take it easy—do you know what comes next? Just this: You can look forward to a dirt-poor life, poverty your permanent houseguest!

Riffraff and rascals . . . their perverse minds are always cooking up something nasty, always stirring up trouble. Catastrophe is just around the corner for them, a total smashup, their lives ruined beyond repair.

Proverbs 6:6–15 MSG

Anyone who has battled ants knows they are industrious and persistent. It's amazing how quickly these teeny insects get into all sorts of items in a pantry or picnic basket. They carry more than their own weight, up to fifty times! They always work as a team for the good of their community. Ants maximize their efforts during harvest-times to prepare for the lean times.

We don't know what challenges we'll face tomorrow, next year, or in another decade, but we can use today's abilities and health to prepare for the future. Our choices should include decisions for the future. We exercise to have a healthier body now and for greater physical strength in the future. We save to create a hedge against future financial burdens. We study and train to prepare for a future career and continue to study to progress in it. We plan meals, shop, and stock a pantry or freezer to provide food for the coming days. We memorize Scripture so God's words will strengthen us when we feel tempted or upset or when we face a crisis. Planning for the future starts with choosing to make the most of every day.

NEVER LOST

You discern my thoughts from afar. You search out my path and my lying down and are acquainted with all my ways. Even before a word is on my tongue, behold, O LORD, you know it altogether. . . .

Where shall I go from your Spirit? Or where shall I flee from your presence? If I ascend to heaven, you are there! If I make my bed in Sheol, you are there! If I take the wings of the morning and dwell in the uttermost parts of the sea, even there your hand shall lead me, and your right hand shall hold me. . . . Even the darkness is not dark to you.

Psalm 139:2–4, 7–10, 12 ESV

It's fun for children to outwit us with a new hiding place. Babies love to play peek-a-boo. Hiding seems natural. But children also hide after they do something naughty. They don't want to admit what they did or face the consequences of their actions.

Adults also try to hide and cover up sins. This started long ago with Adam and Eve. But God sees all and knows all. We can't even hide our thoughts or secret longings from him! During our most joyful, heavenly moments, God is with us. He is also with us in our deepest despair, our failures, and the moments we have sinned.

God's words in this familiar psalm of David bring comfort. God is more than with us—he is also *for* us. He remains close and is always willing to lead us out of trouble. No sin is too dark to remain hidden from God. His forgiveness dispels the darkness of any sin. No matter what we have done, God knows and still wants to be with us. Our choice is to acknowledge that God knows all about us and then to accept his direction and help.

PASSION AND PURITY

The Song—best of all songs—Solomon's song!

Kiss me—full on the mouth! Yes! For your love is better than wine, headier than your aromatic oils. The syllables of your name murmur like a meadow brook. No wonder everyone loves to say your name!

Take me away with you! Let's run off together! An elopement with my King-Lover! We'll celebrate, we'll sing, we'll make great music. Yes! For your love is better than vintage wine. Everyone loves you—of course! And why not?

I am weathered but still elegant, oh, dear sisters in Jerusalem. . . . My brothers . . . made me care for the face of the earth, but I had no time to care for my own face.

Song of Songs 1:1–6 MSG

❋

The Song of Songs is a love song written by King Solomon and full of poetic images. It begins from the woman's perspective, longing for kisses from her man and replaying his name in her mind. The woman is in a vineyard and declares that his love is better than wine, and thus better than anything else she's experienced.

The woman has worked outdoors and is concerned about her tanned skin, weathered from the sun. Somehow when there's a man we desire, there's a need to look our best and we often doubt our appeal.

God wired us to love a man and with passion for sex. This woman asked to elope. She's concerned about purity, even in the height of passion, and believes sex is for marriage.

The work in the vineyard has made the woman disciplined. She understands the problems of letting weeds grow and keeping the vines pure and untangled. Striving for purity, like caring for a weed-free garden, takes work, but the effort is worth it.

Purity begins before a woman meets a man, for it begins with a disciplined life and the choice to be committed to purity.

ANGRY ENOUGH TO KILL

The LORD looked with favor on Abel and his offering, but on Cain and his offering he did not look with favor. So Cain was very angry, and his face was downcast.

Then the LORD said to Cain, "Why are you angry? Why is your face downcast? If you do what is right, will you not be accepted? But if you do not do what is right, sin is crouching at your door; it desires to have you, but you must master it."

Now Cain said to his brother Abel, "Let's go out to the field." And while they were in the field, Cain attacked his brother Abel and killed him.

Then the LORD said to Cain, "Where is your brother Abel?"

"I don't know," he replied. "Am I my brother's keeper?"

Genesis 4:4–9 NIV

Looking at someone else's success can lead to problems. We may think another person is more favored than us, and that leads to jealousy. Cain and Abel, the first sons of Adam and Eve, experienced this. Cain seethed with anger when God accepted Abel's offering and not his own. They both had offered God the fruit of their labor, but Abel gave the best he had and made his offering with faith (see Heb. 11:4), and Cain gave only a token gift. But God didn't treat them differently. Cain gave some produce while Abel gave his best lambs. God told Cain to do what was right and made no mention of Abel's gift. Evidently Cain knew what to do but chose to give in to jealousy and anger. He killed his brother Abel instead of making things right with God. God knew what Cain did.

The Bible doesn't give the reason God rejected Cain's offering but indicates that Cain could give a more acceptable one. God doesn't compare what we do or give to what others do or give. He wants us to do what is right, to listen to him, and to offer him our best.

TASTEFULLY VISIBLE

One day as he saw the crowds gathering, Jesus went up on the mountainside and sat down. His disciples gathered around him, and he began to teach them. . . .

"You are the salt of the earth. But what good is salt if it has lost its flavor? Can you make it salty again? It will be thrown out and trampled underfoot as worthless.

"You are the light of the world—like a city on a hilltop that cannot be hidden. No one lights a lamp and then puts it under a basket. Instead, a lamp is placed on a stand, where it gives light to everyone in the house. In the same way, let your good deeds shine out for all to see, so that everyone will praise your heavenly Father."

Matthew 5:1–2, 13–16 NLT

During one of the most well-known sermons of Jesus, the Sermon on the Mount, Jesus compared believers to salt and light. These analogies bring insight to how we should live.

A little salt flavors and preserves food, but too much can overwhelm the taste. Salt helps maintain the right fluid balance in our bodies, important for many bodily processes. But too much salt increases blood pressure, the risk of eye diseases, and the risk of stroke. Salt loses its flavor when it is diluted or contaminated. Faithful Christians represent truth and act as salt in our families and communities when we do what is right and point to Jesus with our actions and gentle words. Too much "salt"—self-righteous talk and actions—overwhelms and turns others away.

Sunlight energizes us, provides vitamin D, and enhances our immune systems, preventing infections. When we need to see in the dark, light is what we need. God wants Christians to be light to those around us, visible like a beacon that guides a ship or the sun that brings growth.

Salt and light—both add love to the lives of others and bring praise to God, our heavenly Father.

GENEROSITY TRIUMPHS

They gave a dinner for him there. Martha served, and Lazarus was one of those reclining with him at the table. Mary therefore took a pound of expensive ointment made from pure nard, and anointed the feet of Jesus and wiped his feet with her hair. The house was filled with the fragrance of the perfume. But Judas Iscariot, one of his disciples (he who was about to betray him), said, "Why was this ointment not sold for three hundred denarii and given to the poor?" He said this, not because he cared about the poor, but because he was a thief. . . . Jesus said, "Leave her alone, so that she may keep it for the day of my burial. The poor you always have with you, but you do not always have me."

John 12:2–8 ESV

Some people are extravagant with gifts and have a knack for choosing just the right presents to delight those they love. Generous giving expresses our love, honor, or appreciation. Mary gave generously, not just with perfume that cost a year's wages but also with the time and love she spent as she gently massaged the nard on Jesus' feet and dried his feet with her hair. But as the house filled with the scent, Judas sniffed the air and grimaced. Every whiff must have annoyed him. He saw the perfume in terms of money, not love.

For Jesus, the heart and generosity always triumph, especially in giving to God. Throughout the history of the church, the money poured into stained-glass windows and elaborate church architecture comes under scrutiny, as it should. Giving must always be done to express love for God, never for show.

Jesus told Judas to leave Mary alone. He never indulged in comparisons or stopped an expression of love for God. Jesus also knew his crucifixion would come soon, and he approved of Mary's making the most of the time she had left with him. She chose to invest in God.

DIVINE APPOINTMENT

Suddenly Jesus met them. "Greetings," he said. They came to him, clasped his feet and worshiped him. Then Jesus said to them, "Do not be afraid. Go and tell my brothers to go to Galilee; there they will see me." . . .

Then the eleven disciples went to Galilee, to the mountain where Jesus had told them to go. When they saw him, they worshiped him; but some doubted. Then Jesus came to them and said, "All authority in heaven and on earth has been given to me. Therefore go and make disciples of all nations, baptizing them in the name of the Father and of the Son and of the Holy Spirit, and teaching them to obey everything I have commanded you. And surely I am with you always, to the very end of the age."

Matthew 28:9–10, 16–20 NIV

The day Jesus rose from the dead, he met and spoke to women first. He met the women in this passage and gave them a message for the disciples—"Tell them to go to Galilee." He set up a divine appointment with his closest followers.

The women worshipped Jesus and touched his feet. Most women like to touch and be engaged in worship. It's an expression involving mind, body, and soul. They evidently delivered the message; the disciples met with Jesus for one of the most important appointments of their lives. Jesus commissioned them to baptize, teach, and disciple believers. Baptism brings people into the family of God. Teaching shares how to live a Christian life. Discipling trains a follower to maturity. Jesus gave another glimpse of the unity of the Trinity when he named Father, Son, and Holy Spirit. And then he said he would be with them—and thus with us—always.

Some doubted in the very presence of the risen Christ, and Jesus didn't argue with them. Doubting continues today, as does the commission to share the news of Jesus. We can choose to doubt or to believe, worship, and follow God.

CHOOSE HOSPITALITY

A woman named Martha received and welcomed Him into her house.

And she had a sister named Mary, who seated herself at the Lord's feet and was listening to His teaching.

But Martha [overly occupied and too busy] was distracted with much serving; and she came up to Him and said, Lord, is it nothing to You that my sister has left me to serve alone? Tell her then to help me [to lend a hand and do her part along with me]!

But the Lord replied to her by saying, Martha, Martha, you are anxious and troubled about many things. There is need of only one or but a few things. Mary has chosen the good portion [that which is to her advantage], which shall not be taken away from her.

Luke 10:38–42 AMP

The account of Mary and Martha is well-known. Martha, with her type A personality, welcomed Jesus, and then hustled and bustled to serve him a perfect meal. Mary, with the opposite of Martha's personality, sat at Jesus' feet and listened. Martha sought Jesus' help to gain control over her sister, but Jesus didn't fall into Martha's trap.

"Martha, Martha." Jesus called her name twice to get her attention. This busy lady wasn't a good listener. Her goals took all her focus. Jesus acknowledged Martha's feelings of anxiety and worry; then he gently suggested she let go and realize that all her work wasn't necessary. He didn't require a fancy banquet. He wasn't a high-maintenance guest. Quietly he coaxed her into making a better choice, and he used Mary as his example. She sat with him, the guest, and listened.

Hospitality involves having an open heart that listens. How often we invite Jesus into our hearts and lives but then want to manipulate him into solving our problems and responding to our needs. He will help us, of course, but he says the best choice is simply to spend time listening and learning from him.

THE TRUE GIVER

Beware of the scribes, who like to walk about in long robes and love to be saluted [with honor] in places where people congregate and love the front and best seats in the synagogues and places of distinction at feasts. . . .

They will receive the greater condemnation (the heavier sentence, the severer punishment). . . .

Looking up, [Jesus] saw the rich people putting their gifts into the treasury.

And He saw also a poor widow putting in two mites (copper coins).

And He said, Truly I say to you, this poor widow has put in more than all of them; for they all gave out of their abundance (their surplus); but she has contributed out of her lack and her want, putting in all that she had on which to live.

Luke 20:46–47; 21:1–4 AMP

The setting for the event in this passage is the area of the temple called the court of women, near the temple treasury. Several boxes sat in a row to receive offerings. This public spot, where anyone could come, allowed people to be seen as they gave and to watch as others gave. Jesus had just spoken about people who dressed up and enjoyed being honored, whose actions were motivated by the desire to be noticed, when a poor widow tossed in a few small coins.

People who saw the meager offering might have sneered, if anyone besides Jesus noticed her at all, but she gave in spite of anyone seeing her poverty. She gave to God from her heart and not for show. She gave, as Jesus noted, all that she had.

When was the last time you checked your motives for giving or gave anonymously? It's not the amount we give that matters to God, but rather our willingness and spirit when we give. God values the sacrifices we make to give money or time and wants us to give willingly, with our hearts focused on him and not on impressing others.

Choosing to Stay

Near the cross of Jesus stood his mother, his mother's sister, Mary the wife of Clopas, and Mary Magdalene. When Jesus saw his mother there, and the disciple whom he loved standing nearby, he said to his mother, "Dear woman, here is your son," and to the disciple, "Here is your mother." From that time on, this disciple took her into his home.

Later, knowing that all was now completed, and so that the Scripture would be fulfilled, Jesus said, "I am thirsty." A jar of wine vinegar was there, so they soaked a sponge in it, put the sponge on a stalk of the hyssop plant, and lifted it to Jesus' lips. When he had received the drink, Jesus said, "It is finished." With that, he bowed his head and gave up his spirit.

John 19:25–30 NIV

It's hard to watch someone die, especially when death involves great pain. The Bible notes three women and one man who stayed near Jesus on the cross to the end. Jesus saw two of the people dearest to him: his mother and John, his beloved disciple. In his agony he considered his family and loved ones. Jesus asked Mary and John to care for each other as close family, as mother and son. He left this legacy of love as an example to his followers to love and care for one another like family.

Then Jesus returned his focus to his purpose and mentioned his thirst, to fulfill Scripture. He drank the wine vinegar, symbolic of the last cup of the Passover, and said, "It is finished." He had completed his mission.

Those who continued believing soon received a new mission to share all that happened and explain the meaning of Jesus' death and resurrection. Staying power, whether to see a mission through or to keep close to someone experiencing suffering, is a choice. It's not easy to continue on, but commitment calls us to remain hopeful and to stay even during the worst of times.

TALENTS AND CAREERS

All who are skilled among you are to come and make everything the LORD has commanded. . . .

See, the LORD has chosen Bezalel son of Uri, the son of Hur, of the tribe of Judah, and he has filled him with the Spirit of God, with skill, ability and knowledge in all kinds of crafts—to make artistic designs for work in gold, silver and bronze, to cut and set stones, to work in wood and to engage in all kinds of artistic craftsmanship. And he has given both him and Oholiab son of Ahisamach, of the tribe of Dan, the ability to teach others. He has filled them with skill to do all kinds of work as craftsmen, designers, embroiderers in blue, purple and scarlet yarn and fine linen, and weavers— all of them master craftsmen and designers.

Exodus 35:10, 30–35 NIV

※

After the Israelites left Egypt and slavery, God asked them to make him a tent for a dwelling place among them. He provided instructions for the woodworking, embroidery, and other artistic craftsmanship to be used. These requests gave people the opportunity to use their talents for God. He gave some the special skills and knowledge and some the ability to teach others and complete the tasks. Our Creator enjoys seeing us use our creative talents to help one another. Because we are made in his image, we all have creative abilities of one kind or another, and often our talents lead to satisfying careers. But talents have other applications too.

When God asks us to do anything, he will give us ability to perform the tasks. As we create beautiful works of art or decorate a room, we can remember that talent to create, to design, to use our hands comes from God. We glorify God by using our talents and creativity for godly purposes, whether creating games and projects for a Sunday school class or ministry, helping to landscape church grounds, or decorating our homes to reflect his love and blessing.

STRESS & COMMUNITY

Life is seldom without stress or a struggle of some kind. The challenge is to overcome stress or to accept it. People in the Bible found inner strength they didn't know they had and discovered that God always supplied what they needed at just the right moment. As women face stress, we can learn more about God and ourselves, and these discoveries cause us to change for the better.

The best place to handle our stress is in relationship with other people. Women long to belong. We want to be together and build family, nurture friendships, and celebrate life with others. In and through community, we understand the need for lasting connection with God and with other people. Shared laughter, tears, and experiences reveal unique aspects of community.

As pressure and stress bear down on me, I find joy in your commands.

Psalm 119:143 NLT

FACING TROUBLES

Consider it a sheer gift, friends, when tests and challenges come at you from all sides. You know that under pressure, your faith-life is forced into the open and shows its true colors. So don't try to get out of anything prematurely. Let it do its work so you become mature and well-developed, not deficient in any way.

If you don't know what you're doing, pray to the Father. He loves to help. You'll get his help, and won't be condescended to when you ask for it. Ask boldly, believingly, without a second thought. People who "worry their prayers" are like wind-whipped waves. Don't think you're going to get anything from the Master that way, adrift at sea, keeping all your options open.

When down-and-outers get a break, cheer!

James 1:2–9 MSG

After losing a spouse, a woman often becomes more compassionate. She understands grief. As we overcome a problem, we develop our character. It's hard to consider troubles as a gift. We don't think of being robbed, losing a loved one, or being let go from our job as a gift. But God wants us to look through his eyes and see problems as gifts, or opportunities, that allow us to live what we believe and grow our faith.

The Letter of James, one of the earliest New Testament letters, encourages Christians to live faithfully and face persecution with trust in God. James uses the word *when* and not *if* as a reminder that we will all face hardships, or tests. We modify our lives and characters as we face challenges. A widow learns to live without the help of her spouse and develops strength. After a disaster people learn to be more thankful for what they have.

We must believe God will answer our prayers; otherwise we're like jellyfish who can't swim but are tossed around by the waves. We don't need to stress when we believe God is using our challenges to mature us.

Let Not Your Heart Be Troubled

"Do not let your hearts be troubled. Trust in God; trust also in me. In my Father's house are many rooms; if it were not so, I would have told you. I am going there to prepare a place for you. And if I go and prepare a place for you, I will come back and take you to be with me that you also may be where I am. You know the way to the place where I am going."

Thomas said to him, "Lord, we don't know where you are going, so how can we know the way?"

Jesus answered, "I am the way and the truth and the life. No one comes to the Father except through me. If you really knew me, you would know my Father as well."

John 14:1–7 NIV

An expectant mother prepares a room for her baby, wanting a comfortable and secure place for her child before the arrival date. Jesus is also preparing a place for us, making a room for each one of us where we will live with him.

Jesus gave us the ultimate reason not to dwell on trouble. He gave one of the few glimpses into heaven so we could focus on our ultimate joy. Anything else is temporary. We have security because we know where we're going and that we get there through faith in Jesus. This helps us look forward to the results and not the struggles along the way.

This is another well-known and often-memorized passage of the Bible because it so plainly lets us know that faith in Jesus gives us eternal life. We can trust Jesus and his promises because he is the truth. We can follow Jesus because he is the way. He wants us to focus on the eternal, including lasting relationships. He wants us to trust that he and the Father will always be with us. As we get closer to Jesus, we get to know the Father.

Stop Stressing, Start Asking

I tell you the truth, you will weep and mourn while the world rejoices. You will grieve, but your grief will turn to joy. A woman giving birth to a child has pain because her time has come; but when her baby is born she forgets the anguish because of her joy that a child is born into the world. So with you: Now is your time of grief, but I will see you again and you will rejoice, and no one will take away your joy. In that day you will no longer ask me anything. I tell you the truth, my Father will give you whatever you ask in my name. Until now you have not asked for anything in my name. Ask and you will receive, and your joy will be complete.

John 16:20–24 NIV

The fastest way to get a good job at a company where you want to work is through an employee there who gives your résumé to the president of the company. The boss listens to his good employee, so it's a valuable connection. Once hired, you are thankful for your friend and rejoice that your connection was profitable.

Jesus spoke the words in this passage after announcing that he would leave and later return. He had referred to his death and resurrection. The world would rejoice at his death while the disciples would grieve, but the disciples would have joy once Jesus returned.

Jesus did rise, so we know his words are true. He promised that one day we will no longer have to ask for anything, because we will have everything, a reference to heaven. Meanwhile, we don't need to worry because Jesus shared that the most effective way to pray is by using our connection to him. Jesus, as the treasured Son of God, connects us to God the Father, and Jesus' name will impact the Father's decisions and answers. We can freely use his name in prayers for God's will and expect great results.

AGAINST GOD'S WILL

Jonah ran away from the LORD and headed for Tarshish. . . . Then the LORD sent a great wind on the sea, and such a violent storm arose that the ship threatened to break up. . . .

The sailors . . . cast lots and the lot fell on Jonah. So they asked him, "Tell us, who is responsible for making all this trouble for us?" . . . He answered, "I am a Hebrew and I worship the LORD, the God of heaven, who made the sea and the land. . . . Pick me up and throw me into the sea, . . . and it will become calm. I know that it is my fault that this great storm has come upon you." . . . Then they took Jonah and threw him overboard, and the raging sea grew calm. . . .

But the LORD provided a great fish to swallow Jonah, and Jonah was inside the fish three days and three nights.

Jonah 1:3–4, 7–9, 12, 15, 17
NIV

※

When we deliberately turn from what we know God wants us to do, we will struggle and might cause hardships for many other people. This happens, for example, when a spouse or child turns from God and causes heartache and broken relationships.

In the Old Testament, God called Jonah to a mission, but Jonah ran the other way to hide from God. Jonah's choice led to problems for many people. When Jonah accepted the blame and the sailors tossed him into the sea, God calmed the waters and the ship and crew survived. When Jonah admitted his responsibility, he also chose to give his life to save the sailors. The sailors, amazed by God's power, worshipped God. God used Jonah's disobedience to change hearts. Jesus referred to Jonah's time in the fish to illustrate his coming time in the grave.

Jonah's time in the big fish gave him time to pray, think, and choose to obey God. Admitting our responsibility when we have turned away and admitting our sins restores our relationship with God and gives us another chance to obey him, accept his plans for our lives, and do what he calls us to do.

Pity Parties

He sat under [the plant] in [its] shade, till he should see what would become of the city. . . . But when dawn came up the next day, God appointed a worm that attacked the plant, so that it withered. When the sun rose, God appointed a scorching east wind, and the sun beat down on the head of Jonah so that he was faint. And he asked that he might die and said, "It is better for me to die than to live." But God said to Jonah, "Do you do well to be angry for the plant?" And he said, "Yes, I do well to be angry, angry enough to die." And the LORD said, "You pity the plant, for which you did not labor, nor did you make it grow. . . . And should not I pity Nineveh?"

Jonah 4:5, 7–11 ESV

Jonah finally obeyed God and saved the people of Nineveh from destruction and God's wrath. However, Jonah didn't like the Ninevites and was mad that God forgave them! He was so upset that he asked God to take his life. When Jonah had been inside a fish for three days, he prayed and received God's mercy, but he didn't want God's mercy to go to these non-Jewish people even though they repented of their wickedness. Jonah sat alone and held a pity party.

God used a little plant and a worm to illustrate Jonah's heart condition. God wanted Jonah to have compassion for the people and realize God would have been sad if he had destroyed them, especially since he created them. He wants us to understand that his mercy extends to all people.

In a pity party we focus on our feelings, complaints, and not getting what we want. We can look like a child having a temper tantrum. We have no reason for pity parties or desires for God to destroy unbelievers. Instead, God calls us to pray for sinners, love our enemies, share our faith to help save them, and trust in his mercy.

YIELDING TO NAGGING

Samson fell in love with a woman named Delilah, who lived in Sorek Valley. The five Philistine kings went to her and said, "Trick Samson into telling you why he is so strong and how we can overpower him, tie him up, and make him helpless. Each one of us will give you eleven hundred pieces of silver." . . .

So she said to him, "How can you say you love me, when you don't mean it? You've made a fool of me three times, and you still haven't told me what makes you so strong." She kept on asking him, day after day. He got so sick and tired of her bothering him about it that he finally told her the truth. . . .

The Philistines captured him and put his eyes out.

Judges 16:4–5, 15–17, 21 GNT

We often put our trust in the wrong people, forget to ask God for discernment, and yield to nagging. Even within the church, people can wear us down, wanting us to join an outreach project or serve in a ministry that is not where God wants us. We give in, instead of giving the question to God.

Samson was a judge of Israel. At times, his lust controlled him more than his faith. Delilah loved money more than Samson, and she nagged him until he caved in. Their example shows us the importance of making wise decisions in choosing a spouse or friend. Samson wanted to believe Delilah's lies and that she truly loved him. Each time he lied to her, the enemy failed to take away his power after using what Samson told Delilah. But Samson didn't learn from these betrayals. He finally gave in and revealed that his hair gave him strength. He lost his hair, his way, and his strength.

But Samson's hair grew back. He regained his strength, prayed for God's help, and used his might to defeat the enemy. Our failures become new opportunities to trust God!

DISCERNING CONS

Dear friends, do not believe every spirit, but test the spirits to see whether they are from God, because many false prophets have gone out into the world. This is how you can recognize the Spirit of God: Every spirit that acknowledges that Jesus Christ has come in the flesh is from God, but every spirit that does not acknowledge Jesus is not from God. This is the spirit of the antichrist, which you have heard is coming and even now is already in the world.

You, dear children, are from God and have overcome them, because the one who is in you is greater than the one who is in the world. They are from the world and therefore speak from the viewpoint of the world, and the world listens to them. We are from God.

1 John 4:1–6 NIV

Urban legends and scams remind us that people can be gullible. We tend to believe what we hear, and deceivers are happy to tell us what we want to hear. We want to think there is a quick way to get rich, or that this sin or that sin is really OK, so we can do what we want. But God calls us to be wise and not fall prey to scams, especially spiritual ones.

John wrote the letter from which this passage comes at a time when false teachers were spreading untruths, including the teaching that Jesus was not both fully God and fully human. One simple test helps us recognize God's truth: question what is being taught concerning Jesus. The answers should confirm that Jesus is God the Son, that he came to earth as a human being, and that he died and rose again.

Anyone who wants to sin would rather believe a liar than God. Evil is powerful, but God is more powerful. As we hear what seems too good to be true, we must remember that we are Christians and lean on God to discern truth.

SAME OLD PROBLEMS, BETTER HOPE

With most of them God was not pleased, for they were overthrown in the wilderness.

Now these things took place as examples for us, that we might not desire evil as they did. . . . We must not indulge in sexual immorality as some of them did, and twenty-three thousand fell in a single day. We must not put Christ to the test, as some of them did and were destroyed by serpents, nor grumble, as some of them did and were destroyed by the Destroyer. . . . No temptation has overtaken you that is not common to man. God is faithful, and he will not let you be tempted beyond your ability, but with the temptation he will also provide the way of escape, that you may be able to endure it.

1 Corinthians 10:5–6, 8–10, 13 ESV

Incurable sexually transmitted diseases, inability to bear children, and emotional scars can be consequences of sexual immorality, whether a spouse's sin or our own poor choices.

The Old Testament shows God working with his people to teach them about himself and how he responds. These verses refer to a time when the Israelites didn't trust God and feared the enemy. God let all the unbelievers die in the wilderness. When the Israelites followed the Moabites, worshipped with them, and indulged in sexual immorality, God took many Israelite lives. Other times when people complained or tested God's ability, God sent plagues to teach the importance of faithfulness.

We don't need to choose sin or believe lies that say we are too weak to resist. Contraceptives given to teens send a message that we aren't strong enough to resist temptation, but this passage proclaims that God will help us overcome any temptation and that we are strong enough to resist when we rely on him. We must stop when we first think of evil or feel tempted to do something God doesn't want us to do. That's the moment to pray for strength.

LURKING GREEN MONSTERS

You are jealous and argue with each other. This proves that you are not spiritual and that you are acting like the people of this world.

Some of you say that you follow me, and others claim to follow Apollos. Isn't that how ordinary people behave? Apollos and I are merely servants who helped you to have faith. It was the Lord who made it all happen. I planted the seeds, Apollos watered them, but God made them sprout and grow. What matters isn't those who planted or watered, but God who made the plants grow. The one who plants is just as important as the one who waters. And each one will be paid for what they do. Apollos and I work together for God, and you are God's garden and God's building.

1 Corinthians 3:3–9 CEV

Jealousy and arguing reveal that we are self-absorbed. Paul wrote a letter to Christians who argued over petty differences and debated over which Christian leader to follow. Paul had started the church at Corinth, planting seeds of faith. Then Apollos nurtured the growth as the leader who remained at the church. Paul and Apollos had the same goal and both served God. We are not on separate teams as Christians—we all follow God.

Jealousy begins when we make comparisons instead of looking toward the common goal and working together. Each woman is part of God's garden, and God wants her to grow, bloom, and produce fruit and add beauty to the garden. Unity comes when we stop wanting to be the best or believe we have made a better choice and realize we are all working for the same purpose. Unbelievers compete to fulfill personal desires, but Christians should cooperate and be happy for one another.

When personal desires are more important than unity, it shows we are not letting God be in control. We need to look to God for what he wants us to do and be happy to be part of his team.

MURDER IN THE FAMILY

As soon as King Ahaziah's mother Athaliah learned of her son's murder, she gave orders for all the members of the royal family of Judah to be killed. Ahaziah had a half sister, Jehosheba, who was married to a priest named Jehoiada. She secretly rescued one of Ahaziah's sons, Joash, took him away from the other princes who were about to be murdered and hid him and a nurse in a bedroom at the Temple. . . .

After waiting six years Jehoiada the priest decided that it was time to take action. He made a pact with five army officers. . . .

They all gathered in the Temple, and there they made a covenant with Joash, the king's son. Jehoiada said to them, "Here is the son of the late king. He is now to be king."

2 Chronicles 22:10–11; 23:1, 3 GNT

Ahaziah killed her grandchildren when her son, the king, died. She wanted power and the throne. How tragic for Jehosheba, Ahaziah's half sister, to experience such loss and violence! But in spite of her heartache, Jehosheba acted quickly to save one child, her nephew Joash. Their lives remained in danger. She hid Joash in the temple for six years. The temple was large but filled with people coming and going. Keeping a little boy quiet in the temple would have been difficult! At last Jehosheba's husband, the priest Jehoiada, found the courage to form a plan that ended with crowning Joash. How relieved Jehosheba must have felt at the good outcome!

Some people live lives of terrible tragedy within a dysfunctional family. When shocking things happen within families, God gives us comfort and strength. Having a church home also brings comfort. Most of us don't experience such severe violence, but many women live with abuse and need help as they struggle to find solutions. We can volunteer at shelters for women and children to help those who struggle. Giving homemade goodies, clothing, toiletries, and games and toys for children is one way to show we understand and care.

RAPE AND REVENGE

One day Dinah, the daughter of Jacob and Leah, went to visit some of the Canaanite women. When Shechem son of Hamor the Hivite, who was chief of that region, saw her, he took her and raped her. But he found the young woman so attractive that he fell in love with her and tried to win her affection. . . .

Shechem's father Hamor went out to talk with Jacob, just as Jacob's sons were coming in from the fields. When they heard about it, they were shocked and furious that Shechem had done such a thing and had insulted the people of Israel by raping Jacob's daughter. . . .

Three days later . . . two of Jacob's sons, Simeon and Levi, the brothers of Dinah, took their swords, went into the city without arousing suspicion, and killed all the men.

Genesis 34:1–3, 6–7, 25 GNT

Dinah, the only daughter of Jacob, innocently traveled to visit friends, but fun turned to tragedy when she was raped. She didn't cause this to happen, although some people might have said she should not have traveled alone but should have had her brothers or others guard her.

Rape devastates women and their families. Dinah's brothers plotted, deceived Hamor and the town's citizens, and sought revenge. They didn't stop with murder but captured all the women and children in the town and took their possessions as plunder. But such anger isn't a solution either. Their father, Jacob, angrily scolded his sons for taking revenge, but he ignored the rape. God told Jacob to move out of the area where these tragedies occurred.

Families often move away after a rape. Parents may try to cover up the rape in shame and victims avoid discussing or remembering it. Churches need to talk about rape and help women and families cope afterward. Dinah was never mentioned in the Bible again. The silence reflects how many women struggle silently. We need to show compassion for rape victims and encourage churches to offer support groups, counseling services, and classes on rape prevention.

NOT GUILTY, BUT JAILED

His master's wife became infatuated with Joseph and one day said, "Sleep with me."

He wouldn't do it. . . . "You're his wife, after all! How could I violate his trust and sin against God?" . . .

On one of these days he came to the house to do his work and none of the household servants happened to be there. She grabbed him by his cloak, saying, "Sleep with me!" He left his coat in her hand and ran out of the house. . . .

She kept his coat right there until his master came home. . . . She said, "The Hebrew slave, the one you brought to us, came after me and tried to use me for his plaything. When I yelled and screamed, he left his coat with me and ran outside." . . .

Joseph's master took him and threw him into the jail.

Genesis 39:7–9, 11–12, 16–18, 20 MSG

Many men, including pastors and church leaders, have fallen prey to seduction, resulting in immorality, broken families, and destroyed careers, but lust is not a sin only of men. Joseph, sold into slavery by his brothers, worked for Potiphar, whose beautiful wife lusted after Joseph. Joseph failed to convince her to stop chasing him, but as a slave he couldn't leave. Potiphar's wife went further when she was alone with Joseph. Feeling unloved can trigger lust in women.

Movies, romance novels, and love songs tempt women to look and lust, but God calls us to remain pure. For some women, it's a great struggle to see good-looking men and not fantasize. Once lust takes root, arguments and appeals to purity seldom work.

Commit to purity and avoid looking. Practice "bouncing" your eyes away from temptation. That's hard in our culture with images everywhere that entice women to look. If needed, find an accountability partner. If you're married, commit to avoid being alone with a man who is not your husband. The battle is best won by remembering you're loved and valued—let the Bible remind you how much God loves and treasures us.

RESTORING LOST YEARS

Be glad, O children of Zion, and rejoice in the LORD your God, for he has given the early rain for your vindication; he has poured down for you abundant rain, the early and the latter rain, as before.

The threshing floors shall be full of grain; the vats shall overflow with wine and oil. I will restore to you the years that the swarming locust has eaten, the hopper, the destroyer, and the cutter, my great army, which I sent among you.

You shall eat in plenty and be satisfied, and praise the name of the LORD your God, who has dealt wondrously with you. And my people shall never again be put to shame.

Joel 2:23–26 ESV

God sent Joel to prophesy coming disaster. The Israelites had become wealthy and relied on their money. They forgot God and turned to idolatry and sin. God planned to punish them for their sins. But God also gave Joel a message of future restoration.

Terrorism, violence, and divorce destroy families and lives. Restoration takes a long time and hard work. We suffer the consequences of living in a world where evil often reigns, and we also suffer the consequences of our own actions, whether having an affair or going alone somewhere dangerous at night. We have seasons of brokenness and seasons of restoration. God forgives and restores us when we desire to follow him.

God can restore broken relationships and help us overcome fear. He also will restore loss due to devastation we suffered. He can refill our lives with love and joy and help us rebuild finances. He wants us to once again enjoy life.

When we struggle with great loss or ruin, we can cling to the promises of God for restoration. God wants to restore our hearts first, and that means we must open up and accept God's love as well as confess all sin.

NOT YOUR BATTLE

After King Josiah had done all this for the Temple, King Neco of Egypt led an army to fight at Carchemish on the Euphrates River. Josiah tried to stop him, but Neco sent Josiah this message: "This war I am fighting does not concern you, King of Judah. I have not come to fight you, but to fight my enemies, and God has told me to hurry. God is on my side, so don't oppose me, or he will destroy you."

But Josiah was determined to fight. He refused to listen to what God was saying through King Neco, so he disguised himself and went into battle on the plain of Megiddo.

During the battle King Josiah was struck by Egyptian arrows. . . .

He died and was buried in the royal tombs.

2 Chronicles 35:20–24 GNT

Parents try to tell grown children how to raise their children, women try to tell others how to dress, and sometimes we try to get between fighting friends to help settle the dispute. But we have enough battles of our own without getting into somewhere we don't belong.

King Josiah, the sixteenth king of Judah, became king when he was only eight. He was one of the southern kingdom's best kings. He wholeheartedly obeyed God's laws throughout his thirty-one-year reign. Tragically, his end came when he stressed over going into battle with the pharaoh of Egypt against God's message to stay out of the battle. He fought a battle that wasn't his and died doing it.

Josiah might have worried that the soldiers would march across his land, win their battle, and then fight his people. Josiah didn't pray and ask God to confirm King Neco's message but went into action himself. Impulsiveness can be costly; stress causes us to leap when we should pray and think. When you start to worry and stress, decide to stop, look, and listen. Evaluate the situation and decide if it's your battle. Enter in only where you belong.

MARITAL STRIFE

David, wearing only a linen cloth around his waist, danced with all his might to honor the LORD. And so he and all the Israelites took the Covenant Box up to Jerusalem with shouts of joy and the sound of trumpets. As the Box was being brought into the city, Michal, Saul's daughter, looked out of the window and saw King David dancing and jumping around in the sacred dance, and she was disgusted with him. . . .

Afterward, when David went home to greet his family, Michal came out to meet him. "The king of Israel made a big name for himself today!" she said. "He exposed himself like a fool in the sight of the servant women of his officials!"

David answered, "I was dancing to honor the LORD.". . .

Michal, Saul's daughter, never had any children.

2 Samuel 6:14–16, 20–21, 23 GNT

❋

My husband always ruins the laundry." "My husband sits on the coach and gets fatter." "My husband is lazy and will never get a good job." Ridiculing our husbands shows lack of faith in them and disrespect.

Michal, daughter of King Saul and wife of David, struggled with anger. Her father had taken her from David and given her to another man; David later took her from that husband, reclaiming her for himself, but not necessarily because he loved her. She privately ridiculed her husband. David responded with remarks that reminded her that God chose him as king of the people and he would honor God for all to see. He would set an example of sharing joy in the Lord. Releasing emotions can be done appropriately, but it's more important to communicate to resolve issues.

Michal's barrenness also reflected the strain her anger put on her marriage. Men don't need a wife to ridicule them. She did it privately, but many women do it publicly. Listen to yourself. Are you too critical? Calling a spouse names or berating him for his actions reveals a resentful heart.

No Comparison

We are not bold to class or compare ourselves with some of those who commend themselves; but when they measure themselves by themselves and compare themselves with themselves, they are without understanding. But we will not boast beyond our measure, but within the measure of the sphere which God apportioned to us as a measure, to reach even as far as you.

For we are not overextending ourselves, as if we did not reach to you, for we were the first to come even as far as you in the gospel of Christ; not boasting beyond our measure, that is, in other men's labors, but with the hope that as your faith grows, we will be, within our sphere, enlarged even more by you. . . .

But he who boasts is to boast in the LORD.

2 Corinthians 10:12–15, 17
NASB

Does your car have a bumper sticker that says your child made the honor roll? Do you have a trophy collection that testifies to your athletic ability? When awards become reasons to boast, we might get caught up in comparisons.

Boasting and making comparisons build our self-esteem at the expense of someone else. Paul's second letter to the Corinthians addressed his own authority and shared how to build unity for ministering together. Paul had numerous reasons to boast, but that wasn't his focus at all. He cared about the people in the Corinthian church and wanted their faith to grow. He wasn't interested in receiving accolades for himself.

Comparisons lead to divisions and competition. We compare our looks and homes with those of other women. Mothers compare their own children to each other and to classmates and teammates. This doesn't help anyone. We need to accept ourselves as God accepts us, feel loved for who God made us to be, and credit God for success.

Could we develop a more inclusive language? "It's good to be in the company of beautiful women." "The whole team worked so hard." Paul urges us to boast in what God does.

TEMPORARY TROUBLES

We are like clay jars in which this treasure is stored. The real power comes from God and not from us. We often suffer, but we are never crushed. Even when we don't know what to do, we never give up. In times of trouble, God is with us, and when we are knocked down, we get up again. We face death every day because of Jesus. Our bodies show what his death was like, so that his life can also be seen in us. . . .

We never give up. Our bodies are gradually dying, but we ourselves are being made stronger each day. These little troubles are getting us ready for an eternal glory that will make all our troubles seem like nothing. Things that are seen don't last forever, but things that are not seen are eternal.

2 Corinthians 4:7–11, 16–18
CEV

❋

Some days we drag ourselves out of bed, already tired. Our busy lives are too full of stress and conflict, making it hard to exercise, eat well, and keep our bodies in shape. We need to draw strength from God and rejoice that he has chosen us, weak as we are, to tell others about him. The image of clay jars holding precious treasure illustrates God's power dwelling within us. Clay jars are fragile and break easily; our bodies get sick and age. In our busy daily lives, we sometimes forget to use the power of God given to us.

How do we continue to get up when we have great conflict in our lives, or get up again after we have failed? One key is noticing how often the word *we* is used in this passage. We don't have to carry our burdens alone. We get up because we know God will help us overcome any failure, because he promises to be with us.

In this passage, Paul reminded his readers—and us—to persevere in our faith. Our struggles and frail bodies are temporary. Lean on girlfriends who will encourage you and pray with you.

CLINGING TO PROMISED COMFORT

A poor beggar named Lazarus was brought to the gate of the rich man's house. He was happy just to eat the scraps that fell from the rich man's table. His body was covered with sores, and dogs kept coming up to lick them. The poor man died, and angels took him to the place of honor next to Abraham. The rich man also died and was buried. He went to hell and was suffering terribly. When he looked up and saw Abraham far off and Lazarus at his side, he said to Abraham, "Have pity on me! Send Lazarus to dip his finger in water and touch my tongue. I'm suffering terribly in this fire." Abraham answered, "My friend, remember that while you lived, you had everything good, and Lazarus had everything bad. Now he is happy and you are in pain."

Luke 16:20–25 CEV

Poverty and hunger are difficult struggles. Worldwide, fifteen million children die of hunger annually, yet people rich enough to have food stored in cupboards and freezers make excuses about sharing resources and money. They fear street beggars might spend handouts on drugs or that once we give, people will beg for more. How often have we relied on social programs to take care of the problem so we don't have to get involved personally, leaving the poor lonely and neglected as well as hungry?

Jesus told this parable to communicate some truths about God and to motivate people to act with love and encourage others to hope in the midst of struggle. The rich man didn't go to hell because of his wealth but because of his selfish attitude regarding money and his lack of compassion toward Lazarus. We know he had seen Lazarus begging on earth, for he identifies him.

We don't know much about the character of Lazarus. But when we suffer pain and illness, we can relate to his suffering and quietly bear the struggle, knowing it's temporary. As believers, we can cling to the knowledge that God will comfort us.

OPPOSITION

I want to do what is good, but I don't. I don't want to do what is wrong, but I do it anyway. But if I do what I don't want to do, I am not really the one doing wrong; it is sin living in me that does it.

I have discovered this principle of life—that when I want to do what is right, I inevitably do what is wrong. I love God's law with all my heart. But there is another power within me that is at war with my mind. This power makes me a slave to the sin that is still within me. Oh, what a miserable person I am! Who will free me from this life that is dominated by sin and death? Thank God! The answer is in Jesus Christ our Lord.

Romans 7:19–25 NLT

Struggling to make the right choice or just trying to figure out what the right choice is can cause great anguish and inner turmoil. Our opposition is sometimes within us, especially when we try to overcome bad habits. Paul wrote to the Romans to give them a clear picture of faith. He also honestly shared his own shortcomings to show how faith helped him in his personal struggles.

Admitting our problems and weaknesses is the start of overcoming challenges. When we confess that we need help, we are then open to receiving support from God and God's people. Loving God's law doesn't make us live it. We are by nature sinful and naturally choose to do wrong. We see this truth operating in young children, who must be taught to share, speak honestly, and be kind.

The struggle between evil and good is ever present. As Paul learned, we have help in our struggle, for Jesus is the answer. He gives us strength and shows us how to live. Each day we can remember that Jesus saved us and set us free from sin. We can make better choices one day at a time.

CONFLICTS AND BITING WORDS

You were doing so well. Who stopped you from being influenced by the truth? The arguments of the person who is influencing you do not come from the one who is calling you. A little yeast spreads through the whole batch of dough. The Lord gives me confidence that you will not disagree with this. However, the one who is confusing you will suffer God's judgment regardless of who he is. . . .

You were indeed called to be free, brothers and sisters. Don't turn this freedom into an excuse for your corrupt nature to express itself. Rather, serve each other through love. All of Moses' Teachings are summarized in a single statement, "Love your neighbor as you love yourself." But if you criticize and attack each other, be careful that you don't destroy each other.

Galatians 5:7–10, 13–15
GOD'S WORD

Criticizing and attacking other people destroys self-esteem and causes divisions. Paul wrote a letter to the church in Galatia to settle controversies among Christians and to help the believers understand freedom in Christ. Some had become legalistic, and Paul strove to correct the false teachings. Legalism fosters criticism as people try to make everyone conform and follow strict rules. Legalism breeds a habit of watching others to find fault. Criticism among Christians confuses unbelievers, who wonder why people can say they follow a God of love yet act so mean.

We should let love rule our hearts and our lives. If you catch yourself being critical, bite your tongue and be quiet or say something kind. Hurtful words cause pain and also cause people to withdraw or leave, destroying relationships. Love frees us and helps us be giving and kind. If we love others, we look for the best in other people instead of finding fault when they don't follow every rule.

When someone criticizes a person, find something good to say about her. Seek reasons to praise people. Greet each person you meet today with a kind word or compliment.

SELF~IMAGE MAKEOVER

He tried to get a look at Jesus, but he was too short to see over the crowd. So he ran ahead and climbed a sycamore-fig tree beside the road, for Jesus was going to pass that way.

When Jesus came by, he looked up at Zacchaeus and called him by name. "Zacchaeus!" he said. "Quick, come down! I must be a guest in your home today."

Zacchaeus quickly climbed down and took Jesus to his house in great excitement and joy. But the people were dis-pleased. "He has gone to be the guest of a notorious sinner," they grumbled.

Meanwhile, Zacchaeus stood before the Lord and said, "I will give half my wealth to the poor, Lord, and if I have cheated people on their taxes, I will give them back four times as much!"

Jesus responded, "Salvation has come to this home today, for this man has shown himself to be a true son of Abraham. For the Son of Man came to seek and save those who are lost."

Luke 19:3–10 NLT

❄

Did you ever sing the song about Zacchaeus, "a wee little man"? He was very short and very rich. Zacchaeus worked for the Roman government as a chief tax collector, a job despised by the Jews because tax collectors were notorious for collecting more than people actually owed. But Jesus singled out Zacchaeus, called him by name, and invited himself to dinner. Jesus didn't act like other religious leaders. His acceptance and his teaching triggered an inner makeover in Zacchaeus and a change of outward behavior too.

Real change starts inwardly but needs to be confirmed by changed behavior. Some people might not believe the change and still talk about our old, bad ways, but Jesus will stand with us. Each day we can examine our actions and words and ask ourselves if we need to change, and then choose to do so.

Do you know someone who has made many mistakes? Speak to her with kindness and acceptance. Your words could start an inner makeover just as Jesus' words did for Zacchaeus.

THE REAL STRUGGLE

We are not fighting against human beings but against the wicked spiritual forces in the heavenly world, the rulers, authorities, and cosmic powers of this dark age. So put on God's armor now! Then when the evil day comes, you will be able to resist the enemy's attacks; and after fighting to the end, you will still hold your ground. So stand ready, with truth as a belt tight around your waist, with righteousness as your breastplate, and as your shoes the readiness to announce the Good News of peace. At all times carry faith as a shield; for with it you will be able to put out all the burning arrows shot by the Evil One. And accept salvation as a helmet, and the word of God as the sword which the Spirit gives you.

Ephesians 6:12–17 GNT

There's an unseen world where fish swim beneath the surface of the water. There's also an unseen world in the heavens, where angels and demons fight. Paul wrote this important passage to be sure Christians understand the reality of evil forces and the need to be prepared to fight them. Our armor and weapons are invisible yet seen through our words and actions.

God's truth is unchanging, even in a world of relativism and redefining meanings. Truth helps us discern reality and not buy into Satan's lies. Righteousness means to be made right or holy before God. Believers are made righteous when we accept Jesus' sacrifice on our behalf. Forgiveness makes us holy, so we confess our sins and ask God to forgive us.

We need to be ready to share the good news about Jesus and the peace he brings and apply our faith to life. The Bible is our offensive weapon for fighting evil, for God's words of truth wound the evil forces. Our minds focus on our salvation, while our hearts must focus on faith that God will help us.

Be aware of spiritual struggles and then apply these methods to win over evil.

START WITH SELF-IMPROVEMENT

Don't pick on people, jump on their failures, criticize their faults—unless, of course, you want the same treatment. Don't condemn those who are down; that hardness can boomerang. Be easy on people; you'll find life a lot easier. Give away your life; you'll find life given back, but not merely given back—given back with bonus and blessing. . . .

It's easy to see a smudge on your neighbor's face and be oblivious to the ugly sneer on your own. Do you have the nerve to say, "Let me wash your face for you," when your own face is distorted by contempt? It's this I-know-better-than-you mentality again, playing a holier-than-thou part instead of just living your own part. Wipe that ugly sneer off your own face and you might be fit to offer a washcloth to your neighbor.

Luke 6:37–38, 41–42 MSG

It's easy to think, *She's heavier than me*, or *She didn't even smile when I said hello*. It's easy to use sarcasm and jokes to pick on someone for her faults, but it's a struggle to see our own faults. We must observe our own actions and words and measure them against those of Christ. Jesus spoke the words in this passage against judging others in his famous Sermon on the Mount.

We can improve our behavior when we honestly evaluate our words and actions. Keep notes on your behavior. Note any negative comments or criticisms you make and people's reactions. Evaluate what Jesus would think about your behavior. Admit any sins and ask for forgiveness. Then decide where you need to improve and start practicing the better behavior.

We improve first by changing our hearts and motivations. Think about the reasons you judge others or think negative thoughts. Do your words make you feel superior? Do your actions show love? The reasons help us find the motivation. Jesus wants us to be motivated by love for God and others, so the real question should be, Did I show love to each person I saw today?

COMPLETE TRUST

Shadrach, Meshach, and Abednego answered, ". . . If our God, whom we honor, can save us from a blazing furnace and from your power, he will, Your Majesty.". . .

The king's order was so urgent and the furnace was so extremely hot that the men who carried Shadrach, Meshach, and Abednego were killed by the flames from the fire. . . .

Then Nebuchadnezzar was startled. He sprang to his feet. He asked his advisers, "Didn't we throw three men into the fire?" "That's true, Your Majesty," they answered. The king replied, "But look, I see four men. They're untied, walking in the middle of the fire, and unharmed. The fourth one looks like a son of the gods.". . .

They saw that the fire had not harmed their bodies. The hair on their heads wasn't singed, their clothes weren't burned, and they didn't smell of smoke.

Daniel 3:16–17, 22, 24–25, 27 GOD'S WORD

✳

If you were told to bow before an idol or wear a new but revealing uniform at work, how would you respond?

In this passage, three men of faith show us how to live boldly. These men lived during the Babylonian exile, when God's people had been conquered and captured as slaves. Jealous leaders tried to use the king's own decree to eliminate these three men who would not worship the huge golden statue of the Babylonian king. Shadrach, Meschach, and Abednego refused to bow before anyone but God, and God rescued these faithful men.

When people persecute God's people, they are touching God with their hatred, and the struggle is greater than they expect. This event showed the power of God and the presence of God in the form of a fourth man who looked like the Son of God. Shadrach, Meschach, and Abednego trusted God completely. They believed in his unlimited power and creativity to help. We build such confidence through trusting God in the everyday moments of our lives and by knowing his words in the Bible.

EXPRESSING EMOTIONS

When I kept silent, my bones wasted away through my groaning all day long. For day and night your hand was heavy upon me; my strength was dried up as by the heat of summer.

I acknowledged my sin to you, and I did not cover my iniquity; I said, "I will confess my transgressions to the LORD," and you forgave the iniquity of my sin.

Therefore let everyone who is godly offer prayer to you at a time when you may be found; surely in the rush of great waters, they shall not reach him. . . .

Many are the sorrows of the wicked, but steadfast love surrounds the one who trusts in the LORD.

Psalm 32:3–6, 10 ESV

If you have ever suppressed your emotions and tried to hide sadness or fear, you understand how that bottles up and can cause physical effects like butterflies in your stomach, sleeplessness, fluttering in your heart, and blockage in your throat. Other times, a great sadness might take away your appetite and desire to live, and you lose weight and energy and feel helpless. King David wrote this psalm, probably after God forgave his sins against Bathsheba and Uriah. David had hidden his sin and deception for a time and kept them bottled up. He understood the physical effects of hidden sin.

Sin eats away at us and keeps us from experiencing joy. We struggle to justify our wrongs and avoid God when we most need to confess to be free of our guilt. God is always willing to forgive us. Nothing we gain from sin is worth keeping, especially our pride.

Whether you find yourself hiding adultery, an abortion, or excessive spending that brings debt, tell God how you feel and what you have done. Admit your fault and resolve to change. Like David, you will feel God's love and forgiveness surrounding you.

LETTING GO OF FEAR

Another of the disciples said to Him, "Lord, permit me first to go and bury my father."

But Jesus said to him, "Follow Me, and allow the dead to bury their own dead."

When He got into the boat, His disciples followed Him. And behold, there arose a great storm on the sea, so that the boat was being covered with the waves; but Jesus Himself was asleep.

And they came to Him and woke Him, saying, "Save us, Lord; we are perishing!"

He said to them, "Why are you afraid, you men of little faith?" Then He got up and rebuked the winds and the sea, and it became perfectly calm.

The men were amazed, and said, "What kind of a man is this, that even the winds and the sea obey Him?"

Matthew 8:21–27 NASB

We can make up excuses or choose to be faithful. But deciding to attend church or make a lifestyle change doesn't mean we won't also react with fear or worry. We can't control our emotional responses when we hear strange noises in the night, strong winds shake our homes, or friends tease us for having faith.

The storm in this passage took place on the Sea of Galilee, which is thirteen miles long, seven miles wide, and 150 feet deep. Storms can come up suddenly as winds rush down from the mountains that surround the sea; twenty-foot waves crashing against a boat cause even experienced sailors to panic. Jesus used this storm to show the disciples his miraculous power.

Our fears are opportunities to trust God and see his power at work. Jesus' question is something we can ask whenever we feel afraid—*Why am I afraid, woman of little faith?* Then remember that Jesus is with you. Remember how he helped the disciples and others. Trust his power. Replace fear with trust. Instead of imagining all the things that can go wrong, which increases fear, think of all the reasons we have to trust.

BLIND OBEDIENCE

Noah was a righteous man, blameless in his generation. Noah walked with God. . . .

Now the earth was corrupt in God's sight, and the earth was filled with violence. . . .

And God said to Noah, "I have determined to make an end of all flesh, for the earth is filled with violence through them. Behold, I will destroy them with the earth. Make yourself an ark of gopher wood. Make rooms in the ark, and cover it inside and out with pitch. . . .

"For behold, I will bring a flood of waters upon the earth to destroy all flesh in which is the breath of life under heaven. Everything that is on the earth shall die. But I will establish my covenant with you, and you shall come into the ark, you, your sons, your wife, and your sons' wives with you."

Genesis 6:9, 11, 13–14, 17–18 ESV

Before the Flood there had been no rain; God watered the earth with streams, or a mist (see Gen. 2:6) that rose from the earth before the flood. Such a large boat would never have been built before Noah built the ark. There had not yet been a formal covenant between God and people, but Noah followed God completely, despite never having seen rain or a boat so big. God kept Noah's focus on God, his family, and animal life.

Noah might have struggled to understand and envision what God spoke about, but he could follow him because he already had a habit of following God and living a holy life. Noah continued to trust God as he built the ark over many years and then filled it with food for his family and the animals.

We don't always understand God or what he asks us to do, but we can follow him obediently. Like Noah, we must first know God to recognize when he is directing us to do something. The more we have the words of the Bible in our hearts and minds, the easier it will be to recognize God's voice.

SPEECHLESS BEFORE GOD

I am sure that what we are suffering now cannot compare with the glory that will be shown to us. . . .

And this hope is what saves us. But if we already have what we hope for, there is no need to keep on hoping. However, we hope for something we have not yet seen, and we patiently wait for it. In certain ways we are weak, but the Spirit is here to help us. For example, when we don't know what to pray for, the Spirit prays for us in ways that cannot be put into words. All of our thoughts are known to God. He can understand what is in the mind of the Spirit, as the Spirit prays for God's people. We know that God is always at work for the good of everyone who loves him.

Romans 8:18, 24–28 CEV

Prayer is talking to God, but we don't always know what to say or how to say it. When we feel pain or grief, it might be hard to talk to God. We may sit speechless or in tears. God helps us in our prayer struggles too. He already knows what we are thinking and feeling. He gives us his Holy Spirit to pray for us. In his letter to the Romans, Paul shared how to live a Christian life and taught about the importance of prayer. He reminded his readers that God is always doing his best for our good. God will provide the best answers for us, especially when we can see only our needs and problems.

Paul was not present at Pentecost when the Holy Spirit came to the disciples and other followers, but he had experienced the Holy Spirit and been guided by the Spirit. Too often we underestimate the Holy Spirit's ability, yet he is the very Spirit of God sent to help us. We cannot understand why God allows a child to be sick, a company to close, or violent acts to harm. Thankfully, the Spirit searches our thoughts, helps us, and prays for us.

VAIN ENVY

I envied the arrogant when I saw the prosperity of the wicked. . . .

Surely in vain have I kept my heart pure; in vain have I washed my hands in innocence. All day long I have been plagued; I have been punished every morning. . . .

I entered the sanctuary of God; then I understood their final destiny. . . .

Whom have I in heaven but you? And earth has nothing I desire besides you. My flesh and my heart may fail, but God is the strength of my heart and my portion forever.

Those who are far from you will perish; you destroy all who are unfaithful to you.

Psalm 73:3, 13–14, 17, 25–27
NIV

Egyptian pharaohs tried to take their wealth with them but failed. The artifacts remained unused in tombs until discovered and displayed in museums. Those treasures remind us that wealth is temporary and not worth envying.

Asaph, a choir director for the temple choir, wrote the psalm from which this passage comes. When he looked around, he felt confused by people who did wrong but lived a great life while faithful people experienced trouble. Asaph entered God's temple, focused on God, and realized that God makes all things right in heaven.

We can become envious of people and their money, looks, or great careers. Such envy is useless, for earthly possessions and looks don't last. Our health will not last forever; we all will die. God will destroy unrepentant, sinful people. God is eternal, and we need to focus on God and living forever with him.

No one can take away our faith or our future. If you struggle with envy, stop as soon as you think how much you wish you had someone's jewelry or thin waist. Stop looking at others and look at God instead, thanking him for his promises of joy in heaven.

DEEP-DOWN CLEANSING

You desire truth and sincerity. Deep down inside me you teach me wisdom. Purify me from sin with hyssop, and I will be clean. Wash me, and I will be whiter than snow. Let me hear sounds of joy and gladness. Let the bones that you have broken dance. . . .

Create a clean heart in me, O God, and renew a faithful spirit within me. . . . Restore the joy of your salvation to me, and provide me with a spirit of willing obedience. . . .

O Lord, open my lips, and my mouth will tell about your praise. . . . The sacrifice pleasing to God is a broken spirit. O God, you do not despise a broken and sorrowful heart.

Psalm 51:6–8, 10, 12, 15, 17
GOD'S WORD

Every day is a new opportunity to let God forgive and renew you. King David wrote this psalm after the prophet Nathan came and reprimanded David for his sins. Hyssop symbolized David's desire to be holy and restored in his relationship with God. Hyssop was used in the ceremonial cleaning at Passover, the feast celebrating God's delivering his people from slavery in Egypt. Hyssop, dipped in the lamb's blood, was used like a brush to sprinkle the blood on doors and doorposts. God also directed the use of hyssop to cleanse people of skin diseases. The sponge soaked in wine and offered to Jesus on the cross was stuck on a hyssop branch.

We are imperfect, and we fail. We give in to temptation and sin. We might tell a little lie, look with lust at someone, or perhaps engage in adultery like David. No matter what we do, we can trust that God is willing to forgive us and change our hearts so that we will be stronger and able to avoid sin. God is touched when someone is sorry and regrets her sins. Like David, let's praise God because he forgives us.

VICTORY AT LAST

There is none holy like the LORD; there is none besides you; there is no rock like our God. Talk no more so very proudly, let not arrogance come from your mouth; for the LORD is a God of knowledge, and by him actions are weighed. The bows of the mighty are broken, but the feeble bind on strength. Those who were full have hired themselves out for bread, but those who were hungry have ceased to hunger. The barren has borne seven, but she who has many children is forlorn. . . . He raises up the poor from the dust; he lifts the needy from the ash heap to make them sit with princes and inherit a seat of honor.

1 Samuel 2:2–5, 8 ESV

If you have ever prayed for years about a need or desire, you understand the joy of a long-awaited answer. Hannah prayed for years to have a child, stressed over her longing, and finally held her first child, Samuel, who became one of Israel's great judges. She prayed the words in this passage after God gave her Samuel. Hannah's prayer gives us hope to persist. In his time God will turn situations around and give generously to faithful people who continue praying. Hannah asked for one child and God gave her six. He can more than answer your prayer too.

Hannah also noted that God reverses the fortunes of unfaithful people who proudly put down the needy. Her husband's other wife had taunted Hannah for being childless, and Hannah let God deal with her. Ask for what you need, and God will give you much more than you dream possible. Don't worry about others who tease you.

If you have debt and little income, if you desire to be married or to have a child, or if you want a better career, don't stop praying. Wait patiently, for God will give you his best.

ALL ARE WELCOME

Peter then said: "Now I am certain that God treats all people alike. God is pleased with everyone who worships him and does right, no matter what nation they come from." . . .

While Peter was still speaking, the Holy Spirit took control of everyone who was listening. Some Jewish followers of the Lord had come with Peter, and they were surprised that the Holy Spirit had been given to Gentiles. Now they were hearing Gentiles speaking unknown languages and praising God.

Peter said, "These Gentiles have been given the Holy Spirit, just as we have! I am certain that no one would dare stop us from baptizing them." Peter ordered them to be baptized in the name of Jesus Christ, and they asked him to stay on for a few days.

Acts 10:34–35, 44–48 CEV

Walking into a new church can be difficult. Sometimes we are greeted and feel welcomed. Other times we feel like outsiders. You might attend for weeks or months before making a friend or fitting in, or you might find a ministry to join, meet people fast, and feel at home. Much of being welcomed depends on the spirit of the people at the church and your own efforts at becoming part of the community.

God had given Peter a dream to show him that the good news of Jesus is not for the Jews only but also for the Gentiles—all non-Jews. Then Peter met Cornelius, a Gentile. Peter preached a good message that God welcomes everyone but still reacted with amazement that God would give the Holy Spirit to Gentiles. What Peter witnessed caused him to baptize the new believers.

We try to welcome one another, but we tend to hold back until we see faith in people's lives or we find a common link. Be willing to accept people and really welcome them, without proof. Talk to new people and find common interests. Trust that God will work in their hearts.

DEVOTED COMMUNITY

"This promise is for you and your children. It is for everyone our Lord God will choose, no matter where they live."

Peter told them many other things as well. Then he said, "I beg you to save yourselves from what will happen to all these evil people." On that day about three thousand believed his message and were baptized. They spent their time learning from the apostles, and they were like family to each other. They also broke bread and prayed together.

Everyone was amazed by the many miracles and wonders that the apostles worked. All the Lord's followers often met together, and they shared everything they had. They would sell their property and possessions and give the money to whoever needed it. . . . Each day the Lord added to their group others who were being saved.

Acts 2:39–45, 47 CEV

Have you attended a conference or large retreat where people showed excitement and had a great time worshipping together? Have you heard a speaker who got the crowd excited about their faith? That's what happened on the day the church began.

The synergy of three thousand believers must have been amazing. Peter and the other disciples had just received the Holy Spirit. A crowd gathered at the sound of the disciples speaking in a multitude of languages, and Peter preached the first sermon. The new believers couldn't get enough of knowing Jesus and studying God's Word. Their new faith united them into a community that shared everything. Unity and excitement about Jesus bring growth. People gave generously, shared, and felt as close as a healthy, functional family.

God's promises have not changed. He still loves all of us and promises his Holy Spirit to all believers. Be careful not to get so busy that you crowd out time with believing friends. Spend time with new believers too; their excitement will motivate and enthuse you. Spend time with believers, give generously of your time and resources, and you'll develop strong bonds with others in your church family.

COMMUNITY GRAPEVINE

There was a man named Ananias, who with his wife Sapphira sold some property that belonged to them. But with his wife's agreement he kept part of the money for himself and turned the rest over to the apostles. Peter said to him, "Ananias, why did you let Satan take control of you and make you lie to the Holy Spirit by keeping part of the money you received for the property? . . . After you sold it, the money was yours. Why, then, did you decide to do such a thing? You have not lied to people—you have lied to God!" . . .

[Peter said to Sapphira,] "The men who buried your husband are at the door right now, and they will carry you out too!" . . . The whole church and all the others who heard of this were terrified.

Acts 5:1–4, 9, 11 GNT

Finding out that a church leader has had an affair or embezzled money hurts the community and causes some people to lose faith. Rumors spread quickly and can cause those who hear to lose trust in God and the church.

Rumors divide people and destroy community. But when God is the one passing information on, it's to keep the community healthy. Jesus told us he is the Vine and that we must stay connected to him. Peter stayed connected, and the Holy Spirit guided Peter, as part of God's grapevine, to discern the truth when Ananias and his wife lied. That their leaders had such a connection to God frightened people, for it showed that God can reveal hidden sins. After the death of this couple, healings and miracles continued, and the church continued to grow.

As a community of believers, we need a close connection with God, and so do our leaders. We must pray for wholeness and truth to prevail in the church. Spend time praying for your church leaders and Christian friends. Ask God to help you remain honest. Ask God to give his leaders discernment to keep the community healthy.

Community Traditions

Mordecai recorded these events, and he sent letters to all the Jews throughout the provinces of King Xerxes, near and far, to have them celebrate annually the fourteenth and fifteenth days of the month of Adar as the time when the Jews got relief from their enemies, and as the month when their sorrow was turned into joy and their mourning into a day of celebration. He wrote them to observe the days as days of feasting and joy and giving presents of food to one another and gifts to the poor. . . .

(Therefore these days were called Purim, from the word *pur*.) . . . The Jews took it upon themselves to establish the custom [to] without fail observe these two days every year . . . in every generation by every family.

Esther 9:20–22, 26–28 NIV

Every spring in Jewish communities, the celebration of Purim thanks God for his faithfulness in keeping his people from harm, providing a reminder of God's love. The observance involves comic plays, eating *hamantaschen* (a kind of cookie), giving presents, and reading the Purim scroll, or what we call the book of Esther.

Traditions build community. A special sermon repeated yearly, or a Christmas pageant or play, might become a tradition celebrating a community's faith. Traditions can provide identity for people, bridge generations, and reinforce faith. They are great for strengthening families and church communities, as well as reminding us of God's love.

The feasts that celebrate Jesus are natural times to develop or celebrate traditions. The date a church began or something else special happened can be a day to celebrate yearly. Like Purim, with Scripture reading and reenacting how God saved his people, traditions need to reflect what God does in our lives and the meaning of our celebration. Reflect on your favorite tradition, why it's important, and how it can help you share your faith. Make plans to share your tradition within your community and among your friends or family.

ENCOURAGEMENT BUILDS COMMUNITY

Every house has a builder, but the one who built everything is God. . . .

But Christ, as the Son, is in charge of God's entire house. And we are God's house, if we keep our courage and remain confident in our hope in Christ. . . .

Be careful then, dear brothers and sisters. Make sure that your own hearts are not evil and unbelieving, turning you away from the living God. You must warn each other every day, while it is still "today," so that none of you will be deceived by sin and hardened against God. For if we are faithful to the end, trusting God just as firmly as when we first believed, we will share in all that belongs to Christ. Remember what it says: "Today when you hear his voice, don't harden your hearts as Israel did when they rebelled."

Hebrews 3:4, 6, 12–15 NLT

It's hard to see a friend, child, or loved one stop attending church or stop believing in God. She might be angry at God over circumstances or hurt by people within the church. But unresolved problems lead to bitterness or anger.

The church is people, kept together through our common faith in Christ. Any good home needs love. God's "house"—the body of Christ—is not made with walls but with hearts. To stay united we need to lovingly help one another. Our words can give support to others who are lonely or afraid. Words can inspire others with the confidence they need to follow their dreams or develop relationships. Encouragement builds people up, lifts their spirits, and helps them feel appreciated.

Paul viewed encouragement as so important that his letters always included it. Paul noted that sin destroys unity and reminded people that the Israelites' disobedience caused them to wander forty years. Encouraging people helps keep their hearts soft and promotes faithfulness. Use words to express appreciation, ask people how they are doing, support the dreams of others, express acceptance, and be excited for others' good news. Words are the smallest building blocks for uniting us in community.

217

NEIGHBORLINESS

Jesus said: "A man was going down from Jerusalem to Jericho, when he fell into the hands of robbers. They stripped him of his clothes, beat him and went away, leaving him half dead. A priest happened to be going down the same road, and when he saw the man, he passed by on the other side. So too, a Levite, when he came to the place and saw him, passed by on the other side. But a Samaritan, as he traveled, came where the man was; and when he saw him, he took pity on him. He went to him and bandaged his wounds, pouring on oil and wine. Then he put the man on his own donkey, took him to an inn and took care of him."

Luke 10:30–34 NIV

Jesus used this story to illustrate that a neighbor is anyone we encounter who needs our help. Neighborliness is reaching out with love to meet needs. Jesus showed that we shouldn't discriminate based on race, faith, or social background. He broadened the idea of neighbor from people living near us to anyone close enough for us to help.

The beaten man, stripped of clothing, had no identification to show whether he was rich or poor, good or bad. The religious leader and temple worker passed by without helping. If they touched a bleeding man, by Jewish law they would have been unclean until cleared by a priest. They chose pride and isolation by refusing to help. Busyness and "holiness" are poor excuses to avoid helping someone in need.

The pity and compassion of the Samaritan inspired his great generosity and personal care. We can have tender hearts when we are thankful for God's forgiveness and when we practice patience, gentleness, and kindness. Neighborliness can be as simple as helping an elderly woman load her groceries into her car in the parking lot. Each person in need provides an opportunity for us to enlarge our neighborhood.

TOWN PARADE

When the city wall of Jerusalem was dedicated, the Levites were brought in from wherever they were living, so that they could join in celebrating the dedication with songs of thanksgiving and with the music of cymbals and harps. . . .

I assembled the leaders of Judah on top of the wall and put them in charge of two large groups to march around the city, giving thanks to God. . . .

The other group of those who gave thanks went to the left along the top of the wall, and I followed with half of the people. . . .

That day many sacrifices were offered, and the people were full of joy because God had made them very happy. The women and the children joined in the celebration, and the noise they all made could be heard for miles.

Nehemiah 12:27, 31, 38, 43
GNT

※

The entire city paraded on the wide wall of Jerusalem and celebrated the rebuilding of the wall destroyed by the Babylonians decades earlier. Marching to music brought great joy, and the sound filled the community. The Israelites held this parade as part of dedicating the wall to God. They gave their work on the wall and themselves to God and united in praising God.

The event took planning—organizing marchers, preparation by a choir and musicians, and music probably chosen by the choir director. Before the parade the leaders and people purified themselves. We do this by confessing sins and asking for God's forgiveness.

We can praise God as a church community and commit our work and lives to God. We can joyfully sing and thank God for his provisions. In showing their thanks, the Israelites gave generous offerings to God. We can express our thanks through gifts of time and money. We can celebrate accomplishments, especially those through which we've seen God help us persist and overcome adversity. We can dedicate our churches and homes for God's use. Celebrate with friends and help your church plan a celebration or parade with music and thanksgiving.

GETTING ALONG

I appeal to you to be shepherds of the flock that God gave you and to take care of it willingly. . . . Do your work, not for mere pay, but from a real desire to serve. Do not try to rule over those who have been put in your care, but be examples to the flock. . . .

In the same way you younger people must submit yourselves to your elders. And all of you must put on the apron of humility, to serve one another; for the scripture says, "God resists the proud, but shows favor to the humble." Humble yourselves, then, under God's mighty hand, so that he will lift you up in his own good time. Leave all your worries with him, because he cares for you.

1 Peter 5:1–3, 5–7 GNT

Think of your favorite president, church leader, or other leader. What qualities made that person special? Now think of a leader you had trouble following or trusting. What do you think is the biggest difference between good and bad leaders?

As an experienced leader, Peter gave advice to leaders and followers in this passage. He pointed to motivation and attitudes that put others first and show love for the followers. Leaders need to foster a spirit of openness and cooperation, while young people must listen and follow. Have you let pride or selfishness get in the way within your family, church, or local community? Contentiousness—spreading rumors, stirring up resistance, and verbally attacking others—can destroy a community and divide a family or church. If you are a leader, do you really care for your people?

Loving women can nurture others, spread encouragement, and organize support. Choose to serve selflessly. Pray for your leaders and those who follow you. Trust your worries about leaders or followers to God. Express appreciation for the efforts and work of others. Volunteer to lead a ministry or small group or to assist the leader, especially where your talents will help.

HARMONY

Love each other with genuine affection, and take delight in honoring each other. Never be lazy, but work hard and serve the Lord enthusiastically. Rejoice in our confident hope. Be patient in trouble, and keep on praying. When God's people are in need, be ready to help them. Always be eager to practice hospitality.

Bless those who persecute you. Don't curse them; pray that God will bless them. Be happy with those who are happy, and weep with those who weep. Live in harmony with each other. Don't be too proud to enjoy the company of ordinary people. And don't think you know it all!

Never pay back evil with more evil. Do things in such a way that everyone can see you are honorable. Do all that you can to live in peace with everyone.

Romans 12:10–18 NLT

Is your home a place where friends and neighbors drop by for a cup of tea and to chat or discuss their problems? Does the welcome mat or sign at your door reflect your hospitable spirit? These are ways we can show sincere love. A neighborhood that holds block parties, has an e-mail network to let others know if someone needs help, and actually provides help for anyone in need is a thriving community. These people have learned to live together in harmony and care deeply about one another.

Early Christian communities lived these principles, and Paul encouraged them to continue to live their faith through serving one another. Rome was a large city and the Christians there included rich, poor, Jews, and Gentiles. They had learned to share everything with one another and worshipped together.

Encourage harmony within your community. Remain hopeful and patient if neighbors resist your friendly overtures. Walk your neighborhood, praying at each house, greeting anyone you see, and showing concern for people's needs. Open your home and invite neighbors to a party, tea, Bible study, or a play date if you have young children. Ask for e-mail addresses and start an information network.

PEACE-DRIVEN LIFE

Let's stop criticizing each other. Instead, you should decide never to do anything that would make other Christians have doubts or lose their faith. . . .

Don't allow anyone to say that what you consider good is evil. God's kingdom does not consist of what a person eats or drinks. Rather, God's kingdom consists of God's approval and peace, as well as the joy that the Holy Spirit gives. The person who serves Christ with this in mind is pleasing to God and respected by people.

So let's pursue those things which bring peace and which are good for each other. Don't ruin God's work because of what you eat. All food is acceptable, but it's wrong for a person to eat something if it causes someone else to have doubts.

Romans 14:13, 16–20
GOD'S WORD

Don't you think you've had enough to eat?" "Your dress is a little tight. I know a good exercise club." Criticism judges others and says we don't accept or approve of the other person or her actions. Criticism hurts feelings and can cause animosity or resentment.

Paul wrote to the Romans, whom he had not yet met, to explain the Christian faith and encourage unity. Whether to eat meat sold in the marketplace that might have been used in idol worship was causing division within the church. Paul advised his readers to stop focusing on what divides and focus instead on unity, putting strengthening another's faith ahead of their own desires. Constructive criticism helps people change without hurting individuals.

When have you needed to correct someone? Were you prompted more by a desire to show that you knew more or knew best, or did you desire only to build up the other person? The next time you must offer correction, ask yourself first if your critique is so important that you would risk ruining the relationship by hurting the other person's feelings. If you must give correction, also cultivate peace with words that show approval and acceptance.

ACCEPTING OTHERS

If our faith is strong, we should be patient with the Lord's followers whose faith is weak. We should try to please them instead of ourselves. We should think of their good and try to help them by doing what pleases them. Even Christ did not try to please himself. But as the Scriptures say, "The people who insulted you also insulted me." And the Scriptures were written to teach and encourage us by giving us hope. God is the one who makes us patient and cheerful. I pray that he will help you live at peace with each other, as you follow Christ. Then all of you together will praise God, the Father of our Lord Jesus Christ.

Honor God by accepting each other, as Christ has accepted you.

Romans 15:1–7 CEV

Do you have a neighbor you can always call on to help watch your pet or water your plants when you'll be away? She is probably cheerful and kind. That's the type of neighbor we should be.

As Paul wrote the last section of Romans, he continued to encourage unity among believers. Accepting people encourages unity. Going beyond acceptance to actions of pleasing a neighbor creates oneness, because it unites hearts.

We can't control our neighbors, their pets, or their children, but we can choose how to act with love. We can greet them and offer to take in mail or watch pets when they're away. We can bake extra cookies or a loaf of bread for them as a surprise gift. We can also invite a neighbor to sit on our porch or have tea while we get to know each other. We must be willing to put up with the failings of neighbors who have a messy lawn, play loud music, or disturb us in other ways. We can be accepting of people and forgive actions we dislike. Hopefully neighbors will see Christ through our lives and focus on pleasing others.

SOCIAL JUSTICE

The king will say to those on his right, "My father has blessed you! Come and receive the kingdom that was prepared for you before the world was created. When I was hungry, you gave me something to eat, and when I was thirsty, you gave me something to drink. When I was a stranger, you welcomed me, and when I was naked, you gave me clothes to wear. When I was sick, you took care of me, and when I was in jail, you visited me."

Then the ones who pleased the Lord will ask, "When did we give you something to eat or drink?" . . .

The king will answer, "Whenever you did it for any of my people, no matter how unimportant they seemed, you did it for me."

Matthew 25:34–37, 40 CEV

An older widow cooks for two every day and drops off her second meal for a local homeless woman. She serves it on a pretty paper plate and includes plasticware and napkins. She conveys dignity to her homeless friend by treating her with kindness and making the meal attractive. It can be much easier to write a check or box up old clothes, giving anonymously, than to look someone in need in the eye, care for her personally, and converse with her.

Women in jail often wear empty, hopeless-looking expressions. We don't always know what to say, *if* we visit. It can be hard to visit people in hospice care, facing their final days. Yet these are people who need hope, encouragement, and love. Jesus spoke the words in this passage about helping others as he taught about the final judgment.

Volunteering in a soup kitchen, a women's shelter, or a nursing home brings us closer to people who need love and kindness. We touch the heart of God when we bring a smile to the face of someone lonely, hurt, or helpless. The word *social* should remind us to interact with those who need our help.

ENTHUSIASM IS CONTAGIOUS

"Whoever drinks of the water that I will give him will never be thirsty again. The water that I will give him will become in him a spring of water welling up to eternal life."

The woman said to him, "Sir, give me this water, so that I will not be thirsty." . . .

Jesus said to her, "Go, call your husband, and come here." The woman answered him, "I have no husband."

Jesus said to her, "You are right in saying, 'I have no husband'; for you have had five husbands, and the one you now have is not your husband. What you have said is true." . . .

So the woman left her water jar and went away into town and said to the people, "Come, see a man who told me all that I ever did." . . .

John 4:14–18, 28–29 ESV

When we feel parched, we want a cool drink of water. Jesus understood physical thirst. He also understood a greater thirst for water to quench the soul.

Jesus asked a woman at a well for a drink and that surprised her. Jewish men didn't speak to women, and certainly not to a woman like her—married multiple times and currently living with a man without being married. Most women drew water early, before the sun got too hot. This woman came in the middle of the day in order to avoid the other women drawing water; they wouldn't have welcomed her.

But Jesus reached out to people shunned by others. He drew the woman into discussion, offered her living water, and revealed himself to be the Messiah. She left her water jug and ran to tell others, even those who had snubbed her, about Jesus. The people came and invited Jesus to stay, and he visited for two days. Her enthusiasm changed her community as her testimony caused many to believe.

Our words and enthusiasm for Jesus can change our communities. We should tell everyone we meet about Jesus, our Savior.

OPEN TO DEBATE

Immediately when night came, the believers sent Paul and Silas to the city of Berea. When Paul and Silas arrived in the city of Berea, they entered the synagogue. The people of Berea were more open-minded than the people of Thessalonica. They were very willing to receive God's message, and every day they carefully examined the Scriptures to see if what Paul said was true. Many of them became believers, and quite a number of them were prominent Greek men and women.

But when the Jews in Thessalonica found out that Paul was also spreading God's word in Berea, they went there to upset and confuse the people. The believers immediately sent Paul to the seacoast, but Silas and Timothy stayed in Berea. The men who escorted Paul took him all the way to the city of Athens.

Acts 17:10–15 GOD'S WORD

Luke, one of Paul's traveling companions, wrote the book of Acts to record the events during the early time of the Christian church when the faith and persecution both grew rapidly. In this passage, Paul met people willing to listen and debate truth. They didn't let their own lifestyles or beliefs keep them from examining the Scriptures and seeking truth.

When people want to debate us, we might get defensive or worry we won't know what to say. Paul reacted with enthusiasm because anyone willing to listen and debate was open to believing in Jesus. Like Paul, we can rely on Scripture for our defense and not be concerned about someone's education or prominence.

When unbelievers came to confuse people and targeted Paul, Paul got out of the way and left others to continue debating. Sharing faith can be a community effort, with various people continuing the dialogue. You might witness to a woman getting a divorce who then moves away without believing in Jesus. She might later feel confused if others try to dissuade her from believing, but God will send other Christians to share their faith and continue the discussion.

U-Turned

[Suffering] means you have turned from your own desires and want to obey God for the rest of your life. You have already lived long enough like people who don't know God. You were immoral and followed your evil desires. You went around drinking and partying and carrying on. In fact, you even worshiped disgusting idols. Now your former friends wonder why you have stopped running around with them, and they curse you for it. But they will have to answer to God, who judges the living and the dead. . . .

Everything will soon come to an end. So be serious and be sensible enough to pray.

Most important of all, you must sincerely love each other, because love wipes away many sins.

Welcome people into your home and don't grumble about it.

1 Peter 4:2–5, 7–9 CEV

We enjoy our group of girlfriends, but if we stop gossiping, watching X-rated movies, or drinking too much, they might accuse us of turning on them or being "holier-than-thou."

Peter wrote to Christians experiencing persecution of various kinds. He knew that old friends can pressure us to revert to old habits. Peer pressure is still a powerful motivator. If you're a new believer, your commitment to Jesus still means that friends might turn away; you might need to find new friends in your community. You will find the new friends when you see people loving one another sincerely. Continue to love your former friends and forgive them, praying that they will learn to believe in Jesus too. Understand that some people who knew you well won't believe you have really changed.

A U-turn in life means a change of direction and often a change of habits. It's important to find good habits to replace negative habits. Consider joining a Bible study or listening to Christian music, for example. Continue inviting your old friends to visit, shop, or enjoy similar interests that are wholesome. Letting them see your changes in action might influence them to consider Jesus.

FACING THE BULLIES

"Don't be ridiculous!" Saul replied. "There's no way you can fight this Philistine and possibly win! You're only a boy, and he's been a man of war since his youth."

But David persisted. "I have been taking care of my father's sheep and goats," he said. "When a lion or a bear comes to steal a lamb from the flock, I go after it with a club and rescue the lamb from its mouth. If the animal turns on me, I catch it by the jaw and club it to death. I have done this to both lions and bears, and I'll do it to this pagan Philistine, too, for he has defied the armies of the living God! The LORD who rescued me from the claws of the lion and the bear will rescue me from this Philistine!"

1 Samuel 17:33–37 NLT

❋

Every community has its bullies—from playground bullies to street gangs to the office bully. Many have an army of submissive friends behind them. Now we also have cyberbullies. A giant bully terrorized Israel when Saul ruled as king. David's response teaches us a lesson about facing giants—and bullies—in this, one of the most famous Bible stories of the Old Testament. David used just a stone and a slingshot to kill a giant, showing us we simply need a change of perspective—no bully or problem is more powerful than God.

David had trusted God in smaller challenges that gave him courage to face this larger one. Consider keeping a prayer journal. When facing new problems, turn to your journal and be inspired as you review the challenges you've already overcome with God's help.

Is someone at work trying to push you into being submissive, getting him coffee, or doing her work? Stand up for what's right. At church or at school, people might try to control others with veiled threats or verbal attacks. Remember what God has done in your life before and trust that he will help you overcome anything now.

A Richer Life

Timothy, you belong to God, so keep away from all these evil things. Try your best to please God and to be like him. Be faithful, loving, dependable, and gentle. . . .

Warn the rich people of this world not to be proud or to trust in wealth that is easily lost. Tell them to have faith in God, who is rich and blesses us with everything we need to enjoy life. Instruct them to do as many good deeds as they can and to help everyone. Remind the rich to be generous and share what they have. This will lay a solid foundation for the future, so that they will know what true life is like.

Timothy, guard what God has placed in your care! Don't pay any attention to that godless and stupid talk that sounds smart but really isn't.

1 Timothy 6:11, 17–20 CEV

In neighborhoods with high walls and gates, residents shut themselves off from the world to protect their privacy and wealth. But we are called to openness and sharing what God gives us.

In comparison to the rest of world, almost every American is wealthy. If you have a roof over your head, more than one pair of shoes, clothes hanging in the closet, and food stored in cabinets and freezers, you are a wealthy woman.

Paul wrote to Timothy after leaving him to teach the people in the church at Ephesus, a wealthy city. In this passage Paul reminds us that we all can be rich in good deeds and generous with what we have, and he warns against arrogance and clinging to possessions. Like a woman who never has enough shoes, people who trust in money never have enough. We can release the hold money has on us by giving it away. Life is richer with more friends rather than more stuff. Consider a buy-one-get-one-free sale to be God's blessing you with something to give.

If you have a wealthy but miserly neighbor, be generous with love and kindness to demonstrate the joy of giving.

SERVING THE COMMUNITY

After they arrived at Capernaum and settled in a house, Jesus asked his disciples, "What were you discussing out on the road?" But they didn't answer, because they had been arguing about which of them was the greatest. He sat down, called the twelve disciples over to him, and said, "Whoever wants to be first must take last place and be the servant of everyone else."

Then he put a little child among them. Taking the child in his arms, he said to them, "Anyone who welcomes a little child like this on my behalf welcomes me, and anyone who welcomes me welcomes not only me but also my Father who sent me. . . .

"If anyone gives you even a cup of water because you belong to the Messiah, I tell you the truth, that person will surely be rewarded."

Mark 9:33–37, 41 NLT

When we have a heated little discussion with someone, we don't generally want anyone to eavesdrop. If we played back our conversation, we might notice a power struggle to win the debate.

Jesus knew what the disciples were talking about, but his question highlighted their desire for power and position. Each might have felt greater because he knew more Scripture or he thought Jesus turned to him more often. But Jesus embarrassed them all when he caught them in their argument. He countered the craving for greatness with service as the real key to position, using the example of welcoming little children.

Children generally have no ability to empower people. Serving the powerless humbles us. Children are perceptive and recognize someone who genuinely accepts them and wants to help them. When we smile at a child and help a little one, the child's parent might notice, and our action will warm their attitude toward us. So too God's heart is warmed when he sees us accepting children whom he created and serving others.

How do you practice service—by clearing tables, visiting nursing homes, listening to a child? God notices people who help others.

TOGETHER WITHOUT ENVY

I observed all the work and ambition motivated by envy. What a waste! Smoke. And spitting into the wind.

The fool sits back and takes it easy, his sloth is slow suicide.

One handful of peaceful repose is better than two fistfuls of worried work—more spitting into the wind. . . .

It's better to have a partner than go it alone. Share the work, share the wealth. And if one falls down, the other helps, but if there's no one to help, tough! Two in a bed warm each other. Alone, you shiver all night.

By yourself you're unprotected. With a friend you can face the worst. Can you round up a third? A three-stranded rope isn't easily snapped.

Ecclesiastes 4:4–6, 9–12 MSG

❋

Cell phones have become an integral part of our lives, our lifelines to network with family and friends. We text as well as call to stay in touch, ask for advice, and share our lives. One life interacting with another is the heart of community.

Togetherness is good when there's love without envy, when we can really rejoice in our friends' news and blessings. We must connect beyond appearance or circumstances or economic status. Envy wastes our time with focusing on what someone else has instead of being grateful for what we have and spending our time developing bonds of friendships.

Friends visit you when you have a new baby, party with you over a promotion, check out your latest travel photos, and shop with you. Friends sit with you at the hospital during a loved one's operation, or wait in court as your child is sentenced, or listen when your heart is broken by a spouse's betrayal. Friends go through the tough times with us and warm our hearts with their touch. They share the joy of our blessings, but they also are the small community that keeps us from snapping.

Comm~Unity

I am the vine, you are the branches; he who abides in Me and I in him, he bears much fruit, for apart from Me you can do nothing. . . . If you abide in Me, and My words abide in you, ask whatever you wish, and it will be done for you. My Father is glorified by this, that you bear much fruit, and so prove to be My disciples. Just as the Father has loved Me, I have also loved you; abide in My love. If you keep My commandments, you will abide in My love; just as I have kept My Father's commandments and abide in His love. These things I have spoken to you so that My joy may be in you, and that your joy may be made full.

John 15:5, 7–11 NASB

Grape stems branch out and grow from a single vine. One little plant produces bunches of grape clusters. These perennial plants twist and wind around obstacles to keep growing. Water and nutrients flow through the main vine to supply all the branches and fruit.

Jesus invites us to be part of an eternal vine. He wants us closely united with him, for that's what puts *unity* in the church comm*unity*. The love in the church community should grow like a vine, reach out, and spread God's love. A church might sponsor a missionary, send a group to help with disaster relief, work together to build a home for a needy family, or support one another to strengthen members.

Plump, juicy grapes bursting with flavor grow in clusters on the vine. When we serve others together, we can do so much more than when we work alone. God wants the world to see disciples growing together. Jesus will supply all the vine needs. The joy and love are so great that Jesus pointed to this unity as a catalyst for answers to prayer. Come together to worship, serve, and pray—and see unity!

Unity Begins with Two

Some Pharisees wanted to test Jesus. They came up to him and asked, "Is it right for a man to divorce his wife for just any reason?"

Jesus answered, "Don't you know that in the beginning the Creator made a man and a woman? That's why a man leaves his father and mother and gets married. He becomes like one person with his wife. Then they are no longer two people, but one. And no one should separate a couple that God has joined together."

The Pharisees asked Jesus, "Why did Moses say that a man could write out divorce papers and send his wife away?"

Jesus replied, "You are so heartless! That's why Moses allowed you to divorce your wife. But from the beginning God did not intend it to be that way."

Matthew 19:3–8 CEV

Fast food and microwaves promote thinking that everything should be instant and easy. But marriage takes work, commitment, and patience.

The legalistic Pharisees continually tested Jesus and challenged him to answer their trick questions. In this passage, Jesus doesn't dwell on divorce but speaks to the heart of marriage and the mindset of couples who want to stay together. We need to leave our birth families as our prime emotional connection to be free to develop new bonds. Two individuals must get to know each other well enough to become of the same mind. They are to be united, or yoked. Oxen yoked together learn to move together in the same direction. In marriage we need time and practice with one another to develop a lasting attachment.

Divorce means a turning away, or apart, from one another. When one or both spouses start to move away in mind or spirit, they pull and tear apart the oneness. God doesn't want couples breaking apart. He designed marriage, and he is still the glue to join a man and woman in unity. Nurture your togetherness with listening, dating, encouragement, and unselfish acts of kindness.

CHILDREN UNITE A COMMUNITY

[Jesus] said to Philip, "Where can we buy bread to feed these people?" He said this to stretch Philip's faith. He already knew what he was going to do.

Philip answered, "Two hundred silver pieces wouldn't be enough to buy bread for each person to get a piece."

One of the disciples—it was Andrew, brother to Simon Peter—said, "There's a little boy here who has five barley loaves and two fish. But that's a drop in the bucket for a crowd like this."

Jesus said, "Make the people sit down." There was a nice carpet of green grass in this place. They sat down, about five thousand of them. Then Jesus took the bread and, having given thanks, gave it to those who were seated. He did the same with the fish. All ate as much as they wanted.

John 6:5–11 MSG

※

This child's generosity may have reflected faith in Jesus and a child's ability to believe anything is possible. The boy provided an opportunity for Jesus to confirm childlike faith. This account is in three of the four Gospels. Jesus performs miracles even when only a little faith is shown, and that faith is often found in children.

Children bring us hope as we marvel in new life. Children bring us wonder as they express delight and curiosity in the world around them. Children don't see numbers like adults and don't count costs but imagine the impossible. They simply trust. Children easily welcome strangers and other children. They infuse vitality into community.

Children want to belong and interact with people. Andrew brought the boy to Jesus. We don't know how the boy and Andrew became acquainted. The boy must have been hungry too, but he wanted to give what he had to Jesus. Children offer little gifts with their big hearts and believe those gifts will work magic in lives.

Encourage children's curiosity and natural bent to engage people. Encourage their tendency to be generous by giving them things to share.

CHILDREN BELONG

Jesus left Capernaum and went down to the region of Judea and into the area east of the Jordan River. Once again crowds gathered around him, and as usual he was teaching them. . . .

One day some parents brought their children to Jesus so he could touch and bless them. But the disciples scolded the parents for bothering him.

When Jesus saw what was happening, he was angry with his disciples. He said to them, "Let the children come to me. Don't stop them! For the Kingdom of God belongs to those who are like these children. I tell you the truth, anyone who doesn't receive the Kingdom of God like a child will never enter it." Then he took the children in his arms and placed his hands on their heads and blessed them.

Mark 10:1, 13–16 NLT

Some grocery stores have fancy shopping carts with vehicle shapes for kids to ride in. Some bookstores and clothing stores create friendly areas for children. The managers of these stores foster an attitude of acceptance for little ones. Other stores have clerks hovering over children or signs advising shoppers of responsibility for broken items—sending a message to keep children away. Some people also tell us with their body language whether they welcome children.

Jesus made it clear that children are part of God's community. He embraced them, blessed them, welcomed them. God's kingdom reigns on earth in our hearts and actions. We should reach out to help children feel God's acceptance and approval. What message do you give at church or other settings where children are? Do you smile when you see a child? Do you engage children in conversation, or compliment them for their actions? Does your home have a safe area where children are welcome to play?

When you see children today, smile at them. Remember that you are your heavenly Father's child, and he is smiling at you. He's accepted you completely because of the wonderful sacrifice of his Son, Jesus.

LOOK WHO'S MOVING IN

I saw Heaven and earth new-created. Gone the first Heaven, gone the first earth, gone the sea. I saw Holy Jerusalem, new-created, descending resplendent out of Heaven, as ready for God as a bride for her husband. I heard a voice thunder from the Throne: "Look! Look! God has moved into the neighborhood, making his home with men and women! They're his people, he's their God. He'll wipe every tear from their eyes. Death is gone for good—tears gone, crying gone, pain gone—all the first order of things gone." The Enthroned continued, "Look! I'm making everything new. Write it all down—each word dependable and accurate." . . .

The City shimmered like a precious gem, light-filled, pulsing light. She had a wall majestic and high with twelve gates. At each gate stood an Angel.

Revelation 21:1–5, 12 MSG

When a "Sold" sign goes up, we like to try to find out about the prospective new neighbors. When the moving van arrives, we peek to discover who the newcomers are and what they possess. The end of the Bible gives us a glimpse at a new community and one of its residents. God, the neighbor moving in, will dwell among his people, and the city will sparkle. Think of how we will live knowing God is our neighbor!

God gave John a vision that John wrote down; we know it as the book of Revelation, the last book of the Bible. Revelation includes prophecy that gives us great hope for our eternal future. We can live today knowing that God already lives with us and with great hope for our future.

God's Holy Spirit dwells within all Christians, and Jesus has promised he is always with us. Our lives should add sparkle to our community as we let God's love shine through us. We should do what God the Father promises to do, working to dry the tears of lonely and hurt people. Then people will experience a little of heaven on earth.

COMMUNITY REVIVAL

Says the LORD, "I will return to Zion and will dwell in the midst of Jerusalem. Then Jerusalem will be called the City of Truth, and the mountain of the LORD of hosts will be called the Holy Mountain." Thus says the LORD of hosts, "Old men and old women will again sit in the streets of Jerusalem, each man with his staff in his hand because of age. And the streets of the city will be filled with boys and girls playing in its streets. . . .

"These are the things which you should do: speak the truth to one another; judge with truth and judgment for peace in your gates. Also let none of you devise evil in your heart against another, and do not love perjury; for all these are what I hate," declares the LORD.

Zechariah 8:3–5, 16–17 NASB

In unsafe communities mothers shelter their children and keep them indoors, and the elderly shy away from being outside. Gangs fill the streets, especially at night when it's easier not to be identified. The most vulnerable in society need protection. A thriving community has children playing outside, elderly people rocking on porches or sitting and knitting, talking and watching little ones. Mothers can relax and let their children run and play outside.

The prophet Zechariah predicted a future for Jerusalem, also called Zion, of the city filled with life and joyous activities. These words will one day be fulfilled and that city will know peace again. Zechariah ended the chapter from which this passage is taken by describing the future Jerusalem as a place everyone will visit to worship God and seek God's blessings.

For our communities, Zechariah's advice is also true. We must work for peace by treating people fairly. Lies divide and create distrust. Bad intentions cause harm. Truth combined with a desire to help others is the basis of peace. Don't scheme to get your way over a difference with neighbors but seek a resolution that satisfies everyone involved in the dispute.

GRATEFUL REACTIONS

As Jesus came down the mountain, he was followed by large crowds. Suddenly a man with leprosy came and knelt in front of Jesus. He said, "Lord, you have the power to make me well, if only you wanted to." Jesus put his hand on the man and said, "I want to! Now you are well." At once the man's leprosy disappeared. Jesus told him, "Don't tell anyone about this, but go and show the priest that you are well. Then take a gift to the temple just as Moses commanded, and everyone will know that you have been healed." . . .

Jesus went to the home of Peter, where he found that Peter's mother-in-law was sick in bed with fever. He took her by the hand, and the fever left her. Then she got up and served Jesus a meal.

Matthew 8:1–4, 14–15 CEV

It's not fun being sick, and we don't want anyone to see us or ask us to do anything. We seek relief and avoid socializing. Once we're really better we're ready to do anything.

The Bible records many occasions when Jesus healed someone, but in most cases, we don't see the reactions of those he made well. But Peter's mother-in-law got out of bed, completely well, and responded to Jesus by taking her place as hostess, expressing gratitude through her actions. Cooking, serving food, and sharing a meal are part of community and were this woman's return to the community.

Jesus told the healed leper to make his offering so the priest could declare him "clean" according to Jewish law and able to return to society. If you've ever had a contagious disease, spent time in the hospital, or been confined to your bed, you know that with healing we can feel alive again and celebrate by going out or inviting others in. Ask a friend who was sick to tea, lunch, or dessert and invite other mutual friends. Celebrate health. Thank God for your health. Express your gratitude that your friend is healthy again.

Tears for the Treasured City

As He was approaching [the city], at the descent of the Mount of Olives, the whole crowd of the disciples began to rejoice and to praise God [extolling Him exultantly and] loudly for all the mighty miracles and works of power that they had witnessed, crying, Blessed (celebrated with praises) is the King Who comes in the name of the Lord! Peace in heaven [freedom there from all the distresses that are experienced as the result of sin] and glory (majesty and splendor) in the highest [heaven]!

And some of the Pharisees from the throng said to Jesus, Teacher, reprove Your disciples!

He replied, I tell you that if these keep silent, the very stones will cry out.

And as He approached, He saw the city, and He wept [audibly] over it.

Luke 19:37–41 AMP

❋

Tears come after disaster when we realize what has been lost. Oil spills destroy shorelines; tornadoes splinter homes; terrorists attack and kill; illness incapacitates. Disaster can overwhelm us. Jesus wept as he surveyed Jerusalem. No disaster had caused visible damage, but Jesus saw beyond the obvious to the heart of the community and felt great sadness because the people had rejected him as their Messiah.

This happened on the day we sometimes call Palm Sunday. Crowds rejoiced and praised God as they saw Jesus preparing to enter the city. Some of the religious leaders scolded Jesus for allowing the people to praise him as King. They had allowed their hearts to become so hard that they couldn't see God at work among them. Jesus looked at the city and foretold its future destruction, the ravages of war that God would allow because people sought power instead of peace and pride instead of love. Jesus declared it was too late for them to find the way of peace.

We must want peace above our own needs. Peace in a community begins within our hearts, with acknowledging God, and with a desire to make peace with everyone.

Boomerang Living

Don't pick on people, jump on their failures, criticize their faults—unless, of course, you want the same treatment. That critical spirit has a way of boomeranging. It's easy to see a smudge on your neighbor's face and be oblivious to the ugly sneer on your own. Do you have the nerve to say, "Let me wash your face for you," when your own face is distorted by contempt? It's this whole traveling road-show mentality all over again, playing a holier-than-thou part instead of just living your part. Wipe that ugly sneer off your own face, and you might be fit to offer a wash-cloth to your neighbor. . . .

Here is a simple, rule-of-thumb guide for behavior: Ask yourself what you want people to do for you, then grab the initiative and do it for *them*.

Matthew 7:1–5, 12 MSG

What goes up must come down. Every action produces an equal and opposite reaction. These are scientific laws of gravity and motion; actions have consequences. Life has a boomerang effect too, and our actions cause reactions. When we smile at someone, she will normally smile back. When we treat a neighbor with respect, we usually receive respectful treatment. These are the simplest principles of what's called the Golden Rule.

Jesus gave us this principle of treating others the way we want to be treated after talking about not judging others and after prompting people to pray and expect God to respond to our needs. Before speaking or acting, we should think about possible reactions. Instead of looking for faults in others, we should check our own weaknesses and work on self-improvement.

Apply the Golden Rule. If a friend has a difficult child but your child has a more acquiescent personality, don't try to fix your friend's mothering skills. If you have a more organized house, don't make a show of it. Instead, welcome her into your home and accept her as a person unconditionally, letting God point out any needed improvements.

COMMUNITY PRAYER GETS RESULTS

Peter realized what had happened to him, and said, "Now I know that it is really true! The Lord sent his angel to rescue me from Herod's power and from everything the Jewish people expected to happen."

Aware of his situation, he went to the home of Mary, the mother of John Mark, where many people had gathered and were praying. Peter knocked at the outside door, and a servant named Rhoda came to answer it.

She recognized Peter's voice and was so happy that she ran back in without opening the door, and announced that Peter was standing outside. "You are crazy!" they told her. But she insisted that it was true.

So they answered, "It is his angel."

Meanwhile Peter kept on knocking. At last they opened the door, and when they saw him, they were amazed.

Acts 12:11–16 GNT

Prayer takes place everywhere, and many women gather in small or large groups to pray. Excitement comes when prayers are answered. Sometimes we can hardly believe God has answered. An unexpected blessing of a job, a car, or leniency in a court case can amaze us. God is in the business of performing miracles, especially when a community prays.

While Peter spent time in prison for his faith, the church prayed. The Bible doesn't indicate exactly what they prayed—perhaps specifically for Peter's release and more generally that God would receive glory and others would hear of Jesus because of Peter's circumstances. When Peter arrived and knocked and Rhoda announced the news, no one believed her at first.

When you pray with someone, expect answers and look for God's action. The answer might not be what you ask or expect, but God will rock your world. When women pray, things happen. Marriages grow strong, ministries begin and thrive, schools and neighborhoods turn around, people find healing. When you pray, and after you pray, look around you for changes and signs that God is responding, and share your observations and all good news.

241

A GENEROUS CHURCH COMMUNITY

I want to report on the surprising and generous ways in which God is working in the churches in Macedonia province. Fierce troubles came down on the people of those churches, pushing them to the very limit. The trial exposed their true colors: They were incredibly happy, though desperately poor. The pressure triggered something totally unexpected: an outpouring of pure and generous gifts. I was there and saw it for myself.

They gave offerings of whatever they could—far more than they could afford!—pleading for the privilege of helping out in the relief of poor Christians.

This was totally spontaneous, entirely their own idea, and caught us completely off guard. What explains it was that they had first given themselves unreservedly to God and to us. The other giving simply flowed out of the purposes of God working in their lives.

2 Corinthians 8:1–5 MSG

᛭

The generosity of a poor community surprised Paul. No one forced them to give, yet from the little they had, the people gave more than they could afford to give. The women might have had to make their food supply stretch further and mend clothes once again rather than buying fabric to make new.

Unexpected gifts surprise us, especially if we know the giver is financially burdened. A child picks a flower, a woman skips a meal to buy a birthday card or gift for a friend, or a shopper does without a few items on her list and buys lunch for a homeless person in front of a store. It's hard for people with money to understand some of these sacrifices, but imagine giving up a vacation or a new dress and giving the money to a poor family or a ministry. It would help others so much and lift their spirits. Imagine giving your church a large unexpected sum to use to help the poor in the church or community. Your gift might even spark more giving. Generosity shows God at work in our lives, especially when we consider giving a privilege.

LET'S PARTY, GIRLFRIENDS

"In your unfailing love you will lead the people you have redeemed. In your strength you will guide them to your holy dwelling. . . . The LORD will reign for ever and ever."

When Pharaoh's horses, chariots and horsemen went into the sea, the LORD brought the waters of the sea back over them, but the Israelites walked through the sea on dry ground.

Then Miriam the prophetess, Aaron's sister, took a tambourine in her hand, and all the women followed her, with tambourines and dancing. Miriam sang to them: "Sing to the LORD, for he is highly exalted. The horse and its rider he has hurled into the sea."

Exodus 15:13, 18–21 NIV

Moses and the people sang praises to God for delivering them from Pharaoh and four hundred years of slavery in Egypt. God had performed a miracle when he parted the sea to let the people pass into freedom. He roundly defeated their enemies as the Red Sea rolled back and swallowed up the Egyptian soldiers. The people's victory celebration proclaimed God's miracles and answers to their prayers. They sang about God's promise to bring them a new life in a special land.

Miriam listened until she could no longer contain her joy. She grabbed a tambourine and began dancing. Other women followed her and joined in as Miriam sang and danced. This group of people became a united community as they celebrated and interacted. Community begins and is strengthened whenever people get involved and join together, often to celebrate victory or share sorrow. Celebrating together develops a sense of belonging.

Women still revel over triumphs. Spontaneous singing and dancing express joy. It's good to party to rejoice in miracles and to share prayer answers and hope for the future. Is it time to invite friends over for a praise party soon?

Beauty & Health

Women look at the outside and seek beauty that satisfies the eyes. God looks inside to find true beauty, yet he created outward beauty too. Health is necessary for living a full life, and our choices can affect our health. Jesus spent much time healing people, revealing the importance of wholeness. On a deeper level, true wellness comes with a soul that is healed. Viewing beauty and health through God's eyes give us a new perspective.

When Jesus landed and saw a large crowd, he had compassion on them and healed their sick.

Matthew 14:14 NIV

Spa Treatments

This girl, who was also known as Esther, was lovely in form and features, and Mordecai had taken her as his own daughter when her father and mother died. . . .

Esther also was taken to the king's palace and entrusted to Hegai, who had charge of the harem. The girl pleased him and won his favor. Immediately he provided her with her beauty treatments and special food. He assigned to her seven maids selected from the king's palace. . . .

Esther had not revealed her nationality and family background, because Mordecai had forbidden her to do so. . . .

Before a girl's turn came to go in to King Xerxes, she had to complete twelve months of beauty treatments prescribed for the women, six months with oil of myrrh and six with perfumes and cosmetics.

Esther 2:7–10, 12 NIV

Esther, a young Jewish woman living in Persia, grew up as an orphan under her cousin Mordecai's care. The king's men chose Esther to enter a special beauty contest. The shapely and lovely girl who most pleased the king would become his new queen.

Esther's move into the palace with the rest of the contestants came with a spa package—twelve months of expensive and lavish beauty treatments. Esther's treatment included a special diet, perfumes, cosmetics, and oils. The king's servants understood that pampering enhances a woman's beauty—a reminder to us to take time to care for ourselves.

Besides her obvious good looks, Esther also had inner beauty—a calm, quiet spirit interested in serving others. We see her obeying Mordecai and winning favor with the servant in charge of the king's harem. This suggests a pleasant personality.

Inner and outer beauty—neither should be neglected. Do you need to schedule some much-needed time for yourself? While you enjoy soaking in a tub of special oils or surrounded by candlelight and soft music, give some thought to your inner beauty also. Who in your life needs your kindness, gentleness, and love today?

LOOKIN' GOOD

He was pleased with what he saw. Then God said, "And now we will make human beings; they will be like us and resemble us. They will have power over the fish, the birds, and all animals, domestic and wild, large and small." So God created human beings, making them to be like himself. He created them male and female, blessed them, and said, "Have many children, so that your descendants will live all over the earth and bring it under their control. I am putting you in charge of the fish, the birds, and all the wild animals. I have provided all kinds of grain and all kinds of fruit for you to eat." . . . God looked at everything he had made, and he was very pleased. Evening passed and morning came—that was the sixth day.

Genesis 1:25–29, 31 GNT

Oh, I think she has her mother's eyes . . . your grandmother's chin . . . her father's ears." Every new mother hears similar pronouncements. Finding oneself reflected in another person brings joy. Seeing something familiar in the people he created brought delight to God also.

On the first five days of creation, God approved his handiwork; he was pleased. But on the sixth day, after he made a man and a woman, the Bible says he was *very* pleased.

His most splendid, beautiful creation on earth so pleased God that he could hardly stop giving special gifts to the first couple: gifts of food, the ability to have children, and a world full of animals and flowering plants. He didn't want the beauty to stop with two people. He wanted that beauty to continue to fill the entire earth.

God makes each person in his likeness, or image. He sees something of himself when he looks at us. We can feel, reason, and create. We are made to reflect and represent God on earth.

Glance in the mirror at your reflection—you are made in God's image, and he likes what he sees!

No More Bad-Hair Days

Don't be intimidated. Eventually everything is going to be out in the open, and everyone will know how things really are. So don't hesitate to go public now.

Don't be bluffed into silence by the threats of bullies. There's nothing they can do to your soul, your core being. Save your fear for God, who holds your entire life—body and soul—in his hands.

What's the price of a pet canary? Some loose change, right? And God cares what happens to it even more than you do. He pays even greater attention to you, down to the last detail—even numbering the hairs on your head! So don't be intimidated by all this bully talk. You're worth more than a million canaries.

Stand up for me against world opinion and I'll stand up for you before my Father.

Matthew 10:26–32 MSG

The people of Israel understood that God would one day send them a king. They just weren't looking for a king like Jesus. So when Jesus sent his twelve closest friends on a preaching mission, he knew they would run into opposition. He wanted them to remember that God would be paying attention so they wouldn't be afraid.

There's no need for us to focus on the negative opinions others might have of us, as long as we are focused on doing life God's way. God knows when you're facing ridicule for choices you make because of your faith—just like he knows the number of hairs on your head. On average, we've each got over one hundred thousand strands of hair—so that's a lot of counting! You have great value, right down to the roots! You can shrug off your bad-hair days with a laugh.

More important than hair, however, is the body and soul of a woman, and according to this Scripture passage, if you stand up for God, he will stand up for you. Decide to do what he desires. Despite what the world might say, you have nothing to fear.

PEDI-CURE

[Jesus] set aside his robe, and put on an apron. Then he poured water into a basin and began to wash the feet of the disciples, drying them with his apron. When he got to Simon Peter, Peter said, "Master, *you* wash *my* feet?"

Jesus answered, "You don't understand now what I'm doing, but it will be clear enough to you later."

Peter persisted, "You're not going to wash my feet—ever!"

Jesus said, "If I don't wash you, you can't be part of what I'm doing."

"Master!" said Peter. "Not only my feet, then. Wash my hands! Wash my head!"

Jesus said, "If you've had a bath in the morning, you only need your feet washed now and you're clean from head to toe. My concern, you understand, is holiness, not hygiene."

John 13:4–10 MSG

The luxury of a pedicure—what pampering! In Jesus' day, most people wore sandals and walked from place to place. Dust and dirt from unpaved roads stuck to travelers' feet, and a good hostess provided water and towels so visitors could wash it off. If there was a servant in the home, he or she got the job.

It doesn't sound like fun to wash someone's dirty, stinky feet after a long day of walking or working. How amazing that Jesus, knowing he would die the next day, took time to wash his friends' feet! It's also understandable that Peter would object to Jesus' serving him in this way. Why should Jesus do something so trivial? But in the conversation between Jesus and Peter in this passage, Peter missed the point both times.

Jesus wanted to serve his friends with love as an example for them—and us. He was much more concerned with their hearts than their feet. If the Son of God could serve others, whether by washing feet or dying on the cross, how much more should his followers be *holy*—set apart and willing to serve as he did!

Beauty Secret

Let not yours be the [merely] external adorning with [elaborate] interweaving and knotting of the hair, the wearing of jewelry, or changes of clothes; but let it be the inward adorning and beauty of the hidden person of the heart, with the incorruptible and unfading charm of a gentle and peaceful spirit, which [is not anxious or wrought up, but] is very precious in the sight of God.

For it was thus that the pious women of old who hoped in God were [accustomed] to beautify themselves and were submissive to their husbands [adapting themselves to them as themselves secondary and dependent upon them]. . . .

Sarah obeyed Abraham [following his guidance and acknowledging his headship over her by] calling him lord (master, leader, authority). And you are now her true daughters if you do right and let nothing terrify you.

1 Peter 3:3–6 AMP

The apostle Peter wrote this passage in a letter to persecuted Christians not long after the church began. Living among people hostile to faith in God certainly can cause fear and anxiety, but Peter knew the antidote—doing the right thing no matter what the adversity because we know God will eventually right every wrong.

Peter's advice just happens to have a beauty bonus too. True loveliness radiates from inside with charm, peace, and gentleness. But how can you experience peace when the diagnosis is cancer, or you've been laid off, or the car is totaled, or your spouse or a child continues to stubbornly make bad decisions?

Women like Sarah, Abraham's wife, developed inner beauty by basing their actions on trust in God. Even when Abraham acted foolishly, Sarah showed him respect. God's charm school emphasizes considering others' needs before our own. God's daughters have hope because we believe God's promises. When faith lets go of worry, you feel free to smile and let your inner peace shine out to all.

And the beauty bonus? Inner beauty never wrinkles or fades.

PURELY BEAUTIFUL

My dear friends, since you belong to the Lord Jesus, we beg and urge you to live as we taught you. Then you will please God. You are already living that way, but try even harder. Remember the instructions we gave you as followers of the Lord Jesus. God wants you to be holy, so don't be immoral in matters of sex. Respect and honor your wife. Don't be a slave of your desires or live like people who don't know God. You must not cheat any of the Lord's followers in matters of sex. Remember, we warned you that he punishes everyone who does such things. God didn't choose you to be filthy, but to be pure. So if you don't obey these rules, you are not really disobeying us. You are disobeying God, who gives you his Holy Spirit.

1 Thessalonians 4:1–8 CEV

Being desired makes a woman feel happy and loved, but love can be confused with sex. Sex is a beautiful expression of love in married couples committed to one another, but sex itself cannot make a woman beautiful or loved.

Pagan religions often included sexual immorality as part of their rites, and throughout the Roman Empire few boundaries were placed on sexual conduct. The apostle Paul, writing to a young church in a sex-charged culture, encouraged the believers to take a different view of sex—God's view.

God values sexual purity. The word *pure* means "wholesome." *Wholesome* conjures up pictures of healthy foods, rosy cheeks, and happy smiles, but the word also means "to promote good health and well-being." Sex within the boundaries of a committed, loving marriage does just that.

A wholesome woman is healthy in body, mind, and soul. She promotes her own good health and cares for herself in every way, including making wise daily choices.

Each day is a fresh start. Each day is an opportunity to take charge of one's own body and beauty by living with sexual purity.

TIME AND BEAUTY

No more stumbling around. Get on with it! The good, the right, the true—these are the actions appropriate for daylight hours. . . .

Don't waste your time on useless work, mere busywork, the barren pursuits of darkness. Expose these things for the sham they are. It's a scandal when people waste their lives on things they must do in the darkness where no one will see. Rip the cover off those frauds and see how attractive they look. . . . So watch your step. Use your head. Make the most of every chance you get. These are desperate times! Don't live carelessly, unthinkingly. Make sure you understand what the Master wants.

Don't drink too much wine. That cheapens your life. Drink the Spirit of God, huge draughts of him. Sing hymns instead of drinking songs!

Ephesians 5:8–13, 15–19 MSG

This passage speaks of living mindfully—a wide-awake life tuned in to what God wants. Paul was reminding the Christians in Ephesus that their former, aimless way of life—what Paul called living in darkness—had to go. It was no longer appropriate for them—or for us.

Wide-awake women weigh decisions carefully. They choose to work on worthwhile projects and accept opportunities for a fuller life. They don't stumble around doing whatever everyone else wants. They don't party too much or lazily watch hours of TV.

Choosing to use time wisely sounds simple, but it's hard to practice in our busy, materialistic world. We need watchful eyes and attentive ears, reading the Bible and praying, to discover the best opportunities and understand what God wants for us—which is the measuring stick for living well.

Wide-awake living is attractive—much more than any mask of busyness and frantic activity. The wide-awake life means a daily treasure hunt to observe, discover, and grab the opportunities that serve God and make life beautiful.

BETTER THAN PILATES

Exercise daily in God—no spiritual flabbiness, please! Workouts in the gymnasium are useful, but a disciplined life in God is far more so, making you fit both today and forever. You can count on this. Take it to heart. This is why we've thrown ourselves into this venture so totally. We're banking on the living God, Savior of all men and women, especially believers.

Get the word out. Teach all these things. And don't let anyone put you down because you're young. Teach believers with your life: by word, by demeanor, by love, by faith, by integrity. Stay at your post reading Scripture, giving counsel, teaching. And that special gift of ministry you were given when the leaders of the church laid hands on you and prayed—keep that dusted off and in use.

1 Timothy 4:7–14 MSG

米

A good workout stretches the muscles, pumps the heart, and pulls oxygen into the cells. A regular exercise routine invigorates the body, trims flab, keeps the heart beating well, and can add years to a person's life. Exercise might not feel good at the time, as our muscles ache and sweat pours out, but over time we find we've got a beautiful, healthy glow.

Despite all the benefits of physical fitness, Paul wrote to Timothy, his young protégé, that spiritual fitness is a more important goal. Spiritual exercise leads to a healthy soul, the part of a woman that lives forever.

Whether you're young, old, or in between, choose to keep spiritually fit. Stretch by sharing your faith. Each one of us has a unique gift to discover and share—make this your aerobic workout. Spiritual gifts come from God and are meant to be used for the good of other believers. Do strength training by making choices that will please God. Love others as your cooldown.

However you choose to build spiritual fitness, do it wholeheartedly. Spiritual fitness, much more than physical fitness, is a gift of beauty we can give ourselves.

LUMINARIES

We refuse to wear masks and play games. We don't maneuver and manipulate behind the scenes. And we don't twist God's Word to suit ourselves. Rather, we keep everything we do and say out in the open, the whole truth on display, so that those who want to can see and judge for themselves in the presence of God. . . .

All [others] have eyes for is the fashionable god of darkness. . . . They're stone-blind to the dayspring brightness of the Message that shines with Christ, who gives us the best picture of God we'll ever get. . . .

All we are is messengers, errand runners from Jesus for you. It started when God said, "Light up the darkness!" and our lives filled up with light as we saw and understood God in the face of Christ, all bright and beautiful.

2 Corinthians 4:2–6 MSG

A row of luminaries on a driveway lights the night with a welcoming glow. The candles or flashlights inside can't contain the light—it shines out through the openings. Just as God "turned on the light" at Creation, he turns on the light in our lives so we can see him.

In this passage, Paul wanted the Corinthians to understand that this light is for sharing. Like the Corinthians, we are meant to be luminaries, letting others glimpse a bit of heaven, a bit of Christ's love. Love increases a person's glow. A woman in love, a bride, and a mother holding her newborn all radiate with the glow of love.

We have daily opportunities to glow even more. Women don't need to cover up with a mask or play games of pretend. We can be real, open, and truthful because we have a true picture of God, depicted for us in the Bible.

Luminary comes from Anglo-Saxon words meaning "heavenly light" or "window." Are you a luminary? Does Christ's light radiate through you? Let God's beauty shine! Be a window through which others look to find the source of the light.

THE TRUTH ABOUT GOOD HEALTH

Beloved, I pray that all may go well with you and that you may be in good health, as it goes well with your soul. For I rejoiced greatly when the brothers came and testified to your truth, as indeed you are walking in the truth. I have no greater joy than to hear that my children are walking in the truth.

Beloved, it is a faithful thing you do in all your efforts for these brothers, strangers as they are, who testified to your love before the church. . . .

Beloved, do not imitate evil but imitate good. Whoever does good is from God; whoever does evil has not seen God. Demetrius has received a good testimony from everyone, and from the truth itself. We also add our testimony, and you know that our testimony is true.

3 John 2–6, 11–12 ESV

What a joy to wake up feeling good! It's also comforting to hear that someone we prayed for feels great. Answered prayers are wonderful news and confirm our time spent in prayer. Praying for friends benefits their health and encourages their faith.

Prayer, good health, and wellness of the soul go together. There's also a connection noted here between good spiritual health and lifestyle.

Walking is an exercise where we take one step after another in a specific direction. This means we must persist in living our faith and focus on our direction. Choosing truth means to make a choice based on reality. That implies understanding the difference between reality and man-made arguments that truth is relative. We exercise faith as we discern truth and act on it.

Demetrius, an early Christian whom the apostle John praised in this passage, modeled godly behavior and served as a role model for others who observed his life. Who is your Demetrius? Find someone who lives according to biblical principles and follow her example. Good health continues with daily choices that include being honest with yourself and others.

Word Famine

God said, "Right. So, I'm calling it quits with my people Israel. I'm no longer acting as if everything is just fine. . . .

"I'll turn your parties into funerals and make every song you sing a dirge. Everyone will walk around in rags, with sunken eyes and bald heads. Think of the worst that could happen—your only son, say, murdered. That's a hint of Judgment Day. . . .

"I'll send a famine through the whole country. It won't be food or water that's lacking, but my Word. . . . People will . . . go anywhere, listen to anyone, hoping to hear God's Word—but they won't hear it.

"On Judgment Day, lovely young girls will faint of Word-thirst."

Amos 8:2, 10–13 MSG

The people of Israel turned from God's ways numerous times. When that happened, God sent a messenger to call them back to him. This passage comes from the prophet Amos. The word picture Amos presented is not a pretty one. God's patience wouldn't last forever.

Disasters are never pretty. Hurricanes, earthquakes, tsunamis, and drought bring despair, hunger, and poverty. Anyone who has experienced a disaster understands the shock, the hopeless feelings, and the struggle to find basic necessities.

Far worse than any disaster, however, would be a famine, a drought, of hearing from God.

So often we take for granted what is plentiful. The Bible is the most published book throughout history and easily accessible in our world. It's easy to ignore the Bible, but without it, people drift. Imagine everyone drifting, wandering, hoping to hear truth and God's message of love—but finding it nowhere.

This passage is a billboard for what is most vital for inner beauty—knowing God through the Bible, his Word. Wall Street or the fashion industry can't set a devastated world right, but reading and memorizing the Bible will assure that you'll be able to survive any disaster.

BEAUTY BY GOD

All his brothers and sisters and friends came to his house and celebrated. They told him how sorry they were, and consoled him for all the trouble GOD had brought him. Each of them brought generous house-warming gifts.

GOD blessed Job's later life even more than his earlier life. He ended up with fourteen thousand sheep, six thousand camels, one thousand teams of oxen, and one thousand donkeys. He also had seven sons and three daughters. He named the first daughter Dove, the second, Cinnamon, and the third, Darkeyes. There was not a woman in that country as beautiful as Job's daughters. Their father treated them as equals with their brothers, providing the same inheritance.

Job lived on another hundred and forty years, living to see his children and grandchildren—four generations of them!

Job 42:11–16 MSG

Earlier in his life, Job lost all his family except his wife and all his possessions. At this point in Job's story, God had given Job a new family and great wealth. Having lost so much before, Job's new children and fortune must have seemed dearer, especially knowing they were gifts from God.

True beauty comes from God, and he supplied it in Job's daughters. Most parents see beauty in their children, and Job would have loved these new daughters no matter how they looked, but their names reflect a father's love—Dove, a free spirit and symbol for peace; Cinnamon, a fragrant scent and seasoning that adds zest to food; and Darkeyes, someone who captures hearts with her penetrating looks.

And Job, the happy dad, treated his daughters like princesses. He gave them the same inheritance as his sons, something unheard of in biblical days. Through his own misery, Job had searched to know God. Perhaps that's why he valued his daughters as much as his sons.

How well do you know God? As you get to know him more and more, you'll be able to appreciate how highly God values you.

OUTWARDLY UNATTRACTIVE

He grew up before Him like a tender shoot, and like a root out of parched ground; He has no stately form or majesty that we should look upon Him, nor appearance that we should be attracted to Him. He was despised and forsaken of men, a man of sorrows and acquainted with grief; and like one from whom men hide their face He was despised, and we did not esteem Him. . . .

By oppression and judgment He was taken away; and as for His generation, who considered that He was cut off out of the land of the living for the transgression of my people, to whom the stroke was due?

Isaiah 53:2–3, 8 NASB

Beauty is said to be in the eye of the beholder. We see this in little ones who love their elderly grandparents—who might have faces full of wrinkles or be bent, bald, or even scarred from accidents—and mothers who love babies born with defects. Caregivers see the beauty of the person they knew before disease and tragedy marred a loved one. Beauty radiates from within and remains when outer looks fade.

People can seem to age quickly when they are seriously ill or facing difficult circumstances or tragedy. This passage from the prophet Isaiah describes how Jesus looked as he died on the cross. Grief and sorrow changed his appearance. Severe beatings, carrying the heavy cross, and being nailed to the wooden beams marred his body. Onlookers hid their faces or turned away, refusing to look at him.

Jesus didn't cling to outward appearance. Inside he remained the same loving person; his lack of outward beauty on the cross didn't stop him from loving us. His despised appearance actually was a lovely thing—because his suffering on the cross made a beautiful difference in our lives.

ADORNED BY GOD

Instead of your shame you will have a double portion, and instead of humiliation they will shout for joy over their portion. Therefore they will possess a double portion in their land, everlasting joy will be theirs. . . .

Then their offspring will be known among the nations, and their descendants in the midst of the peoples. All who see them will recognize them because they are the offspring whom the LORD has blessed.

I will rejoice greatly in the LORD, my soul will exult in my God; for He has clothed me with garments of salvation, He has wrapped me with a robe of righteousness, as a bridegroom decks himself with a garland, and as a bride adorns herself with her jewels.

Isaiah 61:7, 9–10 NASB

Bridal magazines show full-color beauty of women adorned in the most beautiful fashions with sparkling jewels, headpieces, and shoes that match. There's something radiant about a bride, full of joy, anticipation, and the knowledge that someone cherishes her.

Isaiah prophesied about Jesus and the future restoration of Jerusalem as his bride. He delivered this message long before the destruction of the city and the captivity of the people took place, to give the Israelites hope. Although the city would be destroyed and the people alienated from God, the city would be restored and the people would once again rejoice.

This passage holds a promise for you as well. Your Father in heaven cherishes you and wants each of his daughters to enjoy life with him, now and forever. From the day a woman becomes a Christian, she is adorned like a bride. Envision the love and new garments and walk as though dressed in them already. God already blesses each daughter daily. Smile because God loves you. It's a beauty secret that lets a woman glow even more than a bride!

HEALTHY FOOD CONTEST

Daniel made up his mind that he would not defile himself with the king's choice food or with the wine which he drank; so he sought permission from the commander of the officials that he might not defile himself. . . .

"Please test your servants for ten days, and let us be given some vegetables to eat and water to drink.

"Then let our appearance be observed in your presence and the appearance of the youths who are eating the king's choice food; and deal with your servants according to what you see."

So he listened to them in this matter and tested them for ten days.

At the end of ten days their appearance seemed better and they were fatter than all the youths who had been eating the king's choice food.

Daniel 1:8, 12–15 NASB

A feast fit for a king! All the richness of decadent chocolates, fried specialties, fountain drinks, the house wine, and fancy breads sounds scrumptious. But the king's feast didn't interest Daniel.

During the Israelites' captivity in Babylon, the king chose the brightest and best-looking young men of Judah, including Daniel, to serve him. Daniel followed God wholeheartedly and wanted to obey his laws. He and his friends challenged the servant in charge to allow them to turn down the gourmet banquet.

It's fun to dine on fine foods occasionally, but the best foods for health are still the fruits and vegetables God made. Natural foods for natural good looks and health outperform fad diets and junk food every time.

God cares about our physical appearance and health. The food laws he gave the Israelites helped them eat healthfully and be healthy. Why not try a healthy diet yourself, with plenty of water and fresh produce? See how you feel after ten days. We don't have to follow the eating habits of our culture—we can choose, like Daniel, to live a godly and healthy life.

THE VALUE OF REST

[Moses] told them that the LORD had said, "Tomorrow is the Sabbath, a sacred day of rest in honor of me. So gather all you want to bake or boil, and make sure you save enough for tomorrow."

The people obeyed, and the next morning the food smelled fine and had no worms. "You may eat the food," Moses said. "Today is the Sabbath in honor of the LORD, and there won't be any of this food on the ground today. You will find it there for the first six days of the week, but not on the Sabbath." . . .

The LORD said, ". . . Remember that I was the one who gave you the Sabbath. That's why on the sixth day I provide enough bread for two days. Everyone is to stay home and rest on the Sabbath."

Exodus 16:23–26, 28–29 CEV

Children persistently resist sleeping and battle to stay up. Many adults resist getting needed rest too. God created the Sabbath as a time to focus on him, thank him for his blessings, relax, and refresh. At God's direction, the Israelites observed the Sabbath on the seventh day of the week. Now Christians choose when and how to rest. It might be Sunday, the traditional day of worship, but it doesn't have to be.

No matter what day of the week you celebrate as Sabbath rest, use it for physical and spiritual renewal. The word *Sabbath* means "to cease from work." Real rest begins with slowing down, noting blessings, expressing gratitude to God, releasing stress, and letting go of worries. Preparing the day before with cooking enough for two days is not that difficult. Anticipating leisure is a treat worth planning and scheduling for.

Sabbath rest allows time to release worries, relax muscles, and spend time with loved ones without rushing. Lack of rest shows up in inattentiveness, stress, increased blood pressure, and health problems. Honoring God restores our balance and focus in life so we can relax and let God bless us. And that's beautiful!

The Beauty of God's Love

Moses went up from the plains of Moab to Mount Nebo, to the top of Pisgah, which is opposite Jericho. And the LORD showed him all the land, Gilead as far as Dan. . . . And the LORD said to him, "This is the land of which I swore to Abraham, to Isaac, and to Jacob, 'I will give it to your offspring.' I have let you see it with your eyes, but you shall not go over there." So Moses the servant of the LORD died there in the land of Moab, according to the word of the LORD. . . . Moses was 120 years old when he died. His eye was undimmed, and his vigor unabated. And the people of Israel wept for Moses in the plains of Moab thirty days.

Deuteronomy 34:1, 4–5, 7–8
ESV

Moses spent much of his life outdoors, shepherding for forty years and then wandering the desert with the Israelites for another forty years. A day came when God let Moses know that he was going to die and let him see the Promised Land although he would not enter it. Before his death, Moses gathered his people and reminded them of God's love, blessed them, and proclaimed Joshua as their new leader.

Death stings, no matter what the age of the person who died. The people left feel the loss, especially when they were loved by the person who is gone.

Moses is remembered for facing the most powerful leader on earth at the time, the pharaoh of Egypt, freeing the Israelites from Egyptian slavery, and receiving the Ten Commandments from God. His people mourned his death because they knew he had dearly loved them. Yet Moses, a great man, didn't get to enter the Promised Land.

We may never accomplish all our personal dreams, especially as we balance family with career and helping others. But we can choose to follow God, love at all times, and bring the beauty of God's love into the lives of others.

UNFAILING ENERGY

Have you not known? Have you not heard? The everlasting God, the Lord, the Creator of the ends of the earth, does not faint or grow weary; there is no searching of His understanding.

He gives power to the faint and weary, and to him who has no might He increases strength [causing it to multiply and making it to abound].

Even youths shall faint and be weary, and [selected] young men shall feebly stumble and fall exhausted; but those who wait for the Lord [who expect, look for, and hope in Him] shall change and renew their strength and power; they shall lift their wings and mount up [close to God] as eagles [mount up to the sun]; they shall run and not be weary, they shall walk and not faint or become tired.

Isaiah 40:28–31 AMP

Some days we struggle to get up, simple tasks wear us out, and we feel exhausted rather quickly. Sometimes the cause is physical—lack of sleep, exercise, and good food. Sometimes difficult situations drain emotional energy. Young mothers, working women, students, the aged—we all need more strength and a source of unfailing energy.

When Isaiah spoke the words in this passage, Israel's exile in Babylon would not occur for another 150 years. But God gave his people these comforting words in advance. He wanted them to understand that he would not leave them alone, that he would encourage and energize them physically and emotionally. He would not leave them to languish.

When God gives us passion and purpose, we often also feel an unexplained energy boost. Starting our day with prayer and reading the Bible often brings a surge of joy and strength that keeps us from being worn out by troubles, annoyances, and fears. Anytime you feel drained, pause and ask God for a refill of strength and energy. He is never too tired to listen to your needs or give you more strength and joy from his unlimited supply.

FOOD FOR HEALTH

"I have only a handful of flour left in the jar and a little cooking oil in the bottom of the jug. I was just gathering a few sticks to cook this last meal, and then my son and I will die."

But Elijah said to her, "Don't be afraid! Go ahead and do just what you've said, but make a little bread for me first. Then use what's left to prepare a meal for yourself and your son. For this is what the LORD, the God of Israel, says: There will always be flour and olive oil left in your containers until the time when the LORD sends rain and the crops grow again!" . . .

There was always enough flour and olive oil left in the containers, just as the LORD had promised through Elijah.

1 Kings 17:12–14, 16 NLT

During a five-year famine in Israel, this widow and her son came close to death. She was making a very small fire to cook what she believed would be the last meal she and the son she loved would eat. God knew her situation and chose to send the prophet Elijah to help her. The widow listened to Elijah and believed and acted upon the hope he offered.

Moments earlier, Elijah had asked for a drink of water. The widow gave it to him quickly although water was scarce. Her willingness to help Elijah revealed the inner generosity of a beautiful heart, and God rewarded her with abundance.

Like the widow in this passage, we can willingly respond to needs, especially for the basics that sustain life and health—water, food, clothing, and shelter. A generous woman reaches out with an open hand that reflects a beautiful, trusting heart. Be willing to share what God provides. He is the Creator of heaven and earth, and everything is his. And when you belong to him, everything is yours also. He has promised to take care of you, and he never breaks a promise.

Beautiful Gifts

After Jesus was born in Bethlehem of Judea in the days of Herod the king, magi from the east arrived in Jerusalem, saying, "Where is He who has been born King of the Jews? For we saw His star in the east and have come to worship Him." . . .

After hearing the king, they went their way; and the star, which they had seen in the east, went on before them until it came and stood over the place where the Child was. When they saw the star, they rejoiced exceedingly with great joy. After coming into the house they saw the Child with Mary His mother; and they fell to the ground and worshiped Him. Then, opening their treasures, they presented to Him gifts of gold, frankincense, and myrrh.

Matthew 2:1–2, 9–11 NASB

❋

A lovely gift for a new baby blesses a woman, yet the gifts Mary received for Jesus from these strangers must have puzzled her greatly.

Gold for a poor family would have been a great blessing. Gold also belonged in king's palaces.

Oil distilled from the resin of the frankincense shrub was used to anoint kings to set them apart to rule, and perfumes made use of frankincense because of its pleasing fragrance. A beautiful scent for a newborn King born in a smelly stable!

Mary could use the gift of myrrh for medicinal purposes, as an antiseptic. Yet she would have known that myrrh also was used to prepare a dead body for burial. Babies normally didn't receive a gift of myrrh.

No mother wants to think of her child's death. Yet Mary couldn't help but notice the symbolism of these unusual baby gifts. Her child was no ordinary baby.

The visitors who brought these gifts worshipped Jesus and used their gifts as expressions of honor. The admiration and thought behind costly gifts and perfumes can mean more than the gifts themselves, especially when they celebrate the beauty of a special life.

Beautiful Feet

Scripture says, "Whoever believes in him will not be ashamed."

There is no difference between Jews and Greeks. They all have the same Lord, who gives his riches to everyone who calls on him. So then, "Whoever calls on the name of the Lord will be saved."

But how can people call on him if they have not believed in him? How can they believe in him if they have not heard his message? How can they hear if no one tells the Good News? How can people tell the Good News if no one sends them? As Scripture says, "How beautiful are the feet of the messengers who announce the Good News." But not everyone has believed the Good News.

Isaiah asks, "Lord, who has believed our message?"

Romans 10:11–16 GOD'S WORD

✳

Shoes, nail polish, ankle bracelets, foot scrubs, and massages—beautiful feet require a lot of our attention, whether our feet are petite and dainty or long and elegant. Our feet carry us everywhere and take quite a beating each day. It's nice to put our feet up, stretch them, wiggle our toes, and then rest.

However, this passage tells us that what makes our feet beautiful to God is what we do *with* them, not to them. Feet that go places and tell others who need to hear the good news about Jesus—now those are beautiful feet! Where do your feet go—to the office, the mall, the park, the beach? To the farm or the factory?

God cares about beautiful feet. Rejoice when you soak them, have a professional pedicure, slip into new shoes, or simply go barefoot on the beach and wiggle your toes in the sand. But wherever you go, whether you run, dance, walk, march, or drive, be a messenger for God. Tell those you meet about your faith. You'll have beautiful feet!

THAT TIME OF MONTH

When a woman has a discharge, and the discharge in her body is blood, she shall be in her menstrual impurity for seven days, and whoever touches her shall be unclean until the evening. And everything on which she lies during her menstrual impurity shall be unclean. Everything also on which she sits shall be unclean. . . .

But if she is cleansed of her discharge, she shall count for herself seven days, and after that she shall be clean. And on the eighth day she shall take two turtledoves or two pigeons and bring them to the priest, to the entrance of the tent of meeting. And the priest shall use one for a sin offering and the other for a burnt offering. And the priest shall make atonement for her before the LORD for her unclean discharge.

Leviticus 15:19–20, 28–30
ESV

A young lady feels mixed emotions with her first period. It signals womanhood but can be scary, painful, and messy. Most women remember the first one.

God made us with the ability to bear children, and our cycle is part of our femininity. God cares about the uniqueness of women, our health, our well-being, our purity. To be set apart during a time of moodiness and not be touched while feeling a bit touchy might have been a relief during an era when women labored so hard.

The time of "uncleanness" included a break from work, but it also meant isolation from hugs, kisses, and touching. This passage helps us understand women in the Bible, especially a woman Jesus healed after she'd experienced twelve years of bleeding—twelve years without hugs from her family!

God's laws both promoted healthy habits and protected women in a culture that didn't value women highly. What a relief that we have never had to go through the time of uncleanness, the cleansing ritual, and the pigeon offerings! And what a relief that Jesus sees and understands our every need.

Splendidly Clothed

Don't worry about having something to eat or wear. Life is more than food or clothing. Look at the crows! They don't plant or harvest, and they don't have storehouses or barns. But God takes care of them. You are much more important than any birds. Can worry make you live longer? If you don't have power over small things, why worry about everything else?

Look how the wild flowers grow! They don't work hard to make their clothes. But I tell you that Solomon with all his wealth wasn't as well clothed as one of these flowers. God gives such beauty to everything that grows in the fields, even though it is here today and thrown into a fire tomorrow. Won't he do even more for you? You have such little faith!

Luke 12:22–28 CEV

Fabrics, colors, patterns, and accessories attract the eye. But worrying about our wardrobes can cause us to overspend, incur debt, turn shopping into an addiction, and fuel jealousy. In this faith-building passage, Jesus encouraged his listeners to trust God to provide well for them.

God knows how to create beauty. He made a world of show-stopping flowers, so we know he loves colors and style. But life is more than shopping and clothes. The verses after this passage remind us to seek God and his kingdom.

Flowers have a genetic code within the seed to produce gorgeous blooms. God gave us specific DNA that produced our looks, and he loves how we each look. He also gave us hearts that he fills with love when we seek him. God wants us to stop living shallow lives and start living deeply and passionately. He wants us to dwell on relationships, starting by spending time with him, and to stop fretting about outward appearances.

As God gives exquisite beauty to flowers that fade quickly, so much more will he care for us. Life can be deeper and fuller without preoccupation over styles and trends.

GET MOVING

Near the Sheep Gate in Jerusalem there is a pool with five porches; in Hebrew it is called Bethzatha. A large crowd of sick people were lying on the porches—the blind, the lame, and the paralyzed. A man was there who had been sick for thirty-eight years. Jesus saw him lying there, and he knew that the man had been sick for such a long time; so he asked him, "Do you want to get well?"

The sick man answered, "Sir, I don't have anyone here to put me in the pool when the water is stirred up; while I am trying to get in, somebody else gets there first."

Jesus said to him, "Get up, pick up your mat, and walk." Immediately the man got well; he picked up his mat and started walking.

John 5:2–9 GNT

米

We might think the crippled man in this passage had stopped trying to get well and answered Jesus' question with excuses. But Jesus knew the man's heart, and so he healed him.

Do you want to be well? If so, you must make the effort to eat healthful foods, exercise, and get enough sleep. We all have choices where health is concerned. We can choose the actions that lead to health, or we can offer excuses, complain about our figures, and continue living the same unhealthy lifestyle that seems easier.

Certainly there are circumstances that grab our time and disabilities that make it harder to be active. However, we need to schedule time for ourselves to nurture our own health. One of the best gifts we can give others is to be as healthy as possible, so we will have energy and be around to serve others a long time.

After Jesus healed the man in this passage, he told him to pick up his mat and walk. This implied that the man was now fit to carry his own load and participate in life, a reminder to us to choose health and get moving.

HEALING TOUCH ANY DAY

A woman who was possessed by a spirit was there. The spirit had disabled her for 18 years. She was hunched over and couldn't stand up straight. When Jesus saw her, he called her to come to him and said, "Woman, you are free from your disability." He placed his hands on her, and she immediately stood up straight and praised God.

The synagogue leader was irritated with Jesus for healing on the day of worship. . . .

The Lord said, "You hypocrites! Don't each of you free your ox or donkey on the day of worship? Don't you then take it out of its stall to give it some water to drink? Now, here is a descendant of Abraham. Satan has kept her in this condition for 18 years. Isn't it right to free her on the day of worship?"

Luke 13:11–16 GOD'S WORD

Eighteen years of pain and disability gone instantly! Although she was too bent over to even see Jesus, he spotted her and called her to come. He pronounced her healing and reached out to touch her; she stood tall and straight for the first time in nearly two decades. Jesus' response to the critical religious leader showed that he viewed the day to worship God as the perfect day to heal a child of God.

How do you view time? Too often we let our perceptions get in the way of using God's gift of time in ways that will please him. We are in a rush. We've made commitments. We have responsibilities. The grass needs cutting, the house needs cleaning, the flower beds need weeding—now! We put off helping others for a later date that never comes.

Seize the moment and reach out to help others when you see the need. Stop and chat or call that friend to give a kind, healing word. Don't think you'll magically have time another day; that seldom happens.

Every day offers an opportunity to reach out and touch someone's heart and life. Take time to do it!

Reaching Out for Healing

As Jesus went, the people were crowding around him.

A woman who had been suffering from chronic bleeding for twelve years was in the crowd. No one could cure her. She came up behind Jesus, touched the edge of his clothes, and her bleeding stopped at once.

Jesus asked, "Who touched me?"

After everyone denied touching him, Peter said, "Teacher, the people are crowding you and pressing against you."

Jesus said, "Someone touched me. I know power has gone out of me."

The woman saw that she couldn't hide. Trembling, she quickly bowed in front of him. There, in front of all the people, she told why she touched him and how she was cured at once.

Jesus told her, "Daughter, your faith has made you well. Go in peace!"

Luke 8:42–48 GOD'S WORD

This woman's healing is described in three of the Gospels. One account explains that she had spent all her money on doctors yet had grown worse.

The woman knew the law of Moses forbade women who were bleeding from touching or being touched. Still, she believed that if she could just touch Jesus' coat, she would be healed. She decided to risk it and reach out.

Jesus could have let the woman receive healing without anyone knowing. But he stopped and talked with her. Jesus responded to her need and did more than stop the bleeding. He addressed her with the affectionate term *daughter*, helping others view her as a woman of faith and ending her isolation from society. His words "Go in peace" reveal that he understood her past frustrations and wanted to give her hope for a better future.

Healing begins when we reach out for help. We were meant to live connected to God and to one another. Whether you need physical or emotional healing, whom can you reach out to today? The risk is worth it!

LESS STRESS WITH SHARING

Jesus said, "I praise You, Father, Lord of heaven and earth, that You have hidden these things from the wise and intelligent and have revealed them to infants. Yes, Father, for this way was well-pleasing in Your sight. All things have been handed over to Me by My Father; and no one knows the Son except the Father; nor does anyone know the Father except the Son, and anyone to whom the Son wills to reveal Him.

"Come to Me, all who are weary and heavy-laden, and I will give you rest. Take My yoke upon you and learn from Me, for I am gentle and humble in heart, and you will find rest for your souls. For My yoke is easy and My burden is light."

Matthew 11:25–30 NASB

The members of a support group form a team to encourage one another as they face similar hardships. There's comfort in knowing we are not alone, that someone else understands our problems. Having others hold us accountable helps us to do the sometimes difficult things we need to do to deal with our situations.

Stress and exhaustion are the norm for many women. Pressures at work and at home can create unbearable burdens. In this passage, Jesus shares the ultimate antidote to weariness and stress—a real relationship—being yoked with him.

In many parts of the world today, farmers still slip a wooden yoke over the heads of two oxen. The yoke guides them into moving together in one direction and spreads the weight of the load they pull—heavier than one ox could pull separately. One ox must be the lead, however, to keep the movement steady. Jesus called his invitation to let him share the load his *yoke*—but he will lead.

Being yoked with Jesus means that we are never alone, for he shares the load and walks beside us as we work together with Jesus.

Don't Show Off

Everything they do is just to show off in front of others. They even make a big show of wearing Scripture verses on their foreheads and arms, and they wear big tassels for everyone to see. They love the best seats at banquets and the front seats in the meeting places. And when they are in the market, they like to have people greet them as their teachers. . . .

You Pharisees and teachers are in for trouble! You're nothing but show-offs. You're like tombs that have been whitewashed. On the outside they are beautiful, but inside they are full of bones and filth. That's what you are like. Outside you look good, but inside you are evil and only pretend to be good.

Matthew 23:5–7, 27–28 CEV

Jesus spoke these words to highlight problems of the Jewish religious leaders, the scribes and Pharisees. The Pharisees advocated strict adherence not just to God's law but to their own laws and traditions. These men wore Bible verses for all to see, but they forgot to live them.

Jesus pointed out the ugliness of their inner greed and selfishness. Selfishness is focusing on what we want without regard for others or the hurt we might cause them. Greed is an excessive desire for possessions or position. The Pharisees thought they could win God's favor by doing the "right" things. Their pride became more important to them than God, and they wanted to show off and "look good" to gain the people's attention and praise.

We can't win God's favor or life with him forever by anything we do—only through our faith in Jesus. The first antidote to selfishness, greed, and pride is faith and a humble look at ourselves. Then gratitude and generosity can flow. When we share what we have and share our lives with others, we have no need to show off.

WELLSPRING OF LIFE

My children, listen when your father corrects you. Pay attention and learn good judgment, for I am giving you good guidance. Don't turn away from my instructions. . . .

My child, pay attention to what I say. Listen carefully to my words. Don't lose sight of them. Let them penetrate deep into your heart, for they bring life to those who find them, and healing to their whole body.

Guard your heart above all else, for it determines the course of your life. Avoid all perverse talk; stay away from corrupt speech.

Look straight ahead, and fix your eyes on what lies before you. Mark out a straight path for your feet; stay on the safe path.

Proverbs 4:1–2, 20–26 NLT

A proverb is a wise saying that expresses truth. Solomon wrote the book of Proverbs to share God's wisdom so that people might live wisely. This passage focuses on the heart. The heart determines the course of our lives, for our feelings of love and desire usually dictate our decisions. Some translations state that the heart is the wellspring of life. In this passage the heart means the inner person, so life flows from within us.

Just like our physical hearts need care, so do our spiritual "hearts," our inner beings. We guard our hearts through our senses. This means to listen to good advice and avoid perverse language, including what comes in on television and other media. We are to be intentional and focus on godly goals. We must set boundaries and avoid wandering into places that can tempt us or cause us to sin. Our hearts remain pure when we are careful what we allow to enter and exit, through what we touch, see, hear, speak, and do. God's words should penetrate our hearts because filling our hearts with God's love and wisdom will lead to good choices and create beautiful, healthy hearts.

BOLD FRIENDS PROMOTE HEALING

Jesus returned to Capernaum, and word got around that he was back home. A crowd gathered, jamming the entrance so no one could get in or out. He was teaching the Word. They brought a paraplegic to him, carried by four men. When they weren't able to get in because of the crowd, they removed part of the roof and lowered the paraplegic on his stretcher. Impressed by their bold belief, Jesus said to the paraplegic, "Son, I forgive your sins. . . .

"Get up. Pick up your stretcher and go home." And the man did it—got up, grabbed his stretcher, and walked out, with everyone there watching him. They rubbed their eyes, incredulous—and then praised God, saying, "We've never seen anything like this!"

Mark 2:1–5, 11–12 MSG

The bold friends in this passage didn't let a crowd stop them. We don't know if the paraplegic even believed in Jesus, but his friends believed and creatively made a way to get him help. Their actions must have impressed the crowd, and they certainly got Jesus' attention.

Good friends willingly help one another. We drive friends to doctor appointments, listen to problems and provide encouraging words, help care for children or grandchildren, and pray. We expend time and energy and don't give up.

Friends who care also share their faith in Christ with words as well as actions. Jesus offended the religious leaders by claiming he could forgive sins as well as heal. But his action of healing the paraplegic proved he had power to do both. In the same way, our actions validate our claim of knowing Christ.

People react when they see bold friends. Jesus performed many miracles, but this one caused those in the crowd to rub their eyes and look again. Don't be afraid to act boldly as a representative of Christ. Your actions are part of a process that brings healing and gives people a new life, and that's beautiful.

HOPE & CONTENTMENT

To hope means to expect future good. It's looking for the blessing when we feel only despair. Many passages in the Bible bring women hope for something better to help us persist through hard times. As women seek hope in Scripture, we often discover unexpected twists that make us pause and remember that when we live for God, there is always, always hope.

In a world where inconvenience is equated with discontent, it can be hard to feel satisfied, but having hope for the present and the future makes contentment easier to realize. However, divine discontent—the kind that causes us to seek God and his ways—can inspire us to action. The secret of contentment is to do what we can and then leave the rest to God.

The Scriptures were written to teach and encourage us by giving us hope.

Romans 15:4 CEV

PROMISES OF HOPE

God didn't give him any part of it, not even a square foot. But God did promise to give it to him and his family forever, even though Abraham didn't have any children. . . .

God said to Abraham, "Every son in each family must be circumcised to show that you have kept your agreement with me." So when Isaac was eight days old, Abraham circumcised him. Later, Isaac circumcised his son Jacob, and Jacob circumcised his twelve sons. . . .

Finally, the time came for God to do what he had promised Abraham. By then the number of our people in Egypt had greatly increased. . . .

Later [the tabernacle] was given to our ancestors, and they took it with them when they went with Joshua. They carried the tent along as they took over the land.

Acts 7:5, 8, 17, 45 CEV

God called Abraham to leave his homeland and follow him. He didn't give Abraham the land promised to Abraham's descendants. Instead, God prophesied that Abraham's people would be enslaved for four hundred years and then be brought into the land of Israel.

More than a simple promise, God made a *covenant*—a binding agreement—with Abraham and his descendants. This brought the people into a relationship with God. Circumcision was a sign of the covenant.

God kept his promise. Moses led the people out of slavery in Egypt. Joshua led them into the Promised Land. At God's direction, they built a tent for worship. They called the tent the tabernacle of testimony because it symbolized their covenant with God. The people marched into the land carrying the tent.

The covenant passed from generation to generation as the people hoped and waited for God to keep his promise. God doesn't always act quickly, especially if he's helping us become stronger in hope. Are you hoping for a better tomorrow, a better future? Search out God's promises to you, and count on him to act—he will!

TIMELY HOPE

With the Lord one day is like a thousand years, and a thousand years like one day. The Lord is not slow about His promise, as some count slowness, but is patient toward you, not wishing for any to perish but for all to come to repentance.

But the day of the Lord will come like a thief, in which the heavens will pass away with a roar and the elements will be destroyed with intense heat, and the earth and its works will be burned up.

Since all these things are to be destroyed in this way, what sort of people ought you to be in holy conduct and godliness, looking for and hastening the coming of the day of God, because of which the heavens will be destroyed by burning, and the elements will melt with intense heat!

2 Peter 3:8–12 NASB

A mother knows her baby will someday want a bicycle and later a car. She's not ready to give the child a bicycle at birth. The baby must grow and learn enough to be ready to sit up, pedal, and steer. Waiting is subjective. Some children feel like it's a long wait to get a bike or a driver's license. At the right time, parents bless their children with a bicycle and later help them learn to drive a car. For the parent, the time comes too soon.

Time drags when we wait. God, who lives beyond our finite days, sees the beginning and the end of our activities. Peter wrote this to people suffering persecution to bring hope that Jesus will return in his time. God knows what will happen in the future and the perfect time to answer prayers, bless us with unexpected joys—and send Jesus again.

His delay is because his heart's desire is for everyone to know him, turn to him, and believe in him. When Jesus comes, it will be a spectacular experience for those who hope in him and live godly lives now.

LOFTIER THOUGHTS

Seek the LORD while he may be found; call on him while he is near. Let the wicked forsake his way and the evil man his thoughts. Let him turn to the LORD, and he will have mercy on him, and to our God, for he will freely pardon.

"For my thoughts are not your thoughts, neither are your ways my ways," declares the LORD. "As the heavens are higher than the earth, so are my ways higher than your ways and my thoughts than your thoughts."

Isaiah 55:6–9 NIV

The world's greatest philosophers, scientists, leaders, and kings never had thoughts that matched God's thoughts. As you think and explore, don't you usually find more questions than answers?

The prophet Isaiah prophesied about the coming Messiah and preached to bring the nation of Judah back to following God.

Our ways often cause us struggle. We often turn away from God and impulsively choose to go our own ways, a choice that leads to trouble and pain. We make bad choices, fail, and then tearfully suffer the consequences of our choices.

But God is always holy and perfect. His thoughts are so much grander and complex than ours. His plans for us are far greater than our dreams. He holds the answer key to our lives and has wisdom for the greatest problems we have caused. Whether we have faced financial ruin, a broken marriage, or are unmarried with a child, God forgives us, compassionately loves us, and shows us his ways that will bring hope for a better future. As you seek God, you will find him, and he will direct you with his loftier thoughts to show you the real purpose for your life.

EXPECT CHANGE

Change your life, not just your clothes. Come back to GOD, *your* God. And here's why: God is kind and merciful. He takes a deep breath, puts up with a lot, this most patient God, extravagant in love, always ready to cancel catastrophe. Who knows? Maybe he'll do it now, maybe he'll turn around and show pity. Maybe, when all's said and done, there'll be blessings full and robust for your GOD! . . .

And that's just the beginning: After that—

I will pour out my Spirit on every kind of people: Your sons will prophesy, also your daughters. Your old men will dream, your young men will see visions. . . . I'll set wonders in the sky above and signs on the earth below.

Joel 2:13–14, 28, 30 MSG

❋

When we wake up and get dressed, it feels good to slip into clean clothes and feel the freshness. We also make new choices each day. Some decisions are good and some are bad. The prophet Joel preached the first part of this passage to call people to change—to repent of their sins. He reminded people that God loves them extravagantly. God wants us to make a fresh start by choosing to follow him. If we choose to follow God, we can expect great things.

Joel gave people hope of a future where God would pour out his Spirit upon the people who choose to turn to him. On Pentecost, when the Holy Spirit filled the disciples, Peter quoted part of this passage and declared Jesus had fulfilled it. The message is for us.

Joel declared that young women will see visions and old women will have dreams. Any dreams God gives us—whether a vision or a dream he places in our hearts—will align with the Bible and cause wonder in heaven and on earth. God wants to give us dreams, visions of possibilities, and hope for the future.

Hope for Peace

Our human fathers correct us for a short time, and they do it as they think best. But God corrects us for our own good, because he wants us to be holy, as he is. It is never fun to be corrected. In fact, at the time it is always painful. But if we learn to obey by being corrected, we will do right and live at peace.

Now stand up straight! Stop your knees from shaking and walk a straight path. Then lame people will be healed, instead of getting worse.

Try to live at peace with everyone! Live a clean life. If you don't, you will never see the Lord. Make sure that no one misses out on God's wonderful kindness. Don't let anyone become bitter and cause trouble for the rest of you.

Hebrews 12:10–15 CEV

❊

Do your homework." "Sit up straight." "Chew your food." "No hitting." Parents around the world say things like these. It's part of helping a child become well behaved and mature. Correction improves us, and afterward we are thankful when we have learned to read, ride a bicycle, play a sport, or play an instrument.

The book of Hebrews was written to help Jewish Christians better understand their new faith. This passage encourages believers to endure hardship by grasping the benefits of God's fatherly love. God disciplines us because he sees the bigger picture. Like a father who knows that a child needs to mature into a responsible adult, God knows we need to mature in our faith. God corrects and disciplines us, through the Bible, through the consequences of our actions, and through difficult circumstances. The word *correct* is repeatedly used to impress upon us the fact that we need training. God's correction develops our character, makes us wiser, and helps us live good and peaceful lives.

God loves us and treats us with great kindness. He gives us lasting hope as we are his children, and he promises that we will see him one day.

KNOCK AT NIGHT

Which of you who has a friend will go to him at midnight and say to him, "Friend, lend me three loaves . . ."; and he will answer from within, "Do not bother me; the door is now shut, and my children are with me in bed. I cannot get up and give you anything"? I tell you, though he will not get up and give him anything because he is his friend, yet because of his impudence he will rise and give him whatever he needs.

And I tell you, ask, and it will be given to you; seek, and you will find; knock, and it will be opened to you. For everyone who asks receives, and the one who seeks finds, and to the one who knocks it will be opened.

Luke 11:5–10 ESV

We call a girlfriend for help because we expect her to respond. We hope she has the time and resources to meet our needs. If the answer is no, we might ask again, or ask someone else. Our hope helps us be persistent. The greater the need, the more we persist. We keep asking until the need is met. When we are desperate, we stretch the limits of friendship. A friend might respond from being worn down, but we risk hurting the relationship.

God, on the other hand, expects us to be persistent with him. Jesus told this familiar story of someone pushing the limits of friendship to give us hope—the hope that there is someone who is never too busy or tired to respond to our needs. And there is! God himself invites us to ask, knock, and seek—night or day.

What do you need to ask God for? What does it look like for you to knock and seek? Don't stop now! Continuing to look to God for his help demonstrates your faith, and God promises to reward you. When you seek, you will find!

No-Tears Living

"Who are these people dressed in white robes, and where do they come from?"

"I don't know, sir. You do," I answered.

He said to me, "These are the people who have come safely through the terrible persecution. They have washed their robes and made them white with the blood of the Lamb. That is why they stand before God's throne and serve him day and night in his temple. He who sits on the throne will protect them with his presence. Never again will they hunger or thirst; neither sun nor any scorching heat will burn them, because the Lamb, who is in the center of the throne, will be their shepherd, and he will guide them to springs of life-giving water. And God will wipe away every tear from their eyes."

Revelation 7:13–17 GNT

We post special dates and parties on our calendars as reminders of future joy. Promises of fun offer hope to help us get through tough times.

Revelation, the last book of the Bible, is a prophecy about the resurrected Jesus at the end times. This passage, full of symbolism, lets us glimpse our beautiful future. Jesus called himself the Good Shepherd because he guides us. John the Baptist called him the Lamb of God because he would die as a sacrificial lamb, to save us.

Hope of a better future helps us survive the hardest difficulties. People who come through persecution will be washed and dressed in white robes. They will stand before the throne of God and never suffer again. God will gently wipe away tears caused by abuse, grief, rape, loneliness, depression, and other pain. God will lead us to a life-giving spring that bubbles up and flows freely. Our future joy can bubble up inside us so we will feel alive and well.

God promises us a trouble-free, eternal future. We can trust that any pain we experience on earth is temporary, while joy will last forever.

Hope after Failure

They drew some water and poured it out as an offering to the LORD and fasted that whole day. They said, "We have sinned against the LORD." (It was at Mizpah where Samuel settled disputes among the Israelites.) . . .

While Samuel was offering the sacrifice, the Philistines moved forward to attack; but just then the LORD thundered from heaven against them. They became completely confused and fled in panic. The Israelites marched out from Mizpah and pursued the Philistines almost as far as Bethcar, killing them along the way.

Then Samuel took a stone, set it up between Mizpah and Shen, and said, "The LORD has helped us all the way"—and he named it "Stone of Help." So the Philistines were defeated, and the LORD prevented them from invading Israel's territory as long as Samuel lived.

1 Samuel 7:6, 10–13 GNT

An old word for "stone of help" is *ebenezer*. The song "Come, Thou Fount of Every Blessing" tells of raising an Ebenezer. The thought comes from this passage. The people admitted their sin, gave up their idols, and prayed to God. The enemy started a new battle, but this time the hearts of the people trusted God, and he confused the enemy, allowing the Israelites to triumph. Then in a victory celebration, Samuel set up a special stone as a memorial of the victory.

When God brings victory into our lives, we can set up a "stone of help" to remember what God did. We can sing praises, post a victory sign, and update our friends on social media to share what God did. Prayer God has answered should be remembered. We can journal or use little stones in a jar as a reminder of the answers we receive. The stones or journal of answered prayers will give us courage when we fail, reminding us to turn to God, repent, and try again. Past victories give us hope of future success and show us that failure is an opportunity to trust God.

Rescue from Debts

"Your servant my husband is dead, and you know that your servant feared the Lord, but the creditor has come to take my two children to be his slaves." And Elisha said to her, ". . . Tell me; what have you in the house?" And she said, "Your servant has nothing in the house except a jar of oil." Then he said, ". . . Go in and shut the door behind yourself and your sons and pour into all these vessels. And when one is full, set it aside." . . . When the vessels were full, she said to her son, "Bring me another vessel." And he said to her, "There is not another." Then the oil stopped flowing. . . . [Elisha] said, "Go, sell the oil and pay your debts, and you and your sons can live on the rest."

2 Kings 4:1–4, 6–7 ESV

When the economy is bad, people suffer, especially the poor. A drought and famine caused suffering for this widow. She had lost her husband and her ability to earn money and provide for her family. Without flour and oil she couldn't even make bread, a simple but nourishing meal. This woman faced losing her home and her children—children had to work as slaves to pay their parents' debt. She sought God, her only hope, through his prophet Elisha.

God is greater than famines or debts. He provided a miracle of oil that she could sell. God directed her to help with the solution. This woman still had to work. Elisha had her borrow jars from all her neighbors. Her sons collected the jars and other containers from the neighbors. She poured the oil into containers and sold it to pay her debts. We should trust God for our source of income and be willing to work to pay off our debts. He made the resources and can guide us to solutions.

When we feel hopeless, we can hope in God and trust him to creatively provide a solution.

ANCHORED IN HOPE

He made a promise in his own name when he said to Abraham, "I, the Lord, will bless you with many descendants!" Then after Abraham had been very patient, he was given what God had promised. When anyone wants to settle an argument, they make a vow by using the name of someone or something greater than themselves. So when God wanted to prove for certain that his promise to his people could not be broken, he made a vow. God cannot tell lies! And so his promises and vows are two things that can never be changed.

We have run to God for safety. Now his promises should greatly encourage us to take hold of the hope that is right in front of us. This hope is like a firm and steady anchor for our souls.

Hebrews 6:13–19 CEV

A ship's anchor keeps it from drifting and holds it fast in spite of flowing waters and crashing waves. The anchor's curved ends hook into the ocean bed. The anchor is heavy but not heavier than the ship. Strong chain links attached to the anchor add weight to keep the ship in place.

This passage compares hope in God to a strong anchor. We might still feel waves of trouble crashing against us, but we will stand firm. Abraham's life is a witness to hoping in God. When Abraham finally held his promised son, the nation God had promised had begun.

At the time this passage was written, Jewish Christians faced strong persecution. The book of Hebrews encouraged them to realize that Jesus is the best choice and our hope in Christ is as secure as an anchor that holds firm to the seabed. When you face a stormy relationship or difficult circumstances, trust God to remain with you. Like the links of a chain that add weight to the anchor, we can add chains of hope as we recall what God has done for others and for us.

Reason to Laugh

The Lord said, "I will surely return to you about this time next year, and Sarah your wife shall have a son." And Sarah was listening at the tent door. . . . So Sarah laughed to herself, saying, "After I am worn out, and my lord is old, shall I have pleasure?" The Lord said to Abraham, "Why did Sarah laugh and say, 'Shall I indeed bear a child, now that I am old?' Is anything too hard for the Lord? At the appointed time I will return to you about this time next year, and Sarah shall have a son." But Sarah denied it, saying, "I did not laugh," for she was afraid. He said, "No, but you did laugh." . . .

The Lord did to Sarah as he had promised. . . . And Sarah said, "God has made laughter for me."

Genesis 18:10, 12–15; 21:1, 6 ESV

※

The baby God promised to Abraham and Sarah was a long time coming, and Sarah had abandoned hope. Her words and laughter in the tent revealed her disbelief.

One year later Sarah had a new laugh, the laughter that springs from joy. She laughed with God this time and even gave her son a name that meant "laughter." Sarah's statement that God "made laughter" for her suggests that she had not laughed with joy for a long time and perhaps had even forgotten how to really laugh.

How often do you laugh and look for reasons to rejoice? God is our continual hope and wants us to laugh and be joyful. Laugh when God answers your prayers and rejoice in answered prayers of others. Get together with friends who help you laugh. Watch babies play and laugh at their antics and how God made them so cute. God continually creates new life, and that reminds us that he also continues to answer prayers.

God reminded Sarah that nothing is impossible for him. Sarah and Abraham's long wait for a child encourages us to keep hoping. The God of the impossible is the God of all hope.

HOPE-FILLED TRADITIONS

"You must celebrate this day as a religious festival to remind you of what I, the LORD, have done. Celebrate it for all time to come.". . .

Moses called for all the leaders of Israel and said to them, "Each of you is to choose a lamb or a young goat and kill it, so that your families can celebrate Passover. . . . You and your children must obey these rules forever. When you enter the land that the LORD has promised to give you, you must perform this ritual. When your children ask you, 'What does this ritual mean?' you will answer, 'It is the sacrifice of Passover to honor the LORD, because he passed over the houses of the Israelites in Egypt. He killed the Egyptians, but spared us.'"

The Israelites knelt down and worshiped.

Exodus 12:14, 21, 24–27 GNT

Do you have a favorite holiday food or tradition? Sharing a familiar activity or special meal connects family and friends and brings back memories. God wanted his people to recall their deliverance from slavery in Egypt, and he established the Passover celebration to help them remember how God worked among his people. Retelling the story of their deliverance would remind the people of God's power and provide a way to pass on their testimony of God's greatness to their children. To keep the day from being merely a celebration, God included a child to ask, "What does this ritual mean?" The question caused people to pause, reflect, and respond.

Questions push us beyond mere motions to focus on the hope that what has been done in the past is a glimpse of future possibilities. Dig deeper to understand the spiritual meaning and hope God wants us to discover on special days. Christmas is more than packages as it celebrates God's fulfilling of many prophecies and recalls that Christ chose to become a man to save us. Don't merely celebrate; stop and ask what each day means and what hope it gives you and what it means for your future.

COLORS OF HOPE

"I am making my promise to you. Never again will all life be killed by floodwaters. Never again will there be a flood that destroys the earth."

God said, "This is the sign of the promise I am giving to you and every living being that is with you for generations to come. I will put my rainbow in the clouds to be a sign of my promise to the earth. Whenever I form clouds over the earth, a rainbow will appear in the clouds. Then I will remember my promise to you and every living animal. Never again will water become a flood to destroy all life. Whenever the rainbow appears in the clouds, I will see it and remember my everlasting promise to every living animal on earth."

Genesis 9:11–16 GOD'S WORD

※

Colorful rainbows can appear in the midst of a storm or at the end of one. They seem to pop out of nowhere. In Hawaii, huge rainbows appear almost daily. Each arch paints a picture of hope. The red, yellow, green, blue, indigo, and violet remind us that God never forgets a promise and is faithful through all generations.

God watched as the flood he sent drowned almost all life on earth. Only eight humans were spared—Noah, his wife, his three sons, and their wives. To Noah God stated his promise to all living creatures that he would never again destroy all life with a flood.

Storms and clouds give way to beauty, and that's another message of hope painted in the sky. As we face hardships, we can cling to the hope of color and joy that will come gain, after the floodgates of our tears have dried.

So look for a rainbow the next time it rains! We need to see a rainbow of color in our lives and know God placed it there and remembers all his promises.

MESSIAH'S MISSION

The Spirit of the Lord GOD is upon me, because the LORD has anointed me to bring good news to the afflicted; He has sent me to bind up the brokenhearted, to proclaim liberty to captives and freedom to prisoners; to proclaim the favorable year of the LORD and the day of vengeance of our God; to comfort all who mourn, to grant those who mourn in Zion, giving them a garland instead of ashes, the oil of gladness instead of mourning, the mantle of praise instead of a spirit of fainting. So they will be called oaks of righteousness, the planting of the LORD, that He may be glorified.

Isaiah 61:1–3 NASB

Jesus read the first part of this passage in the synagogue when he launched his preaching and teaching. He finished reading and then stated that the passage had been fulfilled. The "favorable year of the LORD" refers to a jubilee year when people canceled debts and freed slaves, a year of rejoicing.

Jesus came to bring hope and turn lives around. The healings and miracles he did were evidence of the truth that Jesus was the *Messiah*, the hope of all people. *Messiah* means "anointed one." Jesus fulfilled the prophecy in this passage as he brought the good news, healed the sick, and comforted many. This message in Isaiah, written long before Jesus came, gave people hope of a better future. That future arrived.

Jesus still brings hope and reaches out to heal and comfort us. He wants us to see the good within our problems and find joy where there is sorrow. Jesus frees us when we ask for forgiveness and believe in him. A mantle symbolized a spiritual covering. When we feel sorrow, praise will change us and bring us back to hope in Jesus as our spiritual covering.

Hope Springs from God-Given Dreams

Pharaoh said to Joseph, "I have had a dream, but no one can interpret it; and I have heard it said about you, that when you hear a dream you can interpret it." Joseph then answered Pharaoh, saying, "It is not in me; God will give Pharaoh a favorable answer. . . .

"Pharaoh's dreams are one and the same; God has told to Pharaoh what He is about to do. The seven good cows are seven years; and the seven good ears are seven years; the dreams are one and the same. The seven lean and ugly cows that came up after them are seven years, and the seven thin ears scorched by the east wind will be seven years of famine. It is as I have spoken to Pharaoh: God has shown to Pharaoh what He is about to do."

Genesis 41:15–16, 25–28
NASB

We stock our pantries to prepare for the future. God used a dream to prompt needed preparations for a widespread famine. He provided a solution before the catastrophe hit. Ultimately, the famine and Joseph's preparations brought Jacob's father and all his brothers and their families to live in Egypt, where they grew into the people of Israel.

Pharaoh wasn't too proud to seek help from a prisoner. He realized that no one in his court had the knowledge or insight to discern the meaning of his dream. He acknowledged that God had given Joseph a divine spirit.

We too can turn to God for wisdom and understanding for the future. We can ask him to show us what our dreams mean and to guide us even as we shop so we buy things we will need in the future. When we don't understand a situation, we can ask God to show us what we can learn and what he wants us to do. We can seek help from wiser Christians, other "Josephs" who can help us understand. We have hope because God knows the future and knows how to help us prepare for it.

Hidden Face, Hopeful Words

"I will hide my face from this city because of all its wickedness.

"Nevertheless, I will bring health and healing to it; I will heal my people and will let them enjoy abundant peace and security. I will bring Judah and Israel back from captivity and will rebuild them as they were before. I will cleanse them from all the sin they have committed against me and will forgive all their sins of rebellion against me. . . .

"The days are coming," declares the LORD, "when I will fulfill the gracious promise I made to the house of Israel and to the house of Judah.

"In those days and at that time I will make a righteous Branch sprout from David's line; he will do what is just and right in the land."

Jeremiah 33:5–8, 14–15 NIV

Politicians make many false promises. Corrupt leaders prevent their people from living in peace. During difficult times and places, it might seem that God has turned away from the darkness and violence in our world. Yet even in the hard times, God promises to be gracious and help his people. That God chooses to forgive people and rescue us from slavery to sin brings hope for everyone. Still, we might have to suffer the consequences of our sin and turning away from God.

Jeremiah's prophecy in this passage was made before the Babylonians attacked and captured the Israelites. God allowed his people's enemies to conquer them as punishment for their continued severe disobedience. They brought on the problem when they failed to obey God; yet years later God turned back and restored his people. God will forgive anyone who turns to Jesus.

As women we long for security. God will do what is just and right even when leaders and other people do not. Jesus fulfills promises and brings help and healing to all who ask. He gives us hope that we can all start again and be forgiven.

From Despair to Mountaintop

He traveled through the wilderness for a day. He sat down under a broom plant and wanted to die. "I've had enough now, Lord," he said. "Take my life! I'm no better than my ancestors." Then he lay down and slept under the broom plant.

An angel touched him and said, "Get up and eat." When he looked, he saw near his head some bread baked on hot stones and a jar of water. So he ate, drank, and went to sleep again.

The angel of the Lord came back and woke him up again. The angel said, "Get up and eat, or your journey will be too much for you."

He got up, ate, and drank. Strengthened by that food, he traveled for 40 days and nights until he came to Horeb, the mountain of God.

1 Kings 19:4–8 GOD'S WORD

❋

Elijah faced depression and hopelessness even though he served as one of Israel's great prophets and God spoke directly to him! The great despair described in this passage came over Elijah after he orchestrated a contest between God and a false god, Baal, an idol many in Israel were worshipping. The prophets of Baal had been humiliated when God showed up with might and power. Jezebel, the wife of King Ahab, worshipped Baal and wanted to kill Elijah. Rather than die at the hand of the queen, Elijah wanted God to take his life. He wasn't thinking rationally. But God knew and provided what Elijah needed.

When we feel discouraged or at the end of our own strength, deep in despair, we don't think rationally and may not make good choices. That's a time to ask God to renew our energy and strength and direct our steps. He might miraculously provide the help you need through an angel or a friend. Speak up about how you are feeling. Tell God and a friend you can trust. Stop your busyness, refresh, and place your hope in God to remove your despair.

Happy Days Ahead

God blesses those who are poor and realize their need for him, for the Kingdom of Heaven is theirs. God blesses those who mourn, for they will be comforted. God blesses those who are humble, for they will inherit the whole earth. God blesses those who hunger and thirst for justice, for they will be satisfied. God blesses those who are merciful, for they will be shown mercy.

God blesses those whose hearts are pure, for they will see God. God blesses those who work for peace, for they will be called the children of God. God blesses those who are persecuted for doing right, for the Kingdom of Heaven is theirs. . . . Be happy about it! Be very glad! For a great reward awaits you in heaven. And remember, the ancient prophets were persecuted in the same way.

Matthew 5:3–10, 12 NLT

These words of Jesus offered new hope to his listeners—those who persisted in showing love and those who suffered would be blessed! The passage, known as the *Beatitudes*, offers that same new hope to you. *Beatitude* comes from the root word for *beauty*, revealing the value God has for our acts of service.

Jesus spoke these words to a large crowd. He began talking about blessings that explain how God makes our efforts beautiful. This is the opposite reaction of the world, which doesn't value meekness, humility, or pure hearts.

When we focus on actions that please God, then he will bless our work. He brings the beauty of forgiveness to us when we mourn our sins. God blesses us with a heavenly future when we humbly realize our need for God. God blesses us with all he made when we are meek and obey him. God blesses us when we strive for peace by adopting us into his family.

God wants us to look beyond ourselves and respond to him. Today let others go first, don't try to get attention, and examine your words and actions.

GUIDING LIGHT

How sweet are your words to my taste, sweeter than honey to my mouth! . . .

Your word is a lamp to my feet and a light for my path. I have taken an oath and confirmed it, that I will follow your righteous laws. I have suffered much; preserve my life, O LORD, according to your word. Accept, O LORD, the willing praise of my mouth, and teach me your laws. Though I constantly take my life in my hands, I will not forget your law. The wicked have set a snare for me, but I have not strayed from your precepts. Your statutes are my heritage forever; they are the joy of my heart.

Psalm 119:103, 105–111 NIV

The sweet taste of chocolate lingers in our mouths and gives us pleasure. A light in the dark keeps us from stumbling. These analogies remind us that joy is as near as the pages of the Bible. No matter what we suffer, or what scams people try to pull, we can rely on the promises of God.

Psalm 119, the longest psalm, is also the longest chapter of the Bible. Each eight-verse section begins with consecutive Hebrew letters, making the psalm easier to memorize.

The Bible gives us direction and enlightens us better than a flashlight in the dark. These words help us recognize truth and discern goodness—but only if we take the time to read and understand. David's cry to be taught reveals a heart open and willing to listen and learn.

As women we like to talk much more than listen. We react emotionally to stress and situations where God beckons us to recall his wisdom with hope and trust his direction. As Psalm 119 so clearly expresses, our daily practice of following God's Word prepares us to rely on God rather than our own first reactions.

BANNERS UP

May the LORD answer you in the day of trouble! May the name of the God of Jacob set you securely on high! May He send you help from the sanctuary and support you from Zion! May He remember all your meal offerings and find your burnt offering acceptable!

May He grant you your heart's desire and fulfill all your counsel! We will sing for joy over your victory, and in the name of our God we will set up our banners. May the LORD fulfill all your petitions.

Now I know that the LORD saves His anointed; He will answer him from His holy heaven with the saving strength of His right hand.

Psalm 20:1–6 NASB

David wrote this psalm as a prayer before battle, possibly before defeating the Ammonites. Banners were flags the army raised to show victory, and in this case to honor God. These days our "banners" about answered prayers tend to be status updates and comments on social-media networks. We swiftly click them on to girlfriends and they pass around the world in minutes.

Prayer answers remind us that God fulfills our hopes. At the same time we ask, we need to hope—to believe—that God will answer. Our hope should be so positive that we already talk about celebrating the answer! We already anticipate singing with joy and hanging banners proclaiming that God has answered.

This passage also reminds us of our part in the relationship between God and our needs. Burnt offerings were animal sacrifices used to request forgiveness and to express worship. Meal offerings were breads cooked without yeast that expressed thanks. Jesus was the perfect sacrifice, so we no longer need to make sacrificial offerings. We can still come to God for forgiveness and to express thanks that God will give us strength for our struggles and bring us victory over troubles.

CREATION'S REBIRTH

Creation is confused, but not because it wants to be confused. God made it this way in the hope that creation would be set free from decay and would share in the glorious freedom of his children. We know that all creation is still groaning and is in pain, like a woman about to give birth.

The Spirit makes us sure about what we will be in the future. But now we groan silently, while we wait for God to show that we are his children. This means that our bodies will also be set free. And this hope is what saves us. But if we already have what we hope for, there is no need to keep on hoping. However, we hope for something we have not yet seen, and we patiently wait for it.

Romans 8:20–25 CEV

Lovely flowers, a gentle breeze, the taste of ripe fruit. Fallen petals, hurricane winds, and insect-infested fruit trees. The differences clearly show us the imperfections of our world. As God's creations, we also grow old, lose the vitality and beauty of youth, and die. But heaven is on its way.

This part of the book of Romans shares the benefits of the Christian life, including the hope of resurrected bodies. We don't see or experience heaven now, just as a mother doesn't see or hold her child until she gives birth, and waits months for that birth. But the Holy Spirit assures us of the truth of heaven and the truth that we, and all creation, will one day be set free from the limits we experience now. We will no longer grow old, get sick, or suffer pain, for we will have perfect bodies.

The mother experiences the pain of birth, but the pain ends with joy as the mother holds her newborn baby. Our wait will end when we pass from this earth to heaven and experience joy in the arms of God. We wait with hope in God's timing.

A Gleam in His Eye

[Ruth] entered a field and gathered the grain left behind by the reapers. Now it happened that she ended up in the part of the field that belonged to Boaz, who was from Elimelech's family. . . .

Boaz asked the young man in charge of his reapers, "Who is this young woman?"

The young man answered, "She's a young Moabite woman who came back with Naomi from the country of Moab. She said, 'Please let me gather grain. I will only gather among the bundles behind the reapers.' So she came here and has been on her feet from daybreak until now. She just sat down this minute in the shelter."

Boaz said to Ruth, "Listen, my daughter. Don't go in any other field to gather grain, and don't even leave this one. Stay here with my young women."

Ruth 2:3, 5–8 GOD'S WORD

A man turns his head and notices a woman who pleases him by how she looks, walks, or acts. Boaz's interest was peaked quickly when he saw Ruth.

Ruth, a Moabite, came from a foreign country and had been married to the older of Naomi's sons. Naomi and Boaz were close relatives.

Other people gleaned behind the workers, but Boaz asked about only one person who caught his attention. He went beyond a glance and had a gleam in his eye as he looked. He called her by the affectionate term "my daughter" and asked her to glean only in his field, near the other women. Ultimately they married and became the great-grandparents of King David.

A spark of hope began between Ruth and Boaz with a look, kind words, and an invitation. Friendship as well as romance can begin with noticing an individual. Look around today and see if someone is working hard to care for a family; then reach out with kindness. If you are single and a man shows kindness, respond with kindness also. It could become something more.

KINDNESS CHANGES HEARTS

We also once were foolish ourselves, disobedient, deceived, enslaved to various lusts and pleasures, spending our life in malice and envy, hateful, hating one another. But when the kindness of God our Savior and His love for mankind appeared, He saved us, not on the basis of deeds which we have done in righteousness, but according to His mercy, by the washing of regeneration and renewing by the Holy Spirit, whom He poured out upon us richly through Jesus Christ our Savior, so that being justified by His grace we would be made heirs according to the hope of eternal life. This is a trustworthy statement; and concerning these things I want you to speak confidently, so that those who have believed God will be careful to engage in good deeds. These things are good and profitable.

Titus 3:3–8 NASB

Women can be very emotional and react to how people treat us and to our circumstances. Over time a woman can become foolish, angry, envious, and hateful when she feels unloved and hurt. Have you ever been shopping and heard someone's agitated tone and loud complaint as she berated the clerk? Did you wonder what caused her to lash out like that? It could have stemmed from being unloved. In contrast, a woman who feels loved and is treated kindly smiles and speaks gently and graciously and has a joyful bounce in her step.

Paul wrote this passage in a letter to Titus, a friend and leader organizing churches in Crete. Paul emphasized the kindness, love, and mercy of God and encouraged good deeds and kindness among Christians.

Remember when you first realized Jesus loved you. How has his love changed you? Has his forgiveness softened your heart? Has his love changed your words, tone, and actions? Thank God for his love and reach out to a woman you hear lashing out at a store clerk with kind words to show her the hope that she is lovable.

FESTIVE TIMES

Sing and shout for joy, people of Israel! Rejoice with all your heart, Jerusalem! The LORD has stopped your punishment; he has removed all your enemies. The LORD, the king of Israel, is with you; there is no reason now to be afraid. The time is coming when they will say to Jerusalem, "Do not be afraid, city of Zion! Do not let your hands hang limp! The LORD your God is with you; his power gives you victory. The LORD will take delight in you, and in his love he will give you new life. He will sing and be joyful over you, as joyful as people at a festival."

The LORD says, "I have ended the threat of doom and taken away your disgrace. The time is coming!"

Zephaniah 3:14–19 GNT

God and angels often spoke the words "Do not be afraid," each time with a message of hope or combined with a message to have courage. Zephaniah wrote to shake up God's people and urge them to repent and turn away from sin to follow God. He warned that if they continued to worship idols and sin, God would punish them. Zephaniah also promised the people that God would have mercy when they returned to their faith in him. This passage is from that message of hope and God's mercy.

We go through the pain of surgery because of the hope that it will heal us and make us better. We struggle through physical therapy to become stronger and restore health. Hope chases away our fears and helps us look beyond current painful situations. God wants us to trust in him and let hope in him take away fear of any temporary suffering we have on earth. He promises that new life and joy will come. If you are facing surgery or suffering through abuse or divorce, let hope chase away fear. Hope in God and know that the difficulties will end.

A Face Aglow

Jesus' appearance changed in front of them. His face became as bright as the sun and his clothes as white as light. Suddenly, Moses and Elijah appeared to them and were talking with Jesus.

Peter said to Jesus, "Lord, it's good that we're here. If you want, I'll put up three tents here—one for you, one for Moses, and one for Elijah."

He was still speaking when a bright cloud overshadowed them. Then a voice came out of the cloud and said, "This is my Son, whom I love and with whom I am pleased. Listen to him!"

The disciples were terrified when they heard this and fell facedown on the ground. But Jesus touched them and said, "Get up, and don't be afraid!" As they raised their heads, they saw no one but Jesus.

Matthew 17:2–8 GOD'S WORD

Hollywood stars can dazzle us as lights flash at red-carpet events, but nothing can compare to Jesus' appearance in this passage. Stage performers use hidden microphones and speakers to let their voices speak from surprising places, but none would compare to God's voice speaking from a cloud. His voice had thundered from a cloud in the Old Testament in Exodus 19:19.

The event described in this passage is known as the Transfiguration. Jesus' human body took on its heavenly form. Moses and Elijah, long dead, appeared, talked with Jesus, and showed that they exist eternally. The reality of God and eternal life overwhelmed Peter and his friends. They didn't completely understand what they saw. But Peter later recalled that special time in a letter he wrote to the churches. He wrote about seeing Christ's glory; he declared that he and the others had seen Jesus' majesty and heard the voice of God the Father. This memory gave Peter confidence to hope in the prophets and prophecies about Jesus' second coming.

Our experiences and the testimonies of others give us hope. The Transfiguration gives us hope that we too will one day see Christ's glowing face.

COLLECTING LASTING TREASURES

What I'm trying to do here is get you to relax, not be so preoccupied with *getting* so you can respond to God's *giving*. People who don't know God and the way he works fuss over these things, but you know both God and how he works. Steep yourself in God-reality, God-initiative, God-provisions. You'll find all your everyday human concerns will be met. Don't be afraid of missing out. You're my dearest friends! The Father wants to give you the very kingdom itself.

Be generous. Give to the poor. Get yourselves a bank that can't go bankrupt, a bank in heaven far from bankrobbers, safe from embezzlers, a bank you can bank on. It's obvious, isn't it? The place where your treasure is, is the place you will most want to be, and end up being.

Luke 12:29–34 MSG

Jesus frequently taught about money. He wanted his listeners to realize that money is not the most important thing in life. The crowds who heard him would have been of mixed income levels, but many would have been poor. Our level of wealth doesn't matter as much as our perspective on money. Jesus challenges us to decide whether we will place our hope and trust in money or in God.

Our hope guides us in where we spend our time and what we collect, whether it is university degrees, savings accounts, or home furnishings. If we hope in God, then we should invest our time and energy in building a relationship with God. If we truly hope in God, then our calendar and checkbook should reflect that, with time for God scheduled in and money given to help God's people and others.

Jesus reminded us that earthly treasure doesn't last, but God's promises do. Hope placed in people can fail when they die, betray us, or move away. Hope in our money can be lost when financial disaster hits. Evaluate where your hope lies by examining your calendar, journal, and checkbook today.

BOOK OF FAME

[Jesus] said to them, The harvest indeed is abundant [there is much ripe grain], but the farmhands are few. Pray therefore the Lord of the harvest to send out laborers into His harvest. . . .

Behold, I send you out like lambs into the midst of wolves. . . .

The seventy returned with joy, saying, Lord, even the demons are subject to us in Your name!

And He said to them, I saw Satan falling like a lightning [flash] from heaven.

Behold! I have given you authority and power to trample upon serpents and scorpions, and [physical and mental strength and ability] over all the power that the enemy [possesses]; and nothing shall in any way harm you.

Nevertheless, do not rejoice at this, that the spirits are subject to you, but rejoice that your names are enrolled in heaven.

Luke 10:2–3, 17–20 AMP

❋

Jesus sent the disciples out in pairs and with his power. This happened before his death and resurrection. They were sent to the towns where Jesus planned to visit. They performed miracles and experienced God's power. This can happen to us too, and we can expect results.

We need to be sent, and that means we need a calling. Each one called needs a partner, two people God pairs to work together. These are modern-day missionaries. Many go overseas, but many also go into our cities and towns.

Be willing to be called. When called, be bold and brave. Expect God to provide for your needs and to answer prayers. You will work for God with the goal of harvesting souls. Be prepared to go. That means knowing God's message of love and salvation. Practice sharing your faith and talking about Jesus. Pray for miracles now so they will abound when you are sent.

Be ready for the opposition, for attackers who argue against the message, for others to mock and make you look foolish. Trust God to overcome such enemies and rejoice at his victories and miracles.

GONE WITH THE WIND

"Teacher, we caught this woman in the act of adultery. In his teachings, Moses ordered us to stone women like this to death. What do you say?" They asked this to test him. They wanted to find a reason to bring charges against him.

Jesus bent down and used his finger to write on the ground. When they persisted in asking him questions, he straightened up and said, "The person who is sinless should be the first to throw a stone at her." Then he bent down again. . . .

One by one, beginning with the older men, the scribes and Pharisees left. . . .

Then Jesus straightened up and asked her, "Where did they go? Has anyone condemned you?"

The woman answered, "No one, sir."

Jesus said, "I don't condemn you either. Go! From now on don't sin."

John 8:4–11 GOD'S WORD

We all fail and sin, but humiliation increases embarrassment and guilt. A humiliated woman often avoids eye contact and looks down.

Jesus bent down and scribbled in the dust. How wonderful that the woman's eyes could rest on someone who didn't accuse her. He did this, lessening her stress first, before responding to the accusers. Jesus' drawings in the dust would eventually be blown away with the wind. No permanent marks would remain for the woman as a reminder of this terrible situation.

Jesus' few words reminded the woman's accusers, and us, that everyone sins. Perhaps the woman continued to look down as Jesus wrote more, still expecting to feel the pounding of rocks against her skin. But there was only the sound of rocks hitting the ground. Then Jesus asked if anyone had condemned her. Maybe only then did she risk a glance up—everyone was gone. Then Jesus said the words that freed her from past actions. He would not condemn her. She was free.

Jesus cares about our stress. He wants to be our buffer and offers to free us from sin.

More Precious Than Gold

Blessed be the God and Father of our Lord Jesus Christ, who according to His great mercy has caused us to be born again to a living hope through the resurrection of Jesus Christ from the dead, to obtain an inheritance which is imperishable and undefiled and will not fade away, reserved in heaven for you, who are protected by the power of God through faith for a salvation ready to be revealed in the last time. In this you greatly rejoice, even though now for a little while, if necessary, you have been distressed by various trials, so that the proof of your faith, being more precious than gold which is perishable, even though tested by fire, may be found to result in praise and glory and honor at the revelation of Jesus Christ.

1 Peter 1:3–7 NASB

※

Gold shines and lasts a long time. In the securities industry gold is called nonperishable. Yet to God, even gold is perishable and will not last. Fire is still used to test the purity of gold and to differentiate it from fool's gold and other imitations. This method melts the gold so it no longer retains its original shape and becomes liquid and moldable instead.

Peter wrote to encourage Christians being persecuted by unbelievers. He compared the mistreatment of Christians to the process of purifying gold.

Our trials and difficult situations are like fire testing our faith. The testing is for a little while. Our reactions as we pass through problems prove that our faith is real and pure as gold. The testing softens us so we are moldable by God.

We are not openly persecuted in America as Christians were during the time Peter lived, but we are pushed to accept certain unbiblical behavior as good and laws that try to keep us from speaking out against sin. We must not fear imprisonment or the anger of those who oppose God but hope in God as we stand for his truth.

Hopeless without God

When neither sun nor stars appeared for many days, and no small tempest lay on us, all hope of our being saved was at last abandoned. . . .

Paul stood up . . . and said, ". . . I urge you to take heart, for there will be no loss of life among you, but only of the ship. For this very night there stood before me an angel of the God to whom I belong and whom I worship, and he said, 'Do not be afraid, Paul; you must stand before Caesar. And behold, God has granted you all those who sail with you.' . . . I have faith in God that it will be exactly as I have been told. But we must run aground on some island." . . .

And so it was that all were brought safely to land.

Acts 27:20–26, 44 ESV

Floundering in darkness on the rough, choppy sea left the sailors in this account feeling hopeless. Experienced in storms at sea, they resigned themselves to doom. However, Paul, traveling as a prisoner on the ship, placed his hope in God, and God did not disappoint. All 270 people on board survived the tempest.

When a natural disaster like a hurricane or tornado strikes, we need to pray for help and not worry. God can guide us to safety. We might face damage to our homes, injury, or death, but we are always safe eternally with God. When other kinds of disasters come—difficult circumstances caused by the sin of others or by our own bad choices—we can still be safe with God if we turn to him for help. In any kind of disaster, we can be the ones who encourage those around us and show them it's an opportunity for hope in God.

We may not see a ray of hope and feel protected when darkness surrounds us in stormy troubles. But God wants us to hope in him instead of letting circumstances and troubles overwhelm us.

Focus for Contentment

I urge Euodia and I urge Syntyche to live in harmony in the Lord. Indeed, true companion, I ask you also to help these women who have shared my struggle in the cause of the gospel, together with Clement also and the rest of my fellow workers, whose names are in the book of life. . . .

Be anxious for nothing, but in everything by prayer and supplication with thanksgiving let your requests be made known to God. And the peace of God, which surpasses all comprehension, will guard your hearts and your minds in Christ Jesus.

Finally, brethren, whatever is true, whatever is honorable, whatever is right, whatever is pure, whatever is lovely, whatever is of good repute, if there is any excellence and if anything worthy of praise, dwell on these things.

Philippians 4:2–3, 6–8 NASB

One woman faces a crisis, such as the death of a loved one or a debilitating illness, while another faces a joy, such as the birth of a child or a promotion at work. Paul urged two women to live in harmony. *Euodia* means "good journey," while *Syntyche* means "fortunate or blessed." Christians struggling with challenges are often said to be on a faith journey. It's good because God will use it for our good. The women's names reflect the idea of one person's struggle while the other receives rich blessings. These situations could change with coming joys and sorrows.

We cannot live dreading trouble will come or fear that good times will end, nor can we envy another person's blessings. Harmony is the pleasing arrangement of at least two notes of a chord to produce a richer sound. When we share our sorrows and joys with our girlfriends, we blend our lives with trust in God, and we produce a harmony. We trust in the future and know that the tough times will end and the blessings are present to enjoy for a season. Friends maintain contentment as we rejoice together over blessings and support one another during hard times.

RENEWED THINKING

Do not conform any longer to the pattern of this world, but be transformed by the renewing of your mind. Then you will be able to test and approve what God's will is—his good, pleasing and perfect will.

For by the grace given me I say to every one of you: Do not think of yourself more highly than you ought, but rather think of yourself with sober judgment, in accordance with the measure of faith God has given you. Just as each of us has one body with many members, and these members do not all have the same function, so in Christ we who are many form one body, and each member belongs to all the others. We have different gifts, according to the grace given us.

Romans 12:2–6 NIV

Listening to the news and following politics can be discouraging. Trying to keep up with ads and the latest trends can be trying. But these are worldly patterns. God calls us to renew our minds, to think more creatively. We need to reprocess what we see and hear through God's perspective, to view everything in a fresh way.

Renewal happens continually to us as Christians. We sin and ask for forgiveness. God forgives us and we are renewed spiritually. In the process we have learned to identify our sins, see our weaknesses, repent, and avoid the temptations in the future. These steps help reprogram our thoughts to be more like Christ's. We continue to change as we study Scripture and discover new knowledge from God that impacts our thinking and renews our minds.

We change and grow as we apply the words in the Bible. As we get together with Christian friends, we see the unique gifts God has given each person and how we can work together within a shared faith to build and renew one another. We enjoy small-group studies to sharpen one another, and these also help to renew our minds.

Developing Confidence

Through Christ we can approach God and stand in his favor. So we brag because of our confidence that we will receive glory from God. But that's not all. We also brag when we are suffering. We know that suffering creates endurance, endurance creates character, and character creates confidence. We're not ashamed to have this confidence, because God's love has been poured into our hearts by the Holy Spirit, who has been given to us.

Look at it this way: At the right time, while we were still helpless, Christ died for ungodly people. Finding someone who would die for a godly person is rare. Maybe someone would have the courage to die for a good person. Christ died for us while we were still sinners. This demonstrates God's love for us.

Romans 5:2–8 GOD'S WORD

When someone expresses approval of us or considers us a favorite friend, it makes us smile and feel happy. We feel at ease around that person, knowing we are accepted. God approves of us and wants us to feel accepted too.

Paul wrote to the Roman church to clearly explain faith and the benefits we receive through faith. Believing with certainty that Christ loves us builds our confidence, and that helps us believe he will take care of us. Confidence in God's power and his ability to supply all we need shapes our contentment.

We really can speak with God and tell him all our worries, fears, and desires! God can help us let go of the anxieties. He can give us what we desire, help us let go of desires, and develop our character. If we go through cancer treatment, God helps us develop empathy, patience, and trust. If we suffer the loss of a home in a flood, we learn to be grateful for our lives and what we still have and discover we can live without as many material things. Our contentment comes from confidence in God, not our possessions or abilities.

I Am What I Am

Last of all he appeared also to me—even though I am like someone whose birth was abnormal. For I am the least of all the apostles—I do not even deserve to be called an apostle, because I persecuted God's church. But by God's grace I am what I am, and the grace that he gave me was not without effect. On the contrary, I have worked harder than any of the other apostles, although it was not really my own doing, but God's grace working with me. . . .

But thanks be to God who gives us the victory through our Lord Jesus Christ! So then, my dear friends, stand firm and steady. Keep busy always in your work for the Lord, since you know that nothing you do in the Lord's service is ever useless.

1 Corinthians 15:8–10, 57–58
GNT

This passage reflects a balance of humility and acceptance. Paul believed himself unworthy because of his past persecution of Christians. He had imprisoned Christians and watched as Stephen was stoned to death. Paul knew his sinful past and that God's grace through Christ—a gift of favor that we don't deserve—forgave his sins. Knowing that God knew all his sins yet had forgiven them kept Paul humble. He focused more on his work than on his shortcomings or needs. He trusted that God had shaped him into the person he had become, so he could state, "I am what I am" and be content, knowing who had made the difference in his character and life.

We can't undo the past, but we can be forgiven, accept today's opportunity, and be confident that God will be pleased with our effort. Whether we lived immoral lives, cheated, stole, or physically hurt others, God can forgive us. We can trust God will be pleased with us and that our work is useful to God, even if we don't see results. Accept yourself as the woman God has helped you become and continue serving God.

Peace of Mind

The Holy Spirit will give you life that comes from Christ Jesus and will set you free from sin and death. The Law of Moses cannot do this, because our selfish desires make the Law weak. But God set you free when he sent his own Son to be like us sinners and to be a sacrifice for our sin. God used Christ's body to condemn sin. He did this, so that we would do what the Law commands by obeying the Spirit instead of our own desires. People who are ruled by their desires think only of themselves. Everyone who is ruled by the Holy Spirit thinks about spiritual things. If our minds are ruled by our desires, we will die. But if our minds are ruled by the Spirit, we will have life and peace.

Romans 8:2–6 CEV

Have you ever watched a selfish person strive to always be first, accumulate things, and rudely grab the best? She seldom has peace as she continually connives to gain more for herself. And she might not have close friends, since she doesn't care about their feelings or needs. That's the type of person Paul stated was ruled by desires.

This passage from the book of Romans helps us understand the consequences of what rules our lives. We can hold on to a me-first attitude or let God's Holy Spirit guide us. When we feel contented, we have peace within our hearts and minds, but peace can seem elusive when conflicts or worries take hold of us. If we worry about paying the bills for all we've bought or about getting more attention, we have no peace. Real peace that lasts comes from accepting guidance from the Holy Spirit.

The Holy Spirit keeps us focused on God and heaven and shows us that our personal desires are not our most important thoughts. Instead we focus on spiritual goals, such as being loving, kind, and patient. This brings us the freedom in our minds that is peace.

GOOD HOUSE BUILDING

Through skillful and godly Wisdom is a house (a life, a home, a family) built, and by understanding it is established [on a sound and good foundation], and by knowledge shall its chambers [of every area] be filled with all precious and pleasant riches. . . .

So shall you know skillful and godly Wisdom to be thus to your life; if you find it, then shall there be a future and a reward, and your hope and expectation shall not be cut off. . . .

These also are sayings of the wise: To discriminate and show partiality, having respect of persons in judging, is not good. . . .

[Put first things first.] Prepare your work outside and get it ready for yourself in the field; and afterward build your house and establish a home.

Proverbs 24:3–4, 14, 23, 27
AMP

If you have ever stayed in a home that is full of peace, where the inhabitants get along, interact, and smile, then you have seen a home built on understanding with skillful work. Maintaining peaceful relationships takes work. There's order and artwork in such a home. The decorations may not be expensive, but the objects are valued by family members and treasured for the sentiments and memories associated with them.

This wise passage, part of the book of Proverbs written by King Solomon, shares insights on how to build such a home. We need to first work and establish income. That provides finances to build the home. Through work we also learn to cooperate and get along with people. Then we can apply those skills to establishing a family. Respect and fairness also are needed. When we show respect to one another, each person feels appreciated, approved, and accepted. These important concepts prevent competition and strife.

A home is *established*—designed with a permanent order by setting rules and building a good foundation of faith in God, wisdom, and respect. The work transforms a house into a home.

UNLIMITED HELP

We've got our hands full continually thanking God for you, our good friends—so loved by God! God picked you out as his from the very start. Think of it: included in God's original plan of salvation by the bond of faith in the living truth. This is the life of the Spirit he invited you to through the Message we delivered, in which you get in on the glory of our Master, Jesus Christ.

So, friends, take a firm stand, feet on the ground and head high. Keep a tight grip on what you were taught, whether in personal conversation or by our letter. May Jesus himself and God our Father, who reached out in love and surprised you with gifts of unending help and confidence, put a fresh heart in you, invigorate your work, enliven your speech.

2 Thessalonians 2:13–17 MSG

Thankfulness helps women look outward and appreciate what we have. It changes our focus from desires to satisfaction. A grateful heart has little room for grumbling or complaining.

In this part of a letter to the Thessalonians, Paul teaches about Christ's second coming and encourages all Christians to remain faithful. He wanted his early readers—and us—to hold on to his teaching and not be led astray. He also models gratitude by expressing his own. His example reminds us to be thankful for God, our friends, and our salvation. These blessings should give us contentment.

We are invited to a life with God—a life worth living—that begins on earth. Gratitude makes us satisfied, or contented, because it helps us focus on what we have and appreciate our blessings. Like Paul, we can start with being thankful for friends, loved ones, and of course God's love. God offers unlimited help in every aspect of our lives. He energizes our work and gives us wonderful thoughts to talk about and good news to share. We continue to discover unlimited reasons to be grateful as God continues to bless our lives with new friends and surprises.

Ups and Downs of Life

The end of something is better than its beginning. It is better to be patient than arrogant. Don't be quick to get angry, because anger is typical of fools. Don't ask, "Why were things better in the old days than they are now?" It isn't wisdom that leads you to ask this! Wisdom is as good as an inheritance. It is an advantage to everyone who sees the sun. Wisdom protects us just as money protects us, but the advantage of wisdom is that it gives life to those who have it. Consider what God has done! Who can straighten what God has bent? When times are good, be happy. But when times are bad, consider this: God has made the one time as well as the other so that mortals cannot predict their future.

Ecclesiastes 7:8–14
GOD'S WORD

❋

Life is always changing, with ups and downs. A loved one dies and a new baby is welcomed into the family. One person loses a job while another gets a promotion. A tornado causes great damage in one part of town while families move into new homes in another. This passage, written by wise King Solomon, encourages us to accept both blessings and hardships and to be ready for the unexpected. The best preparation for the future is wisdom and a good attitude.

Wisdom means to have good judgment and the ability to apply knowledge in life. This develops with experience and learning from the past. Wisdom helps us make good decisions. We can deal with tragedy and problems because wisdom trains us to think and apply knowledge instead of simply reacting to situations. Wisdom helps us trust that whatever God does is beneficial in our lives.

Trouble ends with relief; a good party becomes a happy memory. God doesn't give us predictable lives. If we consider that God is in control when we face hardships, we can trust that he will be with us through them and will give us the wisdom to cope.

SEASONS OF A WOMAN'S LIFE

There is a time for every event under heaven—a time to give birth and a time to die; a time to plant and a time to uproot what is planted. A time to kill and a time to heal; a time to tear down and a time to build up. A time to weep and a time to laugh; a time to mourn and a time to dance. A time to throw stones and a time to gather stones; a time to embrace and a time to shun embracing. A time to search and a time to give up as lost; a time to keep and a time to throw away. A time to tear apart and a time to sew together; a time to be silent and a time to speak.

Ecclesiastes 3:1–7 NASB

One woman gives birth. Another watches her children leave home, all grown. And another launches a new career or rejoins the workforce. Each is in a different season of life, and like the calendar's four seasons, each life season has its share of joy and trouble.

King Solomon wisely noted that timing is important. To be content in the season we are in, we must appreciate God's timing and wisely choose actions in sync with the season. We plant gardens in the spring and uproot them at harvesttime when the produce is ripe. When we resist or deny God's timing, we cause problems. We don't get good results if we plant vegetables in the winter that need the summer's warmth.

Some seasons seem unlikely, such as a season to shun embracing, yet we must shun the embrace of a married man or someone trying to seduce us. A time to weep is a time to be healed, while a time to laugh is a time to rejoice. Each season has a purpose. Contentment comes with being prepared, accepting God's timing, and trusting that as one season ends, a new one will begin.

CELEBRATIONS AND REST

Six days you are to do your work, but on the seventh day you shall cease from labor. . . . Three times a year you shall celebrate a feast to Me. You shall observe the Feast of Unleavened Bread; for seven days you are to eat unleavened bread, as I commanded you, at the appointed time in the month Abib, for in it you came out of Egypt. And none shall appear before Me empty-handed.

Also you shall observe the Feast of the Harvest of the first fruits of your labors from what you sow in the field; also the Feast of the Ingathering at the end of the year when you gather in the fruit of your labors from the field. Three times a year all your males shall appear before the Lord GOD.

Exodus 23:12, 14–17 NASB

God established time and cycles that include rest and celebration. Ceasing from labor means to stop working, taking time to refresh body, mind, and soul. It also offers time to serve God and dwell on God. When we cease from busyness, we can be restored, and that helps us feel better and more satisfied with life.

God gave the Israelites three important feast days to celebrate and every Sabbath for resting and honoring him. The feast days celebrated God's interaction with his people. The Feast of Unleavened Bread reminded them that he is a deliverer. The feast to celebrate the firstfruits of the harvest reminded the people that God causes growth, and the feast of the gathering of crops reminded them that they worked in cooperation with God to satisfy their needs. Celebrations are fun and build memories. There's comfort in familiar traditions and foods.

Celebrations and special days changed when Jesus came, but they still help us focus on God's power. Every day is a day to thank God for salvation. We constantly need to look to God. As we do, we appreciate God's power and trust him to satisfy our needs.

DISCONTENT AND ENVY

When Rachel saw that she bore Jacob no children, she envied her sister, and said to Jacob, Give me children, or else I will die!

And Jacob became very angry with Rachel and he said, Am I in God's stead, Who has denied you children? . . .

And Bilhah, Rachel's maid, conceived again and bore Jacob a second son.

And Rachel said, With mighty wrestlings [in prayer to God] I have struggled with my sister and have prevailed; so she named him [this second son Bilhah bore] Naphtali [struggled]. . . .

Then God remembered Rachel and answered her pleading and made it possible for her to have children. And [now for the first time] she became pregnant and bore a son; and she said, God has taken away my reproach, disgrace, and humiliation.

Genesis 30:1–2, 7–8, 22–23
AMP

✳

Looking at the blessings someone else enjoys can cause envy and discontent. Isaac's son Jacob had two wives who were sisters, and one, Rachel, was barren. In Rachel's day it was a shame not to bear children, and infertility still grieves many women. Rachel used blame, angered her husband, competed through her maid with her sister, and struggled in prayer, pleading with God for children. At last God gave her children, and she praised God for removing her humiliation and disgrace. Jacob and God loved her whether she had children or not, but Rachel focused only on her feelings and her need for a baby.

Women who are discontented make life difficult for the people around them. Nothing satisfies them but the desire triggered by the envy, the need to have what someone else has or to be like someone else. Discontented women, like Rachel, can stir up negative emotions in others and disrupt lives.

After giving birth, Rachel praised God for healing her wounded pride. Discontent selfishly desires something we don't have, instead of trusting God's will and finding satisfaction in the blessings we do have.

MATERIAL OBSESSIONS

Don't be obsessed with getting more material things. Be relaxed with what you have. . . . God assured us, "I'll never let you down, never walk off and leave you." . . .

Appreciate your pastoral leaders who gave you the Word of God. Take a good look at the way they live, and let their faithfulness instruct you, as well as their truthfulness. There should be a consistency that runs through us all. For Jesus doesn't change—yesterday, today, tomorrow, he's always totally himself. . . .

So let's go outside, where Jesus is, where the action is—not trying to be privileged insiders, but taking our share in the abuse of Jesus. This "insider world" is not our home. We have our eyes peeled for the City about to come. Let's take our place outside with Jesus.

Hebrews 13:5, 7–8, 13–15
MSG

Is your home bursting with things and filled with clutter because you keep buying and collecting? What do you love to buy—shoes, china, baskets, porcelain? It takes time to shop and care for what we buy. We rent storage space and build bigger homes and larger closets and still continue to buy. When we can't stop buying or thinking about possessions or desires, it's called obsession. God doesn't want us to think about things. He wants us to fix our minds on what is lasting—our future home in heaven.

The book of Hebrews was written to Jewish Christians suffering persecution for their faith. To "go outside" means to show our faith and willingly suffer. The passage encourages Christians who are mocked or persecuted for faith in Christ to look to Jesus, who never changes and always accepts us.

God wants us to be relaxed, or satisfied, with what we own. Sit back and enjoy the blessings you have, and while outdoors enjoy the world God made. This passage also encourages us to look at the way faithful Christians live. Their example models a passion for living what they believe and also models contentment.

ORDER AND CONTENTMENT

The earth was formless and void, and darkness was over the surface of the deep, and the Spirit of God was moving over the surface of the waters. Then God said, "Let there be light"; and there was light. God saw that the light was good; and God separated the light from the darkness. . . .

God made the expanse, and separated the waters which were below the expanse from the waters which were above the expanse; and it was so. . . .

Then God said, "Let the waters below the heavens be gathered into one place, and let the dry land appear." . . .

Then God said, "Let there be lights in the expanse of the heavens to separate the day from the night, and let them be for signs and for seasons and for days and years."

Genesis 1:2–4, 7, 9, 14 NASB

※

God didn't settle for chaos or a world of darkness. He moved and looked over the void and then got busy turning the void into a beautiful universe. He spent time and energy fashioning the world and creating order. He created time units—years, seasons, days. This passage from the first book of the Bible shows us that God cares about order and beauty. After each day's creative work, God paused and looked at what he had made and said that it was good. God didn't rush around multitasking. Each day he focused on certain aspects of creation, such as light, plants, and animals. Part of creating included organizing and setting things in order.

To live in a void, or have a formless existence, is to live in darkness. We want light to brighten our lives and allow us to see what is around us. When we organize, decorate, or work, we can find goodness in life. If something is good, it is worthwhile and beneficial. Pausing to look at a clean kitchen, a scrapbook album we made, or another completed project helps us appreciate our work and feel contentment in a job well done.

BE HAPPY FOR OTHERS

An argument developed between some of John's disciples and a certain Jew over the matter of ceremonial washing. They came to John and said to him, "Rabbi, that man who was with you on the other side of the Jordan—the one you testified about—well, he is baptizing, and everyone is going to him."

To this John replied, "A man can receive only what is given him from heaven. You yourselves can testify that I said, 'I am not the Christ but am sent ahead of him.' The bride belongs to the bridegroom. The friend who attends the bridegroom waits and listens for him, and is full of joy when he hears the bridegroom's voice. That joy is mine, and it is now complete. He must become greater; I must become less."

John 3:25–30 NIV

If you have ever been a bridesmaid, you understand that the wedding is all about the bride and groom. You served as a helper and background to a lovely ceremony. A good bridesmaid does all she can to make the day special for the wedding couple.

John the Baptist understood his role and felt joy at serving Jesus. The apostle John wrote this passage that describes complaints of the disciples of John the Baptist. God had called John the Baptist to serve Jesus, the real bridegroom. He came to call people to repent of their sins, to baptize them with water, and to tell them the Messiah was coming. John's role would decrease once Jesus came, for the preparations would be done.

John understood the greater joy of the Messiah's presence and rejoiced at his coming. He knew his ministry was not about himself but about Jesus. We should be happy for others who have successful ministries, as they are also working for God. We are part of a team, not competitors. We can be happy doing whatever God wants us to do, no matter how small the task, and rejoice in God's larger plans.

WILD MUSIC

A prayer of Habakkuk the prophet, set to wild, enthusiastic, and triumphal music . . .

I heard and my [whole inner self] trembled; my lips quivered at the sound. Rottenness enters into my bones and under me [down to my feet]; I tremble. . . . Though the fig tree does not blossom and there is no fruit on the vines, [though] the product of the olive fails and the fields yield no food, though the flock is cut off from the fold and there are no cattle in the stalls, yet I will rejoice in the Lord; I will exult in the [victorious] God of my salvation!

The Lord God is my Strength, my personal bravery, and my invincible army; He makes my feet like hinds' feet and will make me to walk [not to stand still in terror, but to walk].

Habakkuk 3:1, 16–19 AMP

✳

The reports of crime and terrorism that fill the news can be depressing. Habakkuk, a prophet who lived several hundred years before the birth of Christ, saw evil people triumphing over others and wickedness increasing. He complained and asked God why evil seemed to be winning. God responded that ultimately justice would prevail because he is always in control and he will punish sin. Habakkuk then said this prayer set to wild, enthusiastic music. The words and music reveal the joy he felt as he realized he didn't need to understand God's ways; he only needed to trust the final outcome to God.

Murder, abuse, theft, bombings—crimes and trouble will continue, but we don't have to fear or be discouraged. When life is hard and things get worse, we can turn on triumphant Christian music, and remember that God is in control. God is not causing the crimes. We can turn to the final chapter in the Bible and know that God will triumph in the end.

"Hind's feet" are the agile feet of a female deer that can jump over rocks and climb high places without slipping. God can help us walk securely.

ROLLER COASTER FROM PAIN TO JOY

They said to her, "Woman, why do you weep?"

"They took my Master," she said, "and I don't know where they put him." After she said this, she turned away and saw Jesus standing there. But she didn't recognize him.

Jesus spoke to her, "Woman, why do you weep? Who are you looking for?"

She, thinking that he was the gardener, said, "Mister, if you took him, tell me where you put him so I can care for him."

Jesus said, "Mary."

Turning to face him, she said in Hebrew, "Rabboni!" meaning "Teacher!"

Jesus said, "Don't cling to me, for I have not yet ascended to the Father." . . .

Mary Magdalene went, telling the news to the disciples: "I saw the Master!" And she told them everything he said to her.

John 20:13–18 MSG

※

Mary Magdalene's emotional ups and downs on the first Easter are a familiar reaction of women to life's circumstances. Jesus had been crucified and buried a few days earlier, and now his tomb was empty. She feared that someone had stolen the body of Jesus. She wept. She tried to coax the man she saw to tell her where he had put the body. In her confused emotional state, she felt pain and missed the obvious. Only when Jesus spoke her name, "Mary!" did she recognize Jesus. Then her source of confusion became her fountain of joy.

Jesus told her not to cling; although he understood her desire to touch him, getting the news out about the Resurrection was more important. He redirected Mary's happiness by asking her to share the news with his disciples. She obeyed and exclaimed the wonder of his resurrection to them with uncontainable joy.

Our first response is often emotional. We don't always see God in our circumstances or recognize miracles around us. Yet if we seek Jesus and listen, even in our most painful and confused times, we will also hear him and find limitless joy to share.

CONTENTED HARMONY

Now you must put them all away: anger, wrath, malice, slander, and obscene talk from your mouth. Do not lie to one another, seeing that you have put off the old self with its practices and have put on the new self, which is being renewed in knowledge after the image of its creator. . . .

Put on then, as God's chosen ones, holy and beloved, compassion, kindness, humility, meekness, and patience, bearing with one another and, if one has a complaint against another, forgiving each other; as the Lord has forgiven you, so you also must forgive. And above all these put on love, which binds everything together in perfect harmony. And let the peace of Christ rule in your hearts, to which indeed you were called in one body. And be thankful.

Colossians 3:8–10, 12–15 ESV

Chalk screeching on a chalkboard, loud crashes, and other disruptive noises hurt our ears. A good conductor can train an orchestra to create beautiful music with various instruments blending together in harmony, but it takes effort and work. In his letter to the Colossian church, Paul confronts the false teaching that had created discord and then in this passage explains how to create harmony among believers.

Words flowing from hearts filled with anger and lacking in love create chaotic noise that hurts others. But when Christ rules the heart, he is the conductor who trains us to blend and harmonize with others. Love is the unifier that creates the harmony. Forgiveness, meekness, kindness, patience, and compassion are the instruments we must learn to play to create a pleasing and peaceful melody that will play in our hearts.

Girlfriends love to talk, but we need to be kind when we talk. We need to bear with one another, just as orchestra members must patiently let various musicians get their instruments in tune with one another. Instead of slandering, gossiping, or lashing out in anger, we can communicate our complaints honestly and forgive one another.

MUSIC SOOTHES THE SAVAGE . . .

Saul's officials told him, "An evil spirit from God is tormenting you. Your Majesty, why don't you command us to look for a man who can play the lyre well? When the evil spirit from God comes to you, he'll strum a tune, and you'll feel better." . . .

One of the officials said, "I know one of Jesse's sons from Bethlehem who can play well. He's a courageous man and a warrior. He has a way with words, he is handsome, and the LORD is with him." . . .

David came to Saul and served him. Saul loved him very much and made David his armorbearer. . . .

Whenever God's spirit came to Saul, David took the lyre and strummed a tune. Saul got relief from his terror and felt better, and the evil spirit left him.

1 Samuel 16:15–16, 18, 21, 23 GOD'S WORD

❋

Temper tantrums, shouting, throwing things—such angry outbursts reveal inner problems. People around King Saul recognized his anguish. Saul's disobedience led God to tear the kingdom away from him and his family, and the Holy Spirit no longer was with Saul. Instead he was left distraught and susceptible to affliction by other spirits. When Saul had bouts of terror, David calmed him with soothing music. Samuel had already secretly anointed David as Israel's new king, yet he humbly played for Saul whenever Saul felt troubled. Music drew them together.

David's melodies touched the king's heart. Both David and Saul were warriors and courageous soldiers, yet they both responded to music.

We play music in our cars, where we often need something to calm us among rude drivers and the frustration of sitting in traffic jams. Young children are calmed down and lulled to sleep with soft music and lullabies. Music is powerful and is used in therapy to reduce stress and depression, reduce pain, and increase pleasure. Slower tempos help people calm down, lower heart rates, and lower blood pressure. We can add peace and contentment to our days by listening to calming music.

HUMBLE PRAYERS BRING CONTENTMENT

To some who were confident of their own righteousness and looked down on everybody else, Jesus told this parable: "Two men went up to the temple to pray, one a Pharisee and the other a tax collector. The Pharisee stood up and prayed about himself: 'God, I thank you that I am not like other men—robbers, evildoers, adulterers—or even like this tax collector. I fast twice a week and give a tenth of all I get.'

"But the tax collector stood at a distance. He would not even look up to heaven, but beat his breast and said, 'God, have mercy on me, a sinner.'

"I tell you that this man, rather than the other, went home justified before God. For everyone who exalts himself will be humbled, and he who humbles himself will be exalted."

Luke 18:9–14 NIV

❋

Jesus spent a great deal of time praying. He understood the joy of communicating with God the Father. He used this story, or parable, to teach about our attitude when we pray.

When we use prayer to brag to God and justify ourselves or our actions, our prayers will not please God and we won't experience peace. But when we come to God sorry for our sins and knowing that we need God's forgiveness and mercy, he will respond and forgive us. The humble man in Jesus' story didn't even list his sins, for he knew God sees everything we do.

Because God sees all we do, he doesn't want us to tell him why we think we are good. He wants us to be honest and share our troubled hearts with him. He wants us to admit that we cheated at work, spread gossip, yelled at our children, or failed to love our spouses. Then he will forgive us, and we will be exalted, or content, because of his comfort. God wants us to lean on him, for that's when we are open to his helping us and changing us to be better.

BEAUTIFUL IN TIME

God has made everything beautiful for its own time. He has planted eternity in the human heart, but even so, people cannot see the whole scope of God's work from beginning to end. So I concluded there is nothing better than to be happy and enjoy ourselves as long as we can. And people should eat and drink and enjoy the fruits of their labor, for these are gifts from God.

And I know that whatever God does is final. Nothing can be added to it or taken from it. God's purpose is that people should fear him. . . .

So I saw that there is nothing better for people than to be happy in their work. That is why we are here! No one will bring us back from death to enjoy life after we die.

Ecclesiastes 3:11–14, 22 NLT

A flower blooms and looks beautiful for a short time. Stars sparkle at night, but not during the day. Each is beautiful according to God's timing.

We don't understand God's eternal plan. We don't even know what might happen tomorrow, but God does. God "planted eternity" in our hearts, and that's why women sense that there is a purpose for life and why we long to know him.

King Solomon observed people and noticed that some activities provide more fulfillment and pleasure than others. We enjoy eating and the fruit of our work. We may not always like the process of labor, but we like the rewards. To have more contentment, it's best if we are happy in our work. Part of being happy with work is to find purpose in what we are already doing. We can seek God, who knows our purpose and what makes us happy, to guide us to the right job if we should change jobs or our mission in life. And we can ask God to help us find purpose in our current situations and trust him to reveal beauty and joy in our work, in his time.

The Heart of Security

A tree is identified by its fruit. . . .

A good person produces good things from the treasury of a good heart, and an evil person produces evil things from the treasury of an evil heart. What you say flows from what is in your heart. . . .

I will show you what it's like when someone comes to me, listens to my teaching, and then follows it. It is like a person building a house who digs deep and lays the foundation on solid rock. When the floodwaters rise and break against the house, it stands firm because it is well built. But anyone who hears and doesn't obey is like a person who builds a house without a foundation. When the floods sweep down against that house, it will collapse into a heap of ruins.

Luke 6:44–45, 47–49 NLT

Jesus frequently used familiar objects to illustrate truths. The tree analogy and the parable of the two builders in this passage are also found in the Gospel of Matthew. They're important enough to be repeated.

Jesus compared our words to good fruit. Once we cultivate a good heart, the outcome will be good, because what is in a woman dominates her words and actions. But it takes more than a good heart to be a strong Christian, so Jesus spoke about building faith. He compared good followers to a wise builder. Jesus told this story by the Sea of Galilee, where people needed to dig below the sand to the bedrock to build homes that would withstand storms and strong winds.

The good builder reflects the time, energy, and focus needed to become a strong Christian. We must dig deep to understand the Bible, know Christ, and build trust in God; then adversity won't shake our faith or cause us to lose hope. Developing solid faith leads to confidence in God that withstands trials and hardships. Just as a good foundation makes a house safe, so a good spiritual foundation makes us secure and content.

A GENEROUS LORD

The workers who had been hired first thought they would be given more than the others. But when they were given the same, they began complaining to the owner of the vineyard. They said, "The ones who were hired last worked for only one hour. But you paid them the same that you did us. And we worked in the hot sun all day long!"

The owner answered one of them, "Friend, I didn't cheat you. I paid you exactly what we agreed on. . . . Don't I have the right to do what I want with my own money? Why should you be jealous, if I want to be generous?"

Jesus then said, "So it is. Everyone who is now first will be last, and everyone who is last will be first."

Matthew 20:10–13, 15–16
CEV

We get annoyed at trivial things, like waiting in line or getting the wrong order in a restaurant. We grumble and complain of unfairness, such as being passed over for a promotion, missing a flight because security delayed us, or not getting the bargain we saw advertised. The men in this famous parable, called the parable of the vineyard workers, felt cheated. They had agreed to a specific payment but complained when they saw others—hired hours later—receive the same pay.

Jesus introduced this story with the words "The kingdom of heaven is like a landowner" (20:1 NIV). He wanted to illustrate to the Jews God's grace, or favor toward all people, including non-Jews, or Gentiles. People who believe at their dying moment will be saved, just like people who believed at a young age and spent their lives serving God.

The workers hired early had the security of a job. The last hired may have worried all day, wondering how they would earn enough for food. They would have been grateful for anything. But God is generous. Rejoice that God has saved you and be happy for all others when they believe.

SHARE CHEERFULLY

The farmer who plants because he has received God's blessings will receive a harvest of God's blessings in return. Each of you should give whatever you have decided. You shouldn't be sorry that you gave or feel forced to give, since God loves a cheerful giver. Besides, God will give you his constantly overflowing kindness. Then, when you always have everything you need, you can do more and more good things. . . .

God gives seed to the farmer and food to those who need to eat. God will also give you seed and multiply it. In your lives he will increase the things you do that have his approval. God will make you rich enough so that you can always be generous. Your generosity will produce thanksgiving to God because of us.

2 Corinthians 9:6–11
GOD'S WORD

※

Seeds kept in a package will never produce a harvest. With God's blessings of rain and sun, seeds planted multiply into an abundant harvest. Paul wrote this passage after reminding the Corinthians that they had promised to give money to help the church in Jerusalem. God never forces us to give but wants us to give willingly, and he rewards generosity.

God gives us wealth so we can be generous and extend his joy of giving to others. When we give, we distribute God's provision, blessing, and love. In return, God wants to give us more blessings. The recipients of our gifts are blessed, and God will be praised. Everyone benefits when we share what we have.

Like any good farmer, we can be intentional about how and what we give. Giving is a way to plant seeds—in a ministry or church or life—that will produce good results. We should give with the joyful contentment of knowing that the gift touches lives. We can give and know that God, who gave us life and all we have, has unlimited resources and can bless us with more to give again.

CAREFREE LIVING

Do not be worried about your life, as to what you will eat or what you will drink; nor for your body, as to what you will put on. Is not life more than food, and the body more than clothing? Look at the birds of the air, that they do not sow, nor reap nor gather into barns, and yet your heavenly Father feeds them. Are you not worth much more than they? And who of you by being worried can add a single hour to his life? . . .

Do not worry then, saying, "What will we eat?" or "What will we drink?" or "What will we wear for clothing?" . . . But seek first His kingdom and His righteousness, and all these things will be added to you.

So do not worry about tomorrow; for tomorrow will care for itself.

Matthew 6:25–27, 31, 33–34
NASB

Birds fill the air with cheerful chirps and tweets that call out for us to be happy and let go of anxiety. We too often listen instead to our worrisome thoughts, dwelling on the negative possibilities of our circumstances or the future. Worry focuses on our own needs. God wants to replace our worries with hope and contentment. Jesus spoke the words in this passage after teaching about a godly attitude toward money. He always challenged his listeners to change their attitudes and think from God's perspective. God wants us to focus on him and trust that he knows what he is doing and knows how to supply our needs.

We cannot know or control the future, but God can. We can learn to control our thoughts, choose our actions, and understand that life on earth is just the beginning of eternal living. Our purpose is to be with God forever, and we should start by getting to know him well now. Whenever you have an anxious thought, make it a habit to pray and seek God's wisdom. Then live carefree as you let go and let God take care of all your tomorrows.

FEELING DOUBLY GOOD

I write this letter to you, Philemon, my good friend and companion in this work—also to our sister Apphia, to Archippus, a real trooper, and to the church that meets in your house. God's best to you! Christ's blessings on you!

Every time your name comes up in my prayers, I say, "Oh, thank you, God!" I keep hearing of the love and faith you have for the Master Jesus, which brims over to other Christians. And I keep praying that this faith we hold in common keeps showing up in the good things we do, and that people recognize Christ in all of it. Friend, you have no idea how good your love makes me feel, doubly so when I see your hospitality to fellow believers.

Philemon 1:1–7 MSG

We experience great joy when we get together with girlfriends and have a happy time. Paul wrote to his friend Philemon, a church leader, to express his thankfulness for their friendship and to encourage Philemon to change his heart attitude about one of his slaves, Onesimus. Paul wanted his friend to love the slave as the Christian brother he had become. Paul viewed all Christians as family united by faith.

Paul's words share the concept of God's love spilling over into relationships with all Christians. Too often we put up walls that divide us, such as status at work, economic class, or denominational differences. Praying for friends and thanking God for them keeps our focus on God's provision of friends and helps us see their positive qualities. These prayers express our joy and contentment in life as we appreciate our friends. Thanking our friends, as Paul did, encourages them and lets them know how much they mean to us.

Every memory of friends should prompt us to pray for them. What friends can you pray for and thank God for today? Express your appreciation for a friend with a note or encouraging words.

You Will Smile Again

I will exalt you, O LORD, for you lifted me out of the depths and did not let my enemies gloat over me. O LORD my God, I called to you for help and you healed me. O LORD, you brought me up from the grave; you spared me from going down into the pit. . . .

For his anger lasts only a moment, but his favor lasts a lifetime; weeping may remain for a night, but rejoicing comes in the morning. . . .

You turned my wailing into dancing; you removed my sackcloth and clothed me with joy, that my heart may sing to you and not be silent.

Psalm 30:1–3, 5, 11–12 NIV

We all have times of grief and mourning the loss of a loved one. When we lose a child or a spouse to death, we experience great pain and shed many tears. This psalm brings a reminder that we will have better times and reasons to rejoice. David sang this song at the dedication of the temple's proposed location. The temple was not built at that time, nor while David lived. David spent years fighting enemies, struggling with family problems, and mourning the loss of his son and Jonathan, his best friend. He had experienced how God made his heart rejoice again and sang to praise God for his help.

The range of emotions David described over one thousand years ago people still experience today. We can feel empty, depressed, defeated, and believe God has abandoned us or punished us.

Grief takes longer to resolve than most people expect. The tears that flow help us release the sorrow. When we call out to God in our heart-wrenching pain, he will lift us out of our pit. The words of this passage comfort us with the promise that we will smile again and music will again touch our hearts. God will give us peace and contentment.

Heart's Desires Fulfilled

Delight yourself in the LORD; and He will give you the desires of your heart. Commit your way to the LORD, trust also in Him, and He will do it. He will bring forth your righteousness as the light and your judgment as the noonday. Rest in the LORD and wait patiently for Him; do not fret because of him who prospers in his way, because of the man who carries out wicked schemes. Cease from anger and forsake wrath; do not fret; it leads only to evildoing. For evildoers will be cut off, but those who wait for the LORD, they will inherit the land. . . .

But the salvation of the righteous is from the LORD; He is their strength in time of trouble.

Psalm 37:4–9, 39 NASB

Not having what we desire often causes discontent. The psalm from which this passage comes, written by King David, is an acrostic poem about trusting God. Each verse begins with a successive letter of the Hebrew alphabet. As we take pleasure in God, we change and reprogram our hearts and minds to be happy. It's a process, and this psalm gives us tools to help us.

We replace our desire with wanting to enjoy God. We delight in God as we praise him and study the Bible. We discover that as we let go and let God take control, we don't need to try to force things to happen, and this helps us relax and wait. An earlier verse in this psalm tells us to trust in God and do good. We switch our actions from impatiently striving to get our way to serving, and we discover patience. We can stop anger by turning away from the source and praying about the problem instead of fuming or arguing. With these choices we can proactively seek contentment. God will bless us with land, salvation, and strength of character—as well as our hearts' desires.

CAN-DO THINKING

I was made very happy in the Lord that now you have revived your interest in my welfare after so long a time. . . .

I have learned how to be content (satisfied to the point where I am not disturbed or disquieted) in whatever state I am.

I know how to be abased and live humbly in straitened circumstances, and I know also how to enjoy plenty and live in abundance. I have learned in any and all circumstances the secret of facing every situation, whether well-fed or going hungry, having a sufficiency and enough to spare or going without and being in want.

I have strength for all things in Christ Who empowers me [I am ready for anything and equal to anything through Him Who infuses inner strength into me; I am self-sufficient in Christ's sufficiency].

Philippians 4:10–13 AMP

Paul wrote to the Philippians to share what he had learned about living as a Christian. Paul had traveled as a missionary, been persecuted, and spent time in jail. As he experienced life, he learned to be content in any situation. His secret was letting Christ strengthen him and help him. He focused on doing what God empowered him to do and didn't worry about the rest. Circumstances change, but God remains constant.

When we are blessed, we should enjoy what God has given us and use what we have. When we have less, we can be thankful for the little we have and realize it's all God has supplied and all that we really need. A time with fewer possessions can give us an opportunity to focus on God and watch how he provides food and shelter. Extra blessings give us more to share and new reasons to be thankful.

Circumstances help us refocus. If a medical condition causes a financial setback, we discover that we can get along with less and things are not so important. A new job with more pay lets us thank God and enjoy extra perks. Contentment is an attitude of acceptance.

DIVINE DISCONTENT

Jesus went into the temple and chased out everyone who was selling or buying. He turned over the tables of the moneychangers and the benches of the ones who were selling doves.

He told them, "The Scriptures say, 'My house should be called a place of worship.' But you have turned it into a place where robbers hide."

Blind and lame people came to Jesus in the temple, and he healed them. But the chief priests and the teachers of the Law of Moses were angry when they saw his miracles and heard the children shouting praises to the Son of David.

The men said to Jesus, "Don't you hear what those children are saying?"

"Yes, I do!" Jesus answered. "Don't you know that the Scriptures say, 'Children and infants will sing praises'?"

Matthew 21:12–16 CEV

Jesus walked into the temple and felt discontent over the way people treated God's house. He wasn't angered about any hurt toward himself or any unsatisfied desire, but by the plight of people's hearts and their actions toward God. His discontent motivated him to act. He restored the temple to a place of worship instead of a marketplace.

A divine discontent about the status quo that hurts God or others causes restlessness. The restlessness motivates us to action, often to bring social justice to God's helpless children or to bring respect to God. This discontent prompted Jesus to respond to the anger of the priests and teachers. He saw the need to clean the inside of their hearts as he affirmed the right of children to praise him as the son of David. Restlessness might be a call to help people get right with God or to invest in ministry that helps others.

Respond to the inner urging of God as he redirects you and challenges you to make a difference in our world. When change starts taking place, people of all ages notice and praise God; they see God's presence in your work.

GET FIRED UP!

I've come to start a fire on this earth—how I wish it were blazing right now! I've come to change everything, turn everything rightside up—how I long for it to be finished! Do you think I came to smooth things over and make everything nice? Not so. I've come to disrupt and confront! From now on, when you find five in a house, it will be—three against two, and two against three. . . .

When you see clouds coming in from the west, you say, "Storm's coming"—and you're right. And when the wind comes out of the south, you say, "This'll be a hot one"—and you're right. Frauds! You know how to tell a change in the weather, so don't tell me you can't tell a change in the season, the God-season we're in right now.

Luke 12:49–56 MSG

Change comes to everyone, and the best way to respond is with enthusiasm. When you know God is bringing change, accept the challenge and get fired up! Jesus spoke about changes coming from God that will disrupt lives and confront us with challenges. We recognize change as a birth or wedding approaches, when an illness is said to be terminal, when a new job takes us to another location, and when we retire. We might also be called to change a ministry or service involvement, as others leave or we feel urged by God to do something different or we receive a new vision from God.

Change can be difficult because we like routines. But challenges can invigorate us if we choose to view them positively, anticipate what we need to help us transition smoothly, and laugh at the little problems that pop up, like losing dishes in a move. We like security and routines, but God pushes us to change and improve. Listing all the positive aspects in a change and praying over the uncertainties can help us enjoy the adjustments and trust the unknown to God with an attitude of contentment.

Faith & Love

Faith is believing that God exists and that what he has told us is true. Faith is also acting upon our beliefs by following God. In the Bible we discover the confidence of even a little faith as well as the desire for faith when it is lacking. We find examples that show us how faith helps us thrive as we find purpose through following God.

God is love, and nothing can separate us from his love! God wired women for love—to love and to be loved by our spouses, family, friends, and church. The Bible helps us understand the varied forms of love and teaches us to view love through the eyes of God instead of a camera lens.

These three remain: faith, hope and love. But the greatest of these is love.

1 Corinthians 13:13 NIV

DOUBTS AND PROOFS

Thomas, one of the twelve apostles, who was called Didymus, wasn't with them when Jesus came. The other disciples told him, "We've seen the Lord."

Thomas told them, "I refuse to believe this unless I see the nail marks in his hands, put my fingers into them, and put my hand into his side."

A week later Jesus' disciples were again in the house, and Thomas was with them. Even though the doors were locked, Jesus stood among them and said, "Peace be with you!" Then Jesus said to Thomas, "Put your finger here, and look at my hands. Take your hand, and put it into my side. Stop doubting, and believe."

Thomas responded to Jesus, "My Lord and my God!"

Jesus said to Thomas, "You believe because you've seen me. Blessed are those who haven't seen me but believe."

John 20:24–29 GOD'S WORD

❋

When something sounds unbelievable, we might check out the story on a website about hoaxes. We don't want to be duped, so we shy away from believing someone telling a miraculous story. We don't want to be gullible or fall prey to people trying to con us.

It's understandable to doubt strangers, but Thomas doubted his close friends when they shared the good news of seeing Jesus again. Thomas believed when he experienced the truth. Doubting is part of our nature. Be patient with people who don't believe your testimony as a Christian or who doubt your word. Pray that Jesus will reveal himself and the truth to them.

Women are less likely than men to have doubts about Jesus and twice as likely as men to attend church. We might have a harder time convincing husbands, dads, and sons to believe in Jesus and overcome their doubts than we do sharing our faith with other women.

When doubt comes to visit you or someone you love, don't be afraid to tell God about it. Then look for ways to experience God again and consider evidences of God. Live your faith so doubters will see faith in action.

BELIEVE, FOR I TOLD YOU SO

I am the way, the truth, and the life; no one goes to the Father except by me. . . .

I will ask the Father, and he will give you another Helper, who will stay with you forever. He is the Spirit, who reveals the truth about God. The world cannot receive him, because it cannot see him or know him. But you know him, because he remains with you and is in you. . . .

I have told you this while I am still with you. The Helper, the Holy Spirit, whom the Father will send in my name, will teach you everything and make you remember all that I have told you. . . .

I have told you this now before it all happens, so that when it does happen, you will believe.

John 14:6, 16–17, 25–26, 29
GNT

Mobile phones hold calendars, photos, notes, and programmable alarms to jog our memories. Jesus offers something better. The power of the Holy Spirit surpasses the best memory techniques and would remind Jesus' disciples of his words and their experiences with him after he returned to heaven. The rush of power that came with the Holy Spirit might have terrified them except that Jesus had told them what to expect. Jesus spoke the words in this passage to the disciples at the Last Supper, after washing their feet, and just before many traumatic events began. Witnessing the Crucifixion could have caused memory problems, but Jesus knew the Helper would restore their memories.

Women tend to remember faces, words, objects, everyday events, and pictures better than men, who remember symbols and nonverbal information better. Our minds function differently, but the Holy Spirit will help us all. We can boost our memories by forming word pictures and by connecting faith experiences to events and people. We don't need photographic memories, fancy gadgets, or a higher education to share truths about Jesus. The Holy Spirit will bring to mind what we need to recall.

Toppled by Obedience

The Lord said to Joshua, "I am about to hand Jericho, its king, and its warriors over to you. All the soldiers will march around the city once a day for six days. Seven priests will carry rams' horns ahead of the ark. But on the seventh day you must march around the city seven times while the priests blow their horns. When you hear a long blast on the horn, all the troops must shout very loudly. The wall around the city will collapse. Then the troops must charge straight ahead into the city." . . .

So the troops shouted very loudly when they heard the blast of the rams' horns, and the wall collapsed. The troops charged straight ahead and captured the city. They claimed everything in it for the Lord.

Joshua 6:2–5, 20–21
GOD'S WORD

❈

Marching around the enemy's fortress walls didn't sound like a battle strategy, but Joshua never questioned God. Guards in Jericho, watching from atop the high city wall, must have laughed at the parade and thought that the Israelites knew little about war. The Israelites had spent forty years wandering in the desert, not drilling and developing battle strategies. However, the people had been learning to obey God and listen to him. They were prepared to follow God's creative battle plan at Jericho.

What are your battles today? Disobedient children who won't pick up after themselves or listen to you? Removing the obstacles to starting a new career? Your best preparation is to develop your faith in God and practice obeying God's laws. Others might laugh or feel sorry for you and not believe you can do what appears impossible, but you can do anything with faith in God.

The collapse of such a strong wall showed the Israelites once again that God is more powerful than man-made structures or armies. He can give us creative ideas for parenting and opportunities for careers. He can give us plans to overcome the seemingly immovable walls we face.

BELIEVING THE MESSAGE

After walking for a day, Jonah warned the people, "Forty days from now, Nineveh will be destroyed!"

They believed God's message and set a time when they would go without eating to show their sorrow. Then everyone in the city, no matter who they were, dressed in sackcloth.

When the king of Nineveh heard what was happening, he also dressed in sackcloth; he left the royal palace and sat in dust. Then he and his officials sent out an order. . . .

"You must also pray to the LORD God with all your heart and stop being sinful and cruel. Maybe God will change his mind and have mercy on us, so we won't be destroyed."

When God saw that the people had stopped doing evil things, he had pity and did not destroy them as he had planned.

Jonah 3:4–7, 9–10 CEV

Jonah preached his message to the Ninevites after three days in the belly of the whale. He must have looked very odd. But the people who heard Jonah paid more attention to his message than his appearance. It took Jonah three days to walk the length of the city of Nineveh, one of the largest and most powerful cities in the world. Everyone listened to Jonah's message that God would destroy the city if the people did not change their ways. Nearly one-quarter million people dressed in sackcloth, even the king. All the men, women, merchants, leaders, and even the children responded to God's message. Centuries later Jesus used Nineveh and its people as an example of faith, because they believed the message and responded to it.

If you have a concern that stirs your heart but you avoid doing anything about it, you might be like Jonah, running away from what God wants you to do. You might be needed to join a ministry or to help at a school or other organization, or to become a speaker. Listen to God and speak up willingly if he calls you to serve or share a message.

EAGER FAITH

I serve God by spreading the Good News about his Son. God is my witness that I always mention you every time I pray. I ask that somehow God will now at last make it possible for me to visit you. I long to see you to share a spiritual blessing with you so that you will be strengthened. What I mean is that we may be encouraged by each other's faith. . . .

That's why I'm eager to tell you who live in Rome the Good News also.

I'm not ashamed of the Good News. It is God's power to save everyone who believes, Jews first and Greeks as well. God's approval is revealed in this Good News. This approval begins and ends with faith as Scripture says, "The person who has God's approval will live by faith."

Romans 1:9–12, 15–17
GOD'S WORD

When we have good news, we want to share it and let everyone know. When we hear about a miracle or listen to a missionary talk, we rejoice for what God has done in the lives of other people. It's exciting to hear a woman speak and share her faith.

Paul's letter to the Romans introduced him to the Christians there. Paul looked forward to an opportunity to meet them and speak to them. He quoted Habakkuk when he wrote about the person who has God's approval. He wanted his readers to approve of his coming to speak, and that phrase helped them know he lived what he preached.

Paul knew that sharing the same faith as others encourages us. When we get together and share what God has done in our lives, we are all inspired. We should be eager to share stories of how our faith has impacted our lives and rejoice at meeting and hearing another Christian woman share her faith. Social networks, letters, and e-mail introduce us but aren't the same as meeting someone personally and seeing her live faithfully. Let people see you live your faith, as that's your best introduction.

LISTEN WITH FAITH

I am the LORD your God, who brought you up out of the land of Egypt. . . .

"But my people did not listen to my voice; Israel would not submit to me. So I gave them over to their stubborn hearts, to follow their own counsels. Oh, that my people would listen to me, that Israel would walk in my ways! I would soon subdue their enemies and turn my hand against their foes. Those who hate the LORD would cringe toward him, and their fate would last forever. But he would feed you with the finest of the wheat, and with honey from the rock I would satisfy you."

Psalm 81:10–16 ESV

Moms and grandmas know that getting children to listen can be a battle. Willful little ones want to have their way and make their own choices, even if the choices are harmful. Anyone watching a strong-willed child understands how a stubborn little one can persist, trying to get her own way.

God faces similar problems with us, his children. He longs for us to listen to him and walk in the path he has prepared for us, yet we often stubbornly do our own thing. Asaph, a temple choir director, wrote this psalm to celebrate God's delivering his people from slavery in Egypt, and reminded people of their unfaithfulness to God.

Some women have left their families for a career or another man; some fall into prostitution or drug use instead of seeking God's solutions for their lives. Others may have families but spend all their time working and having fun and forget to show love and care for their children and spouses. Our desires can become more important than our responsibilities. God wants obedience and love to be our top priorities, not careers, sex, or pleasures. When we are faithful, God will bless us with a sweeter life.

FAITH FOR NEEDS

It was good of you to share in my troubles. Moreover, as you Philippians know, in the early days of your acquaintance with the gospel, when I set out from Macedonia, not one church shared with me in the matter of giving and receiving, except you only; for even when I was in Thessalonica, you sent me aid again and again when I was in need. Not that I am looking for a gift, but I am looking for what may be credited to your account. I have received full payment and even more; I am amply supplied, now that I have received from Epaphroditus the gifts you sent. They are a fragrant offering, an acceptable sacrifice, pleasing to God. And my God will meet all your needs according to his glorious riches in Christ Jesus.

Philippians 4:14–19 NIV

A gift of fragrant flowers lifts our spirits and gives us pleasure. Giving generously to a sister in need is one way to give an offering to God. It pleases God like a fragrant offering, as though we were giving him a beautiful bouquet of flowers.

Paul's friends in Philippi faithfully gave to provide for Paul during his missionary journey to Macedonia and Thessalonica. These early Christians gave to Paul continually, becoming the first church to sponsor a missionary. Paul wanted them to understand that God would meet all their needs because of their faithful giving. Paul saw God interacting with believers in giving and receiving; some of God's blessings will be waiting for us in heaven.

God wants us to focus on the needs of others and let him provide for our needs. Sponsor a missionary, support a hurting neighbor, or help a friend going through a difficult time. You can give time, service, or money. Don't wait for someone to ask for help; offer practical help as you observe needs. God uses his people to meet the needs of others. He will notice your generosity and consider your giving a sweet offering.

PREDICTIONS THAT STIR FAITH

People of Jerusalem, gather your forces! We are besieged! They are attacking the leader of Israel! The LORD says, "Bethlehem Ephrathah, you are one of the smallest towns in Judah, but out of you I will bring a ruler for Israel, whose family line goes back to ancient times."

So the LORD will abandon his people to their enemies until the woman who is to give birth has her son. Then those Israelites who are in exile will be reunited with their own people. When he comes, he will rule his people with the strength that comes from the LORD and with the majesty of the LORD God himself. His people will live in safety because people all over the earth will acknowledge his greatness, and he will bring peace.

Micah 5:1–5 GNT

✳

Women are always interested in news about a baby's birth—weight and length, time of delivery, the baby's name, and even the hospital. In this passage the prophet Micah gave very specific information about the coming of Jesus, the Messiah. Micah lived several hundred years before the birth of Christ. Like all of God's prophets, all his prophecies came true. Fulfilled prophecies like these can stir our faith. God planned the coming of Jesus and kept every promised detail.

Many Israelites confused the message of this passage. They viewed the coming leader as an earthly one who would bring them peace. They missed that Jesus would be God, not like earthly leaders who want power and wealth, and that peace would be offered to all people. They listened selectively to the message. We must listen to all God says and not only what we choose to believe.

We celebrate the fulfillment of this prophecy at Christmas yet get caught up in decorating and presents instead of celebrating what Micah foretold. Micah's words remind us that part of the prophecy is yet to come—the second coming of Christ and the promise of world peace.

SEEDS OF POSSIBILITIES

A man . . . said, "Sir, have mercy on my son. He suffers from seizures. Often he falls into fire or water. I brought him to your disciples, but they couldn't cure him."

Jesus replied, "You unbelieving and corrupt generation! How long must I be with you? How long must I put up with you? Bring him here to me!"

Jesus ordered the demon to come out of the boy. At that moment the boy was cured.

Then the disciples came to Jesus privately and asked, "Why couldn't we force the demon out of the boy?"

He told them, "Because you have so little faith. I can guarantee this truth: If your faith is the size of a mustard seed, you can say to this mountain, 'Move from here to there,' and it will move. Nothing will be impossible for you."

Matthew 17:14–20
GOD'S WORD

❋

A father's plea for his child caught Jesus' attention. This father persisted in seeking help; when the disciples couldn't cast out the demon, the father came straight to Jesus.

A seed does nothing until it is planted. Then it slowly grows and becomes productive, producing the fruit that God designed it to bear. A little mustard seed of faith, something that grows once planted, is all we need. We are designed to grow in faith.

Design is the planning that goes into creating something. God planned when he made you, and his plan includes your ability to nurture and grow your faith. A seed holds the DNA for what the seed will become when it is planted. God has created us to grow and become as well, and he has plans for what we can become. We start small, believing in Jesus. As we learn more about him and discover his power through answers to prayer, our faith grows.

Mountains of doubt in God's healing or mountains of opposition to following God can all be moved with a firm if tiny belief that God can and will make it happen.

SCRAPBOOK OF FAITH

It was faith that kept the prostitute Rahab from being killed with those who disobeyed God, for she gave the Israelite spies a friendly welcome.

Should I go on? There isn't enough time for me to speak of Gideon, Barak, Samson, Jephthah, David, Samuel, and the prophets. Through faith they fought whole countries and won. They did what was right and received what God had promised. They shut the mouths of lions, put out fierce fires, escaped being killed by the sword. They were weak, but became strong; they were mighty in battle and defeated the armies of foreigners. Through faith women received their dead relatives raised back to life.

Others, refusing to accept freedom, died under torture in order to be raised to a better life. Some were mocked and whipped.

Hebrews 11:31–36 GNT

Scrapbooks, family portraits, genealogies, and stories of our heritage give us an identity and teach us lessons of faith and courage. This passage is part of a chapter that's a scrapbook of past deeds God recorded and wants us to remember. Each one comes from a historical account in the Old Testament that showed men and women of faith in action. We can read about the people or deeds named, mostly about judges and prophets of Israel, and discover how each person trusted God and performed mighty deeds. Each one lived significantly for God with faith that serves as a lesson for us. Rahab, for example, changed her life because of her faith when she hid Israelite spies. She could have been executed if her deed had been discovered. God protected her; then she left behind her old life and became an ancestress of Jesus.

Also notice the unsung heroines, women who experienced God's power of resurrection, and people who suffered for their faith. God knows the names and faces of the countless people who have lived faithfully. We too can do what is right and become part of God's scrapbook, encouraging others to be faithful.

PERSISTENT FAITH

He said, "In a certain city there was a judge who neither feared God nor respected man. And there was a widow in that city who kept coming to him and saying, 'Give me justice against my adversary.' For a while he refused, but afterward he said to himself, 'Though I neither fear God nor respect man, yet because this widow keeps bothering me, I will give her justice, so that she will not beat me down by her continual coming.'"

And the Lord said, "Hear what the unrighteous judge says. And will not God give justice to his elect, who cry to him day and night? Will he delay long over them? I tell you, he will give justice to them speedily. Nevertheless, when the Son of Man comes, will he find faith on earth?"

Luke 18:2–8 ESV

Faith means having complete confidence in God. God invites us, through this story Jesus told, to persist in faith with him about our just needs. God, unlike the judge in Jesus' story, is righteous and just. How much more than the unrighteous judge will he be willing to respond when we continually come to him and ask for help? We know he'll answer because he told us he will do it.

We might face unjust lawsuits, unjust pay or other discrimination at work, or unjust property settlements in divorce. God knows our problems. We must not give up pleading with God for a fair response. Keep exercising your faith and plead for God to listen and respond!

This parable follows talks Jesus gave about the coming kingdom of God, and he returns to that thought with a question for his listeners at the end of this story. When Jesus returns, will he find faith on the earth? Jesus understands our weaknesses, our doubting natures, and how easily we forget to pray. What is your answer to Jesus' question going to be? Will you also persist in trusting God no matter how tough life gets?

LEAP OF FAITH

She [Mary] entered Zechariah's home and greeted Elizabeth.

When Elizabeth heard the greeting, she felt the baby kick. Elizabeth was filled with the Holy Spirit. She said in a loud voice, "You are the most blessed of all women, and blessed is the child that you will have. I feel blessed that the mother of my Lord is visiting me. As soon as I heard your greeting, I felt the baby jump for joy. You are blessed for believing that the Lord would keep his promise to you."

Mary said, "My soul praises the Lord's greatness! My spirit finds its joy in God, my Savior, because he has looked favorably on me, his humble servant. From now on, all people will call me blessed because the Almighty has done great things to me. His name is holy."

Luke 1:40–49 GOD'S WORD

All babies growing in the womb move, kick, and roll. Elizabeth felt movement in her womb that she recognized as different. Her baby leaped for joy as Mary greeted Elizabeth.

Elizabeth was old, beyond the age of giving birth, and Mary was a young unmarried virgin. Age didn't matter, but faith did. An angel had told Mary about Elizabeth's pregnancy. The Holy Spirit filled Elizabeth so she understood her son's reaction and Mary's special baby. These two women, used by God, connected in relationship as cousins, faithful believers, and mothers-to-be.

Mary let her joy spill out in a song of praise to God. She knew Elizabeth would listen without disbelief, envy, or doubt. Mary spoke of God's mighty deeds of the past and his mercy for those who trust him.

Find another Christian woman with whom you share a common bond and strengthen that relationship. It's great to have a girlfriend who understands you and your season of life and shares a common belief that God has plans for you both. Share your faith, visions God gives you, and prayer answers. Spending time together with another woman of faith strengthens the faith in both individuals.

ONCE BLIND, NOW SQUINTING

Jesus himself drew near and went with them. But their eyes were kept from recognizing him. . . .

He said to them, "O foolish ones, and slow of heart to believe all that the prophets have spoken! Was it not necessary that the Christ should suffer these things and enter into his glory?" And beginning with Moses and all the Prophets, he interpreted to them in all the Scriptures the things concerning himself. . . .

When he was at table with them, he took the bread and blessed and broke it and gave it to them. And their eyes were opened, and they recognized him. And he vanished from their sight. They said to each other, "Did not our hearts burn within us while he talked to us on the road, while he opened to us the Scriptures?"

Luke 24:15–16, 25–27, 30–32
ESV

Two friends walking to Emmaus stayed blind to the truth until Jesus sat and broke bread with them. While overwhelmed with the reality of the Crucifixion, they let their "mind's eyes" squint. Then something familiar in Jesus' hands, expression, or words opened their eyes. Jesus had explained the Scriptures and gave these two lots of information, but that didn't help them recognize him.

In the busyness of life, as we rush from place to place, we get lots of information. It might not impact our faith, however, because knowledge is different from faith. Jesus is always with us, but we might not recognize his presence until we sit and reflect on what happened during the day. When we sit quietly and let Jesus interact with us, our hearts are more open to understanding, recognizing God, and believing in him. We can hear the still, gentle voice of Jesus or understand that through a prayer answered we encountered Jesus without being aware of him.

We don't always understand as quickly as we'd like. Thankfully we have a God who can open our eyes and minds as we sit, break bread, and let our hearts listen to Jesus.

FAITH MENTOR

You've been a good apprentice to me, a part of my teaching, my manner of life, direction, faith, steadiness, love, patience. . . . Anyone who wants to live all out for Christ is in for a lot of trouble; there's no getting around it. Unscrupulous con men will continue to exploit the faith. They're as deceived as the people they lead astray. . . .

But don't let it faze you. Stick with what you learned and believed, sure of the integrity of your teachers—why, you took in the sacred Scriptures with your mother's milk! There's nothing like the written Word of God for showing you the way to salvation through faith in Christ Jesus. Every part of Scripture is God-breathed and useful one way or another—showing us truth, exposing our rebellion, correcting our mistakes, training us to live God's way.

2 Timothy 3:10, 12–16 MSG

Timothy's mother and grandmother were faithful believers who raised him to know Christ. The apostle Paul met Timothy when he was a young man and became his spiritual mentor—walking alongside him, sharing his own trials and insight, and shaping Timothy's thinking. Paul sent Timothy encouraging letters too. But upbringing and mentoring don't assure that someone will remain faithful to God. Paul knew that God's Word, the Bible, would keep Timothy going in the right direction.

The Bible directs us, points out truth, corrects us, and shows us God's way to live. The Bible is more than a tool, because it is God-breathed and thus living. It's like no other book as it has continued to touch hearts and inform minds throughout the centuries.

Who are the people who have mentored you in your faith? Even more important, how are you letting the Bible mentor you? You can read about women in the Bible to learn how they faced challenges and trusted God. You can study the Bible with other women to share insights that will give you new wisdom. We won't veer off from God's direction if we take time to let the Bible mentor us.

Faith Believes That God Exists

Faith is the assurance (the confirmation, the title deed) of the things [we] hope for, being the proof of things [we] do not see and the conviction of their reality [faith perceiving as real fact what is not revealed to the senses].

For by [faith—trust and holy fervor born of faith] the men of old had divine testimony borne to them and obtained a good report.

By faith we understand that the worlds [during the successive ages] were framed (fashioned, put in order, and equipped for their intended purpose) by the word of God, so that what we see was not made out of things which are visible. . . .

But without faith it is impossible to please and be satisfactory to Him. For whoever would come near to God must [necessarily] believe that God exists.

Hebrews 11:1–3, 6 AMP

As creative women we enjoy scenes and designs in nature that please our senses. This passage paints a picture of faith as a reality we cannot touch or use other senses to experience.

How God interacted with people in the Bible and how he works through people today open our hearts to the reality of God's existence and the possibility of knowing him. As we understand the purpose God had for people in the past, we can believe he has a purpose for us today.

Faith gives us a framework to support our lives, like the framework of a building supports its weight. We would be foolish to ask someone nonexistent to support us. So we must believe God exists before we have faith in him.

If we examine the complexity of nature, DNA, and other aspects of our universe, we see design that is not explained by random coincidence. As we observe answers to prayer, we see evidence of God's existence. When we cry out and ask God to respond to us, he does, for he is a God who pursues. When we discover God in our lives, we can say with conviction, "I believe."

SEEK AND FIND

If you look for the LORD your God when you are among those nations, you will find him whenever you search for him with all your heart and with all your soul. When you're in distress and all these things happen to you, then you will finally come back to the LORD your God and obey him. The LORD your God is a merciful God. He will not abandon you, destroy you, or forget the promise to your ancestors that he swore he would keep.

Search the distant past, long before your time. Start from the very day God created people on earth. Search from one end of heaven to the other. Has anything as great as this ever happened before, or has anything like it ever been heard of?

Deuteronomy 4:29–32
GOD'S WORD

Do you like to travel? Moses invited his listeners to search all the earth for accounts of what God had done. Deuteronomy records the words God gave Moses east of the Jordan River shortly before he died.

Moses had tried to run away from God, but God pursued him and appeared to him in the desert. Moses saw evidence of God's power through the ten plagues God sent the Egyptians and through God's constant care as he led his people in the desert. Here Moses reminded the people that they would find God whenever they searched for him.

If we listen to testimonies of God's existence and activity, we will hear accounts more wonderful than the sights we see as we travel. In our travelogue with God, we will find love, mercy, and a loving Father. Even if we ignore him during happy times and return to him only when we have a great need, God will respond to us. But God doesn't want a casual cry for help; he wants a heart-and-soul search for him, a seeking within the Bible, in nature, and in lives of people.

Small Faith, Big Results

He went to see if there were any figs on the tree. But there were not any, because it wasn't the season for figs. So Jesus said to the tree, "Never again will anyone eat fruit from this tree!" The disciples heard him say this. . . .

As the disciples walked past the fig tree the next morning, they noticed that it was completely dried up, roots and all. Peter remembered what Jesus had said to the tree. Then Peter said, "Teacher, look! The tree you put a curse on has dried up."

Jesus told his disciples: "Have faith in God! If you have faith in God and don't doubt, you can tell this mountain to get up and jump into the sea, and it will. Everything you ask for in prayer will be yours, if you only have faith."

Mark 11:13–14, 20–24 CEV

Women, especially wives and mothers, often feel that few pay attention to our words and others doubt that what we say is true. Jesus understands that sentiment. He called attention to a little fig tree in full leaf but with no fruit. Not one succulent fig hung on any branch. Within one day the tree withered in response to Jesus' curse. Peter seemed amazed by this. Jesus responded with a lesson on the power of faith and prayer to do what seems impossible.

Mother Teresa moved a mountain of apathy by praying and caring for one sick person at a time. Dale Hanson Bourke supports women's health in Africa and began a worldwide bracelet project to help orphans with AIDS and help a continent move a mountain of despair and pain. These women found their strength in faith and prayer. God wants more women to pray and change the world. We can move mountains of apathy around us, energize people to care for the needy, or show faith that helps unbelievers have faith.

Mountainous power exists that we can harness with words. Our prayers will accomplish great things when we believe.

GOD-PREPARED MOVES

This is what the LORD says:

"I will go before you, Cyrus, and level the mountains. I will smash down gates of bronze and cut through bars of iron. And I will give you treasures hidden in the darkness—secret riches. I will do this so you may know that I am the LORD, the God of Israel, the one who calls you by name. . . .

"I am the LORD; there is no other God. I have equipped you for battle, though you don't even know me, so all the world from east to west will know there is no other God. I am the LORD, and there is no other."

Isaiah 45:2–3, 5–6 NLT

Moves can be difficult. They uproot us and take us away from familiar sights and faces. Often we resist change and unknown territory and feel trapped and imprisoned in a new place. A move can divide families and shatter marriages if we face it only from this perspective.

In the words in this passage to King Cyrus of Persia, whom God used to return the Israelites to their homeland after years in exile, God says that he goes before us to make our way smooth. He went before his people in their desert wanderings to lead them to the Promised Land, and now he would lead them home again.

God will open doors and give us new treasure, including new girl-friends, when we move. He goes ahead of us to prepare our way. In any move God calls us to new adventures. He calls us to change and trust him no matter where we live. God promises to be with us anywhere under the sun. He will make moving an adventurous treasure hunt. He is faithful to us everywhere and wants us to faithfully go where he leads.

WINDOWS OF HEAVEN

You, like your ancestors before you, have turned away from my laws and have not kept them. Turn back to me, and I will turn to you. But you ask, "What must we do to turn back to you?" I ask you, is it right for a person to cheat God? Of course not, yet you are cheating me. "How?" you ask. In the matter of tithes and offerings. . . .

Bring the full amount of your tithes to the Temple, so that there will be plenty of food there. Put me to the test and you will see that I will open the windows of heaven and pour out on you in abundance all kinds of good things. . . .

Then the people of all nations will call you happy, because your land will be a good place to live.

Malachi 3:7–8, 10, 12 GNT

Women everywhere care deeply about living in a good place. A relationship where God gives, we give, and then God gives even more sounds too good to be true, but that's what God offers. He calls us to keep his laws and give him what is due him. He gives us everything we have and only asks for us to return to him 10 percent—a *tithe*. And when we faithfully do, he pours out his blessings on us.

Women who tithe find joy in giving and find that giving is better than accumulating things. One woman who continued to tithe when she and her husband had no jobs received gifts of food from friends and unexpected checks in the mail that covered expenses. Another woman who chose to give all the money from her tenth book received unexpected awards as an author. Many women have similar stories of blessings received as they faithfully gave.

A window of heaven is big enough to pour out abundance and provide a glimpse into the wealth of God and his generosity, a peek into what he wants to give his faithful children in eternity.

PRAYER PARTNERS

We prayed to our God and posted a guard day and night to meet this threat. . . . I stationed some of the people . . . by families, with their swords, spears and bows. . . . I stood up and said to the nobles, the officials and the rest of the people, "Don't be afraid of them. Remember the Lord, who is great and awesome, and fight for your brothers, your sons and your daughters, your wives and your homes."

When our enemies heard that we were aware of their plot and that God had frustrated it, we all returned to the wall, each to his own work.

From that day on, half of my men did the work, while the other half were equipped with spears, shields, bows and armor. The officers posted themselves behind all the people of Judah who were building the wall.

Nehemiah 4:9, 13–17 NIV

Faith, a plan, and a leader made a difference in how Nehemiah's people faced their enemies and worked together to rebuild the broken-down walls of Jerusalem. Under Nehemiah half the people worked while half held weapons and guarded their fellow workers. Nehemiah's officers stood guard behind the workers. Read further in the chapter and you'll discover that those who worked held a weapon in one hand and kept their swords at their sides as they worked. Nehemiah saw the plot by Judah's enemies against these builders as a battle against God, a spiritual battle that he trusted God to win.

In all our spheres of influence, whenever we sense spiritual forces of darkness coming against us, women need to stand together armed and trusting God. The New Testament speaks of armor God has given us for this purpose; it includes the Bible, the Word of God. Teaming up in prayer and trusting God is how we fight spiritual battles. Find a girlfriend to team up with. Pray together and pray for each other when you're apart and especially on days you expect to be challenging. Partnering gives us accountability, strength, and courage.

The Gift of Faithful Words

There in the square by the gate he read the Law to them from dawn until noon, and they all listened attentively. . . .

They gave an oral translation of God's Law and explained it so that the people could understand it.

When the people heard what the Law required, they were so moved that they began to cry. So Nehemiah, who was the governor, Ezra, the priest and scholar of the Law, and the Levites who were explaining the Law told all the people, "This day is holy to the LORD your God, so you are not to mourn or cry. Now go home and have a feast. Share your food and wine with those who don't have enough. Today is holy to our Lord, so don't be sad. The joy that the LORD gives you will make you strong."

Nehemiah 8:3, 8–10 GNT

Nehemiah had led the people to rebuild the wall of Jerusalem in fifty-two days, after it lay in ruins for seventy years. After rebuilding the wall and seeing God overcome all enemy plots, the people trusted God and were ready to listen to his law. They grieved over not listening to him in the past, but Nehemiah proclaimed that such understanding is cause for rejoicing, not crying.

The people celebrated the Feast of Booths after listening. That feast celebrated God's protection as he led them through the wilderness. In this passage the people have come through the wilderness of ruin to be restored and found God's protection as they rebuilt the wall.

The law felt precious after the people experienced God's love. When we come through hard times, we can look back and see God's goodness. His words become precious as we feel thankful for what we have experienced and learned. Rebuilding after a disaster, restoring a broken relationship, or coming out of financial debt are times we can look back and see God's goodness and discover how the experience matured us. These are times to rejoice and celebrate as we read the Bible.

DISBELIEF AND TEARS

Martha then said to Jesus, "Lord, if You had been here, my brother would not have died." . . . Jesus said to her, "I am the resurrection and the life; he who believes in Me will live even if he dies." . . .

When Mary came where Jesus was, she saw Him, and fell at His feet, saying to Him, "Lord, if You had been here, my brother would not have died." When Jesus therefore saw her weeping, and the Jews who came with her also weeping, He was deeply moved in spirit and was troubled. . . . Jesus wept. . . .

He cried out with a loud voice, "Lazarus, come forth." The man who had died came forth.

John 11:21, 25, 32–33, 35, 43–44 NASB

※

These snippets of conversation took place over three days. Martha had sent word to Jesus that her brother lay dying. Jesus delayed answering her request for him to come, and when Jesus arrived in Bethany, Lazarus had died and was buried. But Jesus was in control of the situation at every moment. He knew what he would do.

Mary sat at the feet of Jesus, listening to him, and Martha busied herself trying to please Jesus; both had reactions that many women share. When Martha finally saw Jesus arrive, she lamented that he came too late. She believed he could heal the sick but not that he could raise the dead. Then Martha's sister, Mary, ran to Jesus and echoed Martha's concerns.

We can spend our time at church, in Bible studies, and volunteering in ministry but still have problems believing God's power when we face a crisis. Our minds limit what we believe God can do.

Still not believing that Jesus' power could do anything, Mary and Martha led Jesus to the tomb. Then Jesus did what he planned all along: he called Lazarus out of the tomb, alive.

ACTING ON FAITH

The kingdom of heaven is like treasure hidden in a field, which a man found and covered up. Then in his joy he goes and sells all that he has and buys that field.

Again, the kingdom of heaven is like a merchant in search of fine pearls, who, on finding one pearl of great value, went and sold all that he had and bought it.

Again, the kingdom of heaven is like a net that was thrown into the sea and gathered fish of every kind. When it was full, men drew it ashore and sat down and sorted the good into containers but threw away the bad. So it will be at the close of the age. The angels will come out and separate the evil from the righteous.

Matthew 13:44–49 ESV

In these words of Jesus, one person stumbled upon treasure while the other searched for a great pearl. Do you like to search for valuable items in bargain basements and at yard sales? Or is the field where you hunt the mall? We grab what we view as valuable and pay for it on credit, committing future money—and thus future work—to possess what we think is worth too much to let it go. So we understand trading and selling to gather money to buy a valuable treasure or pearl. Jesus' analogy goes further, for he says God's kingdom is worth giving up *everything* we have to possess it.

Historically, many people have clung to faith and given their lives as martyrs. We cannot buy our way into heaven, but we can let go of what we prize to focus on God. We can give up positions and power and discover that being unimportant in God's kingdom is better than earthly accolades. We can stop accumulating possessions and use our money to help others. We can stop all our activity and busyness to seek God once we realize how precious God is to us.

EXTRAVAGANT FAITH

On the Sabbath we went outside the city gate to the river, where we expected to find a place of prayer. We sat down and began to speak to the women who had gathered there. One of those listening was a woman named Lydia, a dealer in purple cloth from the city of Thyatira, who was a worshiper of God. The Lord opened her heart to respond to Paul's message. When she and the members of her household were baptized, she invited us to her home. "If you consider me a believer in the Lord," she said, "come and stay at my house." And she persuaded us. . . .

After Paul and Silas came out of the prison, they went to Lydia's house, where they met with the brothers and encouraged them. Then they left.

Acts 16:13–15, 40 NIV

Lydia sold purple cloth, an expensive and extravagant fabric at the time because of the cost of dying it such a rare and brilliant color. Women still love wearing various hues of purple and lavender, and purple still represents royalty and courage in battle. In the city of Philippi, now in modern Greece, purples and crimsons decorated temples of idols, especially Diana's temple.

Lydia, a Gentile, not a Jew, already worshipped God, but she had not heard of Jesus. She responded to Paul's message and became the first baptized European. In spite of living in a city of idols, Lydia embraced her faith with enthusiasm and challenged Paul to test it. She prevailed upon Paul and his companions to stay in her home.

Within days, men dragged Paul and Silas to prison for preaching about Jesus. Lydia's position and fortune may have been at risk, but she showed extravagant faith as she opened her doors again to these men after their release from prison. Unafraid, she let Paul and Silas hold a meeting in her home before they departed.

Let purple be a colorful reminder to you to have extravagant and courageous faith like Lydia.

RESTORATION TIME

From now on we don't think of anyone from a human point of view. If we did think of Christ from a human point of view, we don't anymore. Whoever is a believer in Christ is a new creation. The old way of living has disappeared. A new way of living has come into existence. God has done all this. He has restored our relationship with him through Christ, and has given us this ministry of restoring relationships. In other words, God was using Christ to restore his relationship with humanity. He didn't hold people's faults against them, and he has given us this message of restored relationships to tell others. Therefore, we are Christ's representatives, and through us God is calling you. We beg you on behalf of Christ to become reunited with God.

2 Corinthians 5:16–20
GOD'S WORD

Have you ever refinished furniture? Sanding and a new finish will restore the piece. You don't hide it in a corner of the garage any longer but put it somewhere in your home where it can add beauty and be useful. The chair, table, or bed is old, yet new again. The basic wood and design have not been altered.

Paul wrote the words of this passage in a letter to defend his ability to preach and serve God. He had a sinful past but God sought him out, changed him, and made him new. That hope of change is for us too. Paul looked the same outwardly, but his faith, attitude, and spirit had changed.

We may search for the perfect table or chair and find an old one that is just right in shape but with gouges, cracks, or stains. We must strip off the old varnish, fill in holes or cracks, sand, and add a new finish to restore the piece to what it was meant to be. God doesn't change us on the outside, but restores our relationship with him so we can be the people he created us to be.

MOLDED BY THE POTTER

No one has ever seen or heard of a God like you. . . . You welcome those who find joy in doing what is right, those who remember how you want them to live. You were angry with us, but we went on sinning; in spite of your great anger we have continued to do wrong since ancient times. All of us have been sinful; even our best actions are filthy through and through. Because of our sins we are like leaves that wither and are blown away by the wind. No one turns to you in prayer; no one goes to you for help. You have hidden yourself from us and have abandoned us because of our sins.

But you are our father, LORD. We are like clay, and you are like the potter. You created us.

Isaiah 64:4–8 GNT

A potter shapes the clay and molds it. She can easily reshape the clay while it's soft. Later, in a kiln, the clay will harden and dry in the shape formed by her hand. Even after it's fired, however, the item can be broken into pieces by the potter, who then pulverizes it and uses the powder for grog to strengthen new clay that she will form into something better.

The second part of the book of Isaiah was written to bring hope to God's people and to help them understand God's promises and future plans. People turn away from God, yet God is the one who made us, and he is compared to a potter here and in another passage of Isaiah.

Like a potter who chose the shape of the items he made, God chose how he formed us. Even if we become broken by sin, God can restore us and strengthen us like a potter who uses the broken and crushed grog to strengthen new clay. God is in control and we, like clay, cannot choose how we are formed. We must trust that God the Potter carefully shapes us.

PASS IT ON

To Timothy, [my] beloved child: Grace (favor and spiritual blessing), mercy, and [heart] peace from God the Father and Christ Jesus our Lord!

I thank God Whom I worship with a pure conscience, in the spirit of my fathers, when without ceasing I remember you night and day in my prayers, and when, as I recall your tears, I yearn to see you so that I may be filled with joy.

I am calling up memories of your sincere and unqualified faith (the leaning of your entire personality on God in Christ in absolute trust and confidence in His power, wisdom, and goodness), [a faith] that first lived permanently in [the heart of] your grandmother Lois and your mother Eunice and now, I am [fully] persuaded, [dwells] in you also.

2 Timothy 1:2–5 AMP

When Paul and Timothy parted, Paul noticed that Timothy shed tears. He longed to be reunited with his friend and bring him joy. He had been a mentor and spiritual father to Timothy. A mentoring or coaching relationship is one to take seriously as we understand what we mean to the people we guide.

Paul wrote this passage in a letter while in prison with only Luke as a visitor. He knew he would die soon and that he had little time left to pass on wisdom and encouragement to Timothy. The memories he mentioned of Timothy's faith would have strengthened Timothy and reminded him of their ties. As Timothy matured, his life showed that he had an unqualified faith, a faith without reservations. Paul's mentoring had produced results.

The individual being mentored should bond with the mentor and desire to spend time with her. The mentor should care deeply for those she influences. There is also a point at which the mentor must encourage her followers they are ready to move on and no longer need her help. As spiritual moms, we can coach others and then encourage them to live what they learned.

Show Your Faith

Suppose you see a brother or sister who has no food or clothing, and you say, "Good-bye and have a good day; stay warm and eat well"—but then you don't give that person any food or clothing. What good does that do?

So you see, faith by itself isn't enough. Unless it produces good deeds, it is dead and useless.

Now someone may argue, "Some people have faith; others have good deeds." But I say, "How can you show me your faith if you don't have good deeds? I will show you my faith by my good deeds." . . .

How foolish! Can't you see that faith without good deeds is useless?

Don't you remember that our ancestor Abraham was shown to be right with God by his actions when he offered his son Isaac on the altar?

James 2:15–18, 20–21 NLT

Compassionate women often reach out to meet needs we see around us. Our actions reveal our hearts. In the same way, the things we do also reveal our faith. Faith should be evident in our actions. No action, argues Paul in this passage, means no faith—dead faith. Paul holds up Abraham as our example of faith in action, especially difficult actions. Abraham's obedience in response to God's command proved that he utterly trusted God to do what he promised. God had given him Isaac, and God could raise Isaac from the dead if need be—the book of Hebrews gives us this insight about Abraham's understanding and faith.

Some women are called to be caregivers as they watch loved ones die. Others fight for freedom in war zones. Others may follow a call to fast or give money saved to the poor.

Our actions also show others what we believe. Serving at shelters for the homeless or at food kitchens is one way we can follow Jesus' call to love others. They see us living our faith, watch what happens, and observe how God works in our lives to see if faith and God are real.

CHAMELEON FAITH SHARERS

I have made myself a slave to all, so that I may win more. To the Jews I became as a Jew, so that I might win Jews; to those who are under the Law, as under the Law though not being myself under the Law, so that I might win those who are under the Law; to those who are without law, as without law, though not being without the law of God but under the law of Christ, so that I might win those who are without law. To the weak I became weak, that I might win the weak; I have become all things to all men, so that I may by all means save some. I do all things for the sake of the gospel, so that I may become a fellow partaker of it.

1 Corinthians 9:19–23 NASB

Have you ever called a girlfriend to find out what she's wearing to a special event? Casual or business casual? Dressy or formal? We want to dress appropriately so that we fit in. A chameleon also changes its "attire" to blend in with its surroundings. It's the protection from predators that God gave this creature.

In this passage, Paul describes himself as something of a chameleon—but not for his own security. Instead, Paul fit in with others in order to try to save them. He showed Jews how he, as a follower of Christ, could live under the law as a Jew. To the weak, he shared his own weaknesses so they saw him as someone imperfect like themselves. And to non-Jews, those who had never known God's law, he shared how his freedom from that law allowed him to live under the new law of Christ—the law of love. Sharing faith starts with meeting people where they live and showing them we care. Paul came alongside people with purpose.

Fit in with girlfriends through mutual activities, such as crafts, exercising, or mutual music interests. Establish a relationship and then share your faith.

BLESSINGS FOR THE FAITHFUL

God appeared to Solomon and said to him, "Ask for whatever you want me to give you." . . .

Solomon answered God, . . . "Give me wisdom and knowledge, that I may lead this people, for who is able to govern this great people of yours?"

God said to Solomon, "Since this is your heart's desire and you have not asked for wealth, riches or honor, nor for the death of your enemies, and since you have not asked for a long life but for wisdom and knowledge to govern my people over whom I have made you king, therefore wisdom and knowledge will be given you. And I will also give you wealth, riches and honor, such as no king who was before you ever had and none after you will have."

2 Chronicles 1:7–8, 10–12 NIV

❋

One of Solomon's first acts as king was to make a thousand freewill offerings to God. He gave because he wanted to honor God and to connect with God. God responded to this faithful king by offering to grant Solomon any desire. Solomon's request for wisdom came from his heart. He could have asked for anything, but he asked for what was best for him as a new leader who wanted to help his people.

What's your heart's desire? Do you want to write a book, be a good mother, earn a degree, or perform your current work better? Think of how your dream could help other people. Then think of what you need to fulfill the dream, especially any needed qualities or virtues. For writing you need discipline and the ability to use language to convey a message. In raising children you need patience. Each dream requires different skills and virtues.

When we freely offer God our talents, hopes, acts of kindness, and even past failures, we show our faith in him. Then we can ask for what we need to perform the tasks necessary to fulfill our dreams or the work God has already given us.

LOVE DEFINED

Love is patient, love is kind. It does not envy, it does not boast, it is not proud. It is not rude, it is not self-seeking, it is not easily angered, it keeps no record of wrongs. Love does not delight in evil but rejoices with the truth. It always protects, always trusts, always hopes, always perseveres.

Love never fails. But where there are prophecies, they will cease; where there are tongues, they will be stilled; where there is knowledge, it will pass away. . . . Now we see but a poor reflection as in a mirror; then we shall see face to face. Now I know in part; then I shall know fully, even as I am fully known.

And now these three remain: faith, hope and love. But the greatest of these is love.

1 Corinthians 13:4–8, 12–13
NIV

Frequently quoted at weddings, this passage reveals the true nature of love. More songs, sonnets, and poems are written about love than any other theme, but often they describe feelings and emotional responses rather than real love. Love involves a decision to put someone first and please that person's best interests through our words and actions. The apostle Paul wrote this passage in a letter to the Christians in Corinth. Because of their lives before hearing about Jesus, many people in the Corinthian church struggled with sexual immorality and confused sex with real love in action. These words reminded them, and us, to persevere to truly love.

Willingness to forgive is a big part of love. When we forgive, we don't keep a record of hurts. This is not a matter of allowing or enabling someone to do wrong, but rather unselfishly wanting the best for the person. Check your attitude and feelings about each person in your address book or social network. Forgive grudges, release jealousies, and commit to encourage people you've enabled to change their behavior.

Love, the greatest of the three virtues of faith, hope, and love, is worth exercising and understanding. Love never fails.

THE MATH OF LOVE

May mercy, peace, and love be multiplied to you. . . .

You must remember, beloved, the predictions of the apostles of our Lord Jesus Christ. They said to you, "In the last time there will be scoffers, following their own ungodly passions." It is these who cause divisions, worldly people, devoid of the Spirit. But you, beloved, build yourselves up in your most holy faith; pray in the Holy Spirit; keep yourselves in the love of God, waiting for the mercy of our Lord Jesus Christ that leads to eternal life. And have mercy on those who doubt. . . . Now to him who is able to keep you from stumbling and to present you blameless before the presence of his glory with great joy, to the only God, our Savior, through Jesus Christ our Lord, be glory, majesty, dominion, and authority.

Jude 2, 17–22, 24 ESV

As love increases, mercy, and peace do too. Mercy is God's forgiveness. Love can multiply—and that's great math.

Jude, an early Christian, traveled with his wife; they ministered to others as a couple. Jude wrote this letter to help others live their Christian faith authentically, encouraging believers then and now to depend on prayer and God's love to develop a strong faith in us that will keep us God-focused in our me-focused world.

When we choose God over living for self-centered desires and the offerings of the world, we receive God's mercy, his tender compassion and desire to free us from suffering. God has compassion for us and wants us to show compassion to people who doubt. These people need God, but doubts keep them from believing and following. Sometimes doubting people mock us. Reaching out with mercy will show them our faith and help them believe.

Forgive someone who abused you or your loved ones. Be generous to an ex-husband regarding visiting with your children. Speak kindly to a critical mother-in-law or boss.

Multiplying love continues when we respond with mercy and love, even to people who mock our faith and us.

A Special Place in Someone's Heart

Whenever I mention you in my prayers, it makes me happy. . . . God is the one who began this good work in you, and I am certain that he won't stop before it is complete on the day that Christ Jesus returns.

You have a special place in my heart. So it is only natural for me to feel the way I do. All of you have helped in the work that God has given me, as I defend the good news and tell about it here in jail. God himself knows how much I want to see you. He knows that I care for you in the same way that Christ Jesus does.

I pray that your love will keep on growing and that you will fully know and understand how to make the right choices.

Philippians 1:4, 6–10 CEV

When we think of someone we love, we smile and recall happy memories. Paul began a letter to the Christians in Philippi by reminding them of his joy when he thought of them and prayed for them. The love connection between them linked their hearts across distance. They had helped him during difficult times and were now supporting him while he was imprisoned. Paul had ministered in Philippi twice, where Lydia and many others became believers. Paul had been an instrument to connect these people to Jesus, and he wanted their love for Jesus to grow. He had invested time in these relationships and continued to keep in touch.

How wonderful to have a special place in someone's heart and know the individual cares for us! We can call or e-mail and trust our loved one will be happy to hear from us. These relationships began and grew as we spent time with one another. Is there someone who needs time from you today? Love and understanding grow stronger when you continue to spend time together, stay connected, and communicate the special place you hold for someone in your heart.

AWESOME LOVE

One of the scribes . . . asked him, "Which commandment is the most important of all?" Jesus answered, "The most important is, 'Hear, O Israel: The Lord our God, the Lord is one. And you shall love the Lord your God with all your heart and with all your soul and with all your mind and with all your strength.' The second is this: 'You shall love your neighbor as yourself.' There is no other commandment greater than these." And the scribe said to him, "You are right, Teacher. You have truly said that he is one, and there is no other besides him. And to love him with all the heart and with all the understanding and with all the strength, and to love one's neighbor as oneself, is much more than all whole burnt offerings and sacrifices."

Mark 12:28–33 ESV

A scribe listening to Jesus asked him about a point of law. He wanted Jesus to name the most important commandment. The scribes in Jesus' time were lawyers, accustomed to mulling over legal issues. This scribe probably viewed even God's law as a set of rules to debate and argue. But Jesus gave him an answer that focused on love, not law. Jesus summed up all God's law in these two greatest commandments—love God first and completely, and then love everyone else.

The answer more than satisfied the scribe. He showed he "got it" by his response. Under the law, offerings and sacrifices were designated to be made to thank God, honor God, make amends for sin, and accompany specific requests. But love brings us into a stronger relationship with God than following rules about how to behave.

When we say, "I've done more good than bad," we are trying to win approval by being good enough. Keeping the commandments, such as not lying or stealing, but twisting words and deceiving people follows the rules but doesn't show love.

Focus on loving God and others with your thoughts, actions, and energy every day.

Love's Request

From the church leader. To a very special woman and her children. I truly love all of you, and so does everyone else who knows the truth. We love you because the truth is now in our hearts, and it will be there forever. I pray that God the Father and Jesus Christ his Son will be kind and merciful to us! May they give us peace and truth and love. . . .

Dear friend, I am not writing to tell you and your children to do something you have not done before. I am writing to tell you to love each other, which is the first thing you were told to do. Love means that we do what God tells us. And from the beginning, he told you to love him.

2 John 1:1–3, 5–6 CEV

※

When we bring a new friend to meet our family and friends, we want them all to get along and love one another. We want to bring the person into our circle; we're not replacing an old friend with a new one. John, known as the beloved disciple or the disciple whom Jesus loved, felt so loved by God that love defined him. In this letter, John asked a special friend and her children to love the people he loved and to love God as he loved God. John underscored the importance of this by identifying himself as the church leader, or elder. He put his authority behind his request that we love God and one another.

Understanding the truth in the Bible and obeying it helps love grow and remain loyal. God helps us do what he wants us to do. Sometimes loving others is hard, but it is God's command to us.

We are all special women, for we are all beloved of God. If we love God, we will want to please God by loving others. What new friend is on the horizon for you to introduce to the love of God?

SOCIALLY NETWORKED

I commend to you our sister Phoebe, who is a servant of the church which is at Cenchrea; that you receive her in the Lord in a manner worthy of the saints, and that you help her in whatever matter she may have need of you; for she herself has also been a helper of many, and of myself as well.

Greet Prisca and Aquila, my fellow workers in Christ Jesus, who for my life risked their own necks, to whom not only do I give thanks, but also all the churches of the Gentiles; also greet the church that is in their house. Greet Epaenetus, my beloved, who is the first convert to Christ from Asia. Greet Mary, who has worked hard for you. . . . Greet Ampliatus, my beloved in the Lord.

Romans 16:1–6, 8 NASB

The new online social networks help us stay connected and increase our circle of friends; they make it easier to introduce our friends to one another too. Networking isn't new, as people have connected friends for centuries, but technology makes it faster to connect with and find help for our friends.

At the end of his letter to the Christians in Rome, and in his other encouraging letters, Paul promoted a kind of social networking among his friends. In this passage he introduces the Romans to Phoebe and speaks highly of her, encouraging his friends in Rome to treat her well. Some scholars believe that Phoebe might have been the one to carry Paul's letter to the church at Rome.

Discovering someone we meet is a friend of one of our friends is exciting and quickly builds a bond. When the mutual friend is someone we love and respect, it makes it easy to welcome the new person into our life. Keep introducing your friends to others and let your friendship circle grow. Like Paul, recommend your friends and their attributes to others.

REAL LOVE

God is love. If we keep on loving others, we will stay one in our hearts with God, and he will stay one with us. If we truly love others and live as Christ did in this world, we won't be worried about the day of judgment. A real love for others will chase those worries away. The thought of being punished is what makes us afraid. It shows that we have not really learned to love.

We love because God loved us first. But if we say we love God and don't love each other, we are liars. We cannot see God. So how can we love God, if we don't love the people we can see? The commandment that God has given us is: "Love God and love each other!"

1 John 4:16–21 CEV

Romance and fairy-tale endings don't last. We can find real and lasting love only when we find the source of love. This passage reveals that source with the words "God is love." We need to plug into God and experience his love for us, and then our hearts will respond with love for God. John says our love for other people accurately measures our love for God.

So how does your love for God measure up? How are you doing at loving the people close to you? People in need, whether near or far? People who annoy or trouble you? Ask God to show you how to love the people he made that you meet and know. Look and listen to discover the talents, qualities, and lovable gifts God gave each person who comes into your life.

If you have ever had someone tell you they love your friend, spouse, or child, you know how that warms your heart. It's the same with God. When we love the people he loves, we make God happy. God knows what we need most is love—and to be loved, we need to love others.

Love Goes Round and Round

Beloved, let us love one another, for love is from God, and whoever loves has been born of God and knows God. Anyone who does not love does not know God, because God is love. In this the love of God was made manifest among us, that God sent his only Son into the world, so that we might live through him. In this is love, not that we have loved God but that he loved us and sent his Son to be the propitiation for our sins. Beloved, if God so loved us, we also ought to love one another. No one has ever seen God; if we love one another, God abides in us and his love is perfected in us.

By this we know that we abide in him and he in us, because he has given us of his Spirit.

1 John 4:7–13 ESV

✳

Christmas gift exchanges with loved ones. Valentine cards and candy. Expressions of love for each other can be fun and meaningful. But the true gift of love is better than beribboned packages or Valentine cards. God got the giving going. In this letter the beloved disciple John tells us how: God loved us so much that he gave us what he valued most, his Son, to rescue us from our sin.

God wants the giving of love to continue. As we share God's love, we are completing, or perfecting, God's will that we love others. We put God's love into action, and he responds by abiding, or living, with us. Love creates an unending circle.

Have you been hurt by someone you love? Maybe a spouse betrayed you, or an employer let you go unfairly, or a child refuses to do what is right, or a friendship has gone awry. Loving someone who has caused us pain is hard. Sometimes we feel grief, and sometimes anger. Remember that God loves us continually. His love will renew our love for others and help us act in love—with the best interest of the other person as our desire.

LOVE IS A CIRCLE OF GIVING

This is how we know what love is: Christ gave his life for us. We too, then, ought to give our lives for others! If we are rich and see others in need, yet close our hearts against them, how can we claim that we love God? My children, our love should not be just words and talk; it must be true love, which shows itself in action.

This, then, is how we will know that we belong to the truth; this is how we will be confident in God's presence. . . .

We receive from him whatever we ask, because we obey his commands and do what pleases him. What he commands is that we believe in his Son Jesus Christ and love one another, just as Christ commanded us. Those who obey God's commands live in union with God.

1 John 3:16–19, 22–24 GNT

Laws forcing citizens to provide for others can't solve all societal problems, because laws don't change hearts. Telling people God loves them and we love them is useless without actions of love as well. This letter of John is considered a great discourse that reveals how to love unconditionally.

How can you put feet and hands onto your love, with deeds that show you care? A smile, listening, and kind words are the first actions. When we respond to others' needs and share what God gives us, with clothes or food for the needy or hugs and understanding for the hurting, we show that we belong to God. Our lives of service and love for others will reflect Jesus' sacrifice of his life for us and draw others in to be part of the lasting circle of God's love as we respond to their needs.

Being part of God's family builds our confidence that God will answer our prayers. But God is not a genie. We choose to please God; then he willingly responds to our prayers. That's a loving relationship. We please God when we believe in Jesus, his Son, and love the people he created.

GENUINE LOVE

"No!" the other woman shouted. "He was your son. My baby is alive!"

"The dead baby is yours," the first woman yelled. "Mine is alive!"

They argued back and forth in front of Solomon, until finally he said, "Both of you say this live baby is yours. Someone bring me a sword. . . . Cut the baby in half! That way each of you can have part of him."

"Please don't kill my son," the baby's mother screamed.

"Your Majesty, I love him very much, but give him to her. Just don't kill him."

The other woman shouted, "Go ahead and cut him in half. Then neither of us will have the baby."

Solomon said, "Don't kill the baby." Then he pointed to the first woman, "She is his real mother. Give the baby to her."

1 Kings 3:22–27 CEV

❋

This famous narrative shows us Solomon, the wisest king of Israel and named the wisest man on earth by God, testing the love of two mothers. The baby's real mother offered to give up her child so he could live. Genuine love wants the absolute best for the person loved. This woman passionately revealed her love when she declared she loved her infant enough to give him up.

The mother who had stolen the baby in her grief over her own son's death didn't care if her choice caused pain to another mother or the death of another child.

We will feel pain when we experience loss, but our pain is never an excuse to hurt anyone else. It's so easy, however, to lash out in anger at others when we are frustrated or grieving. When we are in that state, we need wise women around us. And when we see another woman grieving, we can reach out with comfort.

Genuine love means choosing to do the right thing and what's best for others. Love others and be wise. Consider what will most help someone and then do it.

The Example of Love

God is pleased if a person is aware of him while enduring the pains of unjust suffering. What credit do you deserve if you endure a beating for doing something wrong? But if you endure suffering for doing something good, God is pleased with you.

God called you to endure suffering because Christ suffered for you. He left you an example so that you could follow in his footsteps. Christ never committed any sin. He never spoke deceitfully. Christ never verbally abused those who verbally abused him. When he suffered, he didn't make any threats but left everything to the one who judges fairly. Christ carried our sins in his body on the cross so that freed from our sins, we could live a life that has God's approval. His wounds have healed you.

1 Peter 2:19–24 GOD'S WORD

※

Christ divided history and made a difference in countless lives because he loved us enough to suffer and die for us. The apostle Peter watched all that Jesus endured and how he reacted. In this passage, Peter encouraged believers who were suffering because of their faith to look to Jesus as their example. God is pleased when we think of him as we suffer for doing what is good and right and continue to do good even when others hurt us.

It's easy to respond with anger or aggression when we're taken advantage of, or accused unjustly. It can be hard to work where we have been passed over for promotion due to a coworker's lies or cheating. It's difficult to be teased—or worse, to be abused—by a spouse, a parent, or a sibling while we remain calm, control our instincts to fight back, and continue to be kind and loving.

If you or your children are in an abusive situation, you must seek help and protection. God notices our pain and will heal our wounds, and focusing on God's love and approval when we suffer helps ease the pain.

BROKEN HEARTS

When the soldiers came to the place called "The Skull," they nailed Jesus to a cross. They also nailed the two criminals to crosses. . . .

Jesus said, "Father, forgive these people! They don't know what they're doing." . . .

The soldiers made fun of Jesus and brought him some wine. . . .

Around noon the sky turned dark and stayed that way until the middle of the afternoon. The sun stopped shining, and the curtain in the temple split down the middle.

Jesus shouted, "Father, I put myself in your hands!" Then he died.

When the Roman officer saw what had happened, he praised God and said, "Jesus must really have been a good man!"

A crowd had gathered to see the terrible sight. Then after they had seen it, they felt brokenhearted and went home.

Luke 23:33–34, 36, 44–48 CEV

The death of Jesus is recorded in all four books of the Bible called the Gospels, but only this passage from the Gospel of Luke records the reactions of the crowd of onlookers. Luke, a physician accustomed to observing people, tells us how immediately Christ's death impacted people. A Roman officer praised God as he saw how Jesus trusted his Father as he died. But the sight of Jesus dead on the cross broke the hearts of onlookers, and Luke tells us they returned to the safety of their homes.

When a woman loses someone she loves, especially a child, spouse, or close friend, it breaks her heart. If someone close to us experiences such a loss, we feel it too. How much more, however, should we also feel the same pain that onlookers at the Crucifixion felt as they gazed on Jesus' beaten body on the cross? Our sin helped put him there, after all.

We all need a safe place to go when our hearts are broken after experiencing great loss. The safest place to be is in a relationship of love with God our Father, through Jesus who gave his life for us.

MENDING HEARTS

I wrote to you out of much affliction and anguish of heart and with many tears, not to cause you pain but to let you know the abundant love that I have for you.

Now if anyone has caused pain, he has caused it not to me, but in some measure—not to put it too severely—to all of you. For such a one, this punishment by the majority is enough, so you should rather turn to forgive and comfort him, or he may be overwhelmed by excessive sorrow. So I beg you to reaffirm your love for him. For this is why I wrote, that I might test you and know whether you are obedient in everything. Anyone whom you forgive, I also forgive. What I have forgiven, if I have forgiven anything, has been for your sake.

2 Corinthians 2:4–10 ESV

❋

Diplomats delicately solve relationships between people to bring a peaceful outcome. It's not an easy task to reinstate someone who has caused hurt. In this passage, Paul indicates his anguish as he acted in the role of diplomat. He understood that when one believer sins, everyone in the church is affected.

Paul used the Greek word *charizomai*, meaning "to give freely," for *forgive*. The church Paul wrote to had followed his earlier directions about how to discipline a believer who was engaging in sexual sin and bragging about it. Now Paul pleaded for the discipline to end and reconciliation and forgiveness for the sinner to begin.

When we correct someone, we must do it with love, a focus on improving the person, and a desire for unity to be preserved as much as possible. When there is repentance, reconciliation and restoration can follow.

As women we long to live in peace and harmony, but sometimes that requires tears of anguish over the division the sin has caused and careful diplomacy. This example of mediating shows how to reunite loved ones through love that forgives.

INSEPARABLE LOVE

He who did not spare His own Son, but delivered Him over for us all, how will He not also with Him freely give us all things? . . .

Who will separate us from the love of Christ? Will tribulation, or distress, or persecution, or famine, or nakedness, or peril, or sword? Just as it is written, "For Your sake we are being put to death all day long; we were considered as sheep to be slaughtered."

But in all these things we overwhelmingly conquer through Him who loved us. For I am convinced that neither death, nor life, nor angels, nor principalities, nor things present, nor things to come, nor powers, nor height, nor depth, nor any other created thing, will be able to separate us from the love of God, which is in Christ Jesus our Lord.

Romans 8:32, 35–39 NASB

❋

When we attend a wedding, we listen to two people pledge to stay faithful and together no matter what happens. Alas, that commitment does not always hold over time and troubles. But when we attend a twenty-fifth or fiftieth anniversary and see loving people who *have* kept that commitment, we renew our hope in love that unites.

God's love is stronger than the best and longest-lasting marriage. His love is inseparable and multidimensional. These words from Paul's letter to the Christians in Rome are among the most powerful and comforting words for women in the Bible because they promise enduring love throughout any circumstances and forever. Paul wrote his letter shortly before the church of Rome underwent great persecution.

These words from Paul are words to cling to during hard times. What difficulties are you experiencing today? Where are you looking for help, for love? When we face hardships or feel separated from love, hurt or abandoned by loved ones, or experience loss of love through death, this passage brings hope and the commitment that God still loves us and will keep loving us.

THE HEIGHTS OF LOVE

As high as the sky is above the earth, so great is his love for those who honor him. As far as the east is from the west, so far does he remove our sins from us. As a father is kind to his children, so the LORD is kind to those who honor him. He knows what we are made of; he remembers that we are dust.

As for us, our life is like grass. We grow and flourish like a wild flower; then the wind blows on it, and it is gone—no one sees it again. But for those who honor the LORD, his love lasts forever, and his goodness endures for all generations.

Psalm 103:11–17 GNT

A dad is often tough, brave, and strong but also kind and loving. If you grew up with a dad like that, you might understand something about God as a kind, loving Father. All women who love God are daddy's little girl to him. This passage is from a psalm written by King David that tells us what this "dad" is like. The key theme of the psalm is God's mercy, which can also be translated as "loyal love."

A good dad knows his children well. God knows his daughters well too—he knows that we are "but dust" and can crumble like a clump of garden dirt without his love to keep us strong and on the right path. Because of his mercy, God removes our sins completely when we come to him.

Some have flown through outer space, but no one has reached the end of space or understands the expanse of God's love. It's available to all but given to those who obey his commands and stay true to the relationship he wants with us—daughters who trust their heavenly Father to do what is best for them and love them always.

COMFORTING LOVE

A big crowd was going along with them. As they came near the gate of the town, they saw people carrying out the body of a widow's only son. Many people from the town were walking along with her.

When the Lord saw the woman, he felt sorry for her and said, "Don't cry!"

Jesus went over and touched the stretcher on which the people were carrying the dead boy. They stopped, and Jesus said, "Young man, get up!" The boy sat up and began to speak. Jesus then gave him back to his mother.

Everyone was frightened and praised God. They said, "A great prophet is here with us! God has come to his people."

News about Jesus spread all over Judea and everywhere else in that part of the country.

Luke 7:11–17 CEV

In Bible times the dead were never buried inside a city. The townspeople would walk with the body through the city gate and outside the town. Jesus and his friends walked to the city of Nain and encountered a funeral procession as they entered the gate.

The woman had already lost her husband, and now she had lost her only son. This meant she no longer had any financial support; as well as grieving another loss, she was also destitute. Jesus felt sorry for her and reached out to comfort her and refill her life with love. The widow must have been stunned by the sight of her son alive again. Jesus actually had to bring her son to her. The news of the miracle amazed people; they couldn't stop talking about it. The news spread and showed that Jesus is compassionate and reaches out to help us.

Telling others about God's loving compassion still amazes people. News of compassionate people, like Mother Teresa, spreads too, and reveals God's love. When we see grieving women, we can follow Christ's example and reach out to fill their emptiness with compassion and love.

Love among Friends

The greatest way to show love for friends is to die for them. And you are my friends, if you obey me. Servants don't know what their master is doing, and so I don't speak to you as my servants. I speak to you as my friends, and I have told you everything that my Father has told me.

You did not choose me. I chose you and sent you out to produce fruit, the kind of fruit that will last. Then my Father will give you whatever you ask for in my name. So I command you to love each other. . . .

If you belonged to the world, its people would love you. But you don't belong to the world. I have chosen you to leave the world behind, and that is why its people hate you.

John 15:13–17, 19 CEV

✵

At some point in our relationships we take a new step and we move from being acquaintances to friendship. This happens as we share from the depths of our hearts and give more than surface information to the other person. Jesus spoke the memorable words in this passage after washing his disciples' feet as an object lesson on serving others before his arrest and crucifixion. He had spent three years sharing much about himself and God the Father with these men, with the result that he could now call them friends. Friendship can take time to build.

Jesus also chose us to be his friends and to reveal to us, through the Bible, what he heard from God, just as he shared that with his disciples. Jesus wants us, like the disciples, to bear lasting fruit—loving actions, sharing faith, productive deeds that make an eternal difference.

Build relations: treat a girlfriend to a movie or ask a friend how you can pray for her; host a family gathering or shop with your in-laws; buy groceries or a gift card for someone in need; and spend time with Jesus by listening to worship songs and taking prayer walks.

Unloved by Men, Loved by God

The Lord saw that Leah was unloved, and He opened her womb, but Rachel was barren. Leah conceived and bore a son and named him Reuben, for she said, "Because the Lord has seen my affliction; surely now my husband will love me." Then she conceived again and bore a son and said, "Because the Lord has heard that I am unloved, He has therefore given me this son also." So she named him Simeon.

She conceived again and bore a son and said, "Now this time my husband will become attached to me, because I have borne him three sons." Therefore he was named Levi. And she conceived again and bore a son and said, "This time I will praise the Lord." Therefore she named him Judah. Then she stopped bearing.

Genesis 29:31–35 NASB

Unfortunately, some women end up in a loveless marriage. Sometimes we are simply ignored. When this happens, it's tempting to try to earn love by pleasing the one we want to love us.

Jacob wanted to marry Rachel, but her father tricked him into first marrying his older daughter, Leah, before he also gave Rachel to Jacob as his wife. God noticed that Leah was unloved by Jacob and gave her children. Leah hoped that giving Jacob sons to carry on his legacy would turn her husband's heart toward her. She gave the first three sons names that meant "Behold a son," "Hearing," and "Joined." The names show Leah's hope that Jacob would appreciate her, love her, and realize they were joined in marriage in hope of being joined in love.

At last, Leah gave up and looked to God for love instead of to Jacob. She named her fourth son Judah, which means "Let God be praised." God chose Judah to be an ancestor of Christ.

If you've tried to earn love through gifts, children, or actions, release those efforts. Turn to prayer and ask for God's love. Like Leah, we can count on God's love.

WOMAN WITH A PAST

The LORD said to me, "Go again, love a woman who is loved by her husband, yet an adulteress, even as the LORD loves the sons of Israel, though they turn to other gods and love raisin cakes." So I bought her for myself for fifteen shekels of silver and a homer and a half of barley. Then I said to her, "You shall stay with me for many days. You shall not play the harlot, nor shall you have a man; so I will also be toward you." For the sons of Israel will remain for many days without king or prince, without sacrifice or sacred pillar and without ephod or household idols. Afterward the sons of Israel will return and seek the LORD their God and David their king.

Hosea 3:1–5 NASB

If you have a promiscuous past, you might not view yourself as lovable. You might wonder, *How could a godly man want a woman with a sinful past or sexual addiction?*

When Hosea was prophesying in Israel, the people had been repeatedly untrue to God. God used Hosea and Gomez, a prostitute whom Hosea took as his wife, as an example of how he loves us when we are sinful and unlovable. Through Hosea God proclaimed a time when Israel would be without leaders but also without idols. This would allow the people time to recover from their idolatry and realize their need for God.

When Gomez returned to prostitution after her marriage, Hosea went after her and took her back. He redeemed her and brought her home. He set a time for refraining from sex, because sex without love can dull a woman's ability to discern real love. Abstinence would allow Gomez to withdraw from sexual addictions and heal.

God's love and his actions toward us, regardless of the nature of our mistakes or rebellion, are like Hosea's. God, the best matchmaker, can always guide women to someone who will love them—and especially to himself.

BELIEVE IN TRUE LOVE

God loved the world this way: He gave his only Son so that everyone who believes in him will not die but will have eternal life. God sent his Son into the world, not to condemn the world, but to save the world. Those who believe in him won't be condemned. But those who don't believe are already condemned because they don't believe in God's only Son.

This is why people are condemned: The light came into the world. Yet, people loved the dark rather than the light because their actions were evil. People who do what is wrong hate the light and don't come to the light. They don't want their actions to be exposed. But people who do what is true come to the light so that the things they do for God may be clearly seen.

John 3:16–21 GOD'S WORD

The beginning of this passage is perhaps the most memorized and quoted verse in the Bible. Yet the event recorded here took place in the dark. A respected Jewish teacher snuck out at night, when his peers would not see him, to question Jesus. Jesus spoke the words in this passage as he and Nicodemus stood in the dark. And in the dark Jesus first proclaimed God's love and then addressed the ideas of judgment, truth, and light.

We must let our faith show in the light. We can't worship on Sunday and spend the rest of the week in the dark, seeking to meet our own wants our own way, such as wearing revealing clothing, flirting, or drinking excessively.

Nicodemus's curiosity concerning miracles Jesus performed drew him to seek Jesus, but he strove to keep the meeting secret, avoiding the judgment of other leaders. God's love should encourage our willingness to be seen as believers. Let your love be visible as you help disabled or jobless neighbors. As you work openly and speak the truth in the light, God's work will be accomplished—you will show God's love to the world.

In His Loving Hands

The LORD called me before my birth; from within the womb he called me by name. He made my words of judgment as sharp as a sword. He has hidden me in the shadow of his hand. I am like a sharp arrow in his quiver. . . .

Yet Jerusalem says, "The LORD has deserted us; the Lord has forgotten us."

"Never! Can a mother forget her nursing child? Can she feel no love for the child she has borne? But even if that were possible, I would not forget you! See, I have written your name on the palms of my hands. . . . All your children will come back to you. . . . They will be like jewels."

Isaiah 49:1–2, 14–16, 18 NLT

Anyone who ever waited for her mother to pick her up might have wondered if her mother had forgotten her. Anyone who has been the daughter in a divorce and then saw one of her parents less and less, or maybe not at all, understands feeling abandoned. And mothers with grown children who seldom call or visit understand the pain of being forgotten.

In this passage Isaiah addressed God's people in exile. He addressed the people as Zion, a name that means "highest point," in contrast to their complaint that God had abandoned them and their feeling at their lowest point. Then he proclaimed how much God loved Israel, more than a nursing mother who feels the suck and tug of the baby at her breast so she cannot forget the infant.

God has engraved us, his people, on the palm of his hand, ever near him. The city of Jerusalem and the nation of Israel, empty and abandoned by God's children, would be restored and filled by them. God never forgets us or leaves us empty. His promise and power to restore is for women today too. When you feel low, trust that God will lift your spirit and refill your life.

MULTIDIMENSIONAL LOVE

I ask God from the wealth of his glory to give you power through his Spirit to be strong in your inner selves, and I pray that Christ will make his home in your hearts through faith. I pray that you may have your roots and foundation in love, so that you, together with all God's people, may have the power to understand how broad and long, how high and deep, is Christ's love. Yes, may you come to know his love—although it can never be fully known—and so be completely filled with the very nature of God.

To him who by means of his power working in us is able to do so much more than we can ever ask for, or even think of: to God be the glory in the church and in Christ Jesus.

Ephesians 3:16–21 GNT

❋

Have you ever received a gift that surprised you and showed that the giver cared more about you than you suspected? Have you loved someone for years and still find new depth to their love? These experiences remind us of what Paul hoped believers would discover about God's love.

Paul wrote this part of a letter to the believers in Ephesus as a prayer for God's Spirit to empower his people and Christ's love to dwell in their hearts. The more our heart is Christ's home, the more we discover about his love—it's all-encompassing height, depth, and breadth.

How deep do your roots go into the love God has for you? Have you opened up every area of your life to Jesus, or do you still have a few walled-off rooms in your heart where he isn't welcome to live? He wants to be family, not an occasional invited guest.

Jesus' love is wide enough to embrace us and help us in all our troubles. It's high enough to reach heaven's ear for us. It's deep enough to satisfy our longings because this love knows us completely.

391

LUST OR LOVE?

In the course of time, Amnon son of David fell in love with Tamar, the beautiful sister of Absalom son of David. . . .

Then Amnon said to Tamar, "Bring the food here into my bedroom so I may eat from your hand." And Tamar took the bread she had prepared and brought it to her brother Amnon in his bedroom. But when she took it to him to eat, he grabbed her and said, "Come to bed with me, my sister."

"Don't, my brother!" she said to him. "Don't force me. Such a thing should not be done in Israel! Don't do this wicked thing." . . . But he refused to listen to her, and since he was stronger than she, he raped her.

Then Amnon hated her with intense hatred. In fact, he hated her more than he had loved her.

2 Samuel 13:1, 10–12, 14–15
NIV

A man may take advantage of a woman and want to possess her, but never really know how to love her. Amnon, one of King David's sons, thought he loved his half sister Tamar, but he really only lusted after her beauty and her body. She responded to him with kindness and sisterly love and said no when he propositioned her. But lust is not satisfied with rejection, so Amnon raped Tamar. Sin and sex don't bring love. Once he satisfied his lust, Amnon hated Tamar instead of hating and admitting his sin.

Rape hurts women and leaves them emotionally wounded. With support and help to recover, healing can begin. All women, however, can learn from Amnon's example about the connection of lust and hate. Lust is never satisfied and never satisfies, and because of this, the object of our lust becomes hateful to us, whether we crave another person, a promotion, or applause.

Avoid looking at the object of your lust, fill your time with wholesome activities, and find an accountability partner. Meet with someone regularly who can encourage you to avoid temptation and whom you can call for support when needed.

THE MONEY TRAP

These people always cause trouble. Their minds are corrupt, and they have turned their backs on the truth. To them, a show of godliness is just a way to become wealthy.

Yet true godliness with contentment is itself great wealth. After all, we brought nothing with us when we came into the world, and we can't take anything with us when we leave it. So if we have enough food and clothing, let us be content.

But people who long to be rich fall into temptation and are trapped by many foolish and harmful desires that plunge them into ruin and destruction. For the love of money is the root of all kinds of evil. And some people, craving money, have wandered from the true faith and pierced themselves with many sorrows.

1 Timothy 6:5–10 NLT

We work hard for money for food, shelter, and luxuries. Shopping with girlfriends and celebrating a raise or other financial blessing can be fun. God, who blessed King Solomon with great wealth, is not against wealth; however, he is opposed to people who love money instead of loving God and other people.

Paul's letter to Timothy, a young minister and Paul's protégé, is full of practical advice on living a Christian life. This passage reminds us that we can't take money or what it buys with us when we die. We need to keep money and our use of money in line with what God desires. Don't let your desire for fashions and jewelry that enhance your looks or decorating your home to beautify it become more important than people or God—these things then become idols and interfere with relationships. Cravings for things can pull us away from faith, especially if we start living as though money will solve all our problems and buy us happiness.

The next time you think, *I have to get that now*, or when you don't have the money but want to purchase an item anyway, stop and consider: what do you love the most?

SELFISH LOVE

Samuel [said,] "He sent you out with orders to destroy those wicked people of Amalek. He told you to fight until you had killed them all. Why, then, did you not obey him? Why did you rush to grab the loot, and so do what displeases the LORD?"

"I did obey the LORD," Saul replied. "I went out as he told me to, brought back King Agag, and killed all the Amalekites. But my men did not kill the best sheep and cattle that they captured; instead, they brought them here to Gilgal to offer as a sacrifice to the LORD your God."

Samuel said, "Which does the LORD prefer: obedience or offerings and sacrifices? It is better to obey him than to sacrifice the best sheep to him."

1 Samuel 15:18–22 GNT

H ave it your way" and "do your own thing" have become mantras for many in our world. We like to change the rules of games, or drive above the speed limit, as though rules are merely guidelines we don't have to actually obey. But the Bible is not a buffet where we can pick and choose what we'd like to believe.

Saul, Israel's first king, disobeyed God, and God expressed his displeasure to Samuel, Israel's judge, priest, and prophet at that time. Samuel was grieved at God's stance; he might even have pleaded with God to be flexible and bend his rules for Saul. But God is holy and unchanging. He sent Samuel to announce to Saul that the kingdom would not continue under the rule of Saul's family. Although Saul would remain in power until he died, God's choice of a new king would be anointed. Samuel struggled in prayer all night and then accepted God's decision.

Saul argued that he had only bent the rules a little. Samuel then posed the question we need to ask ourselves also: is it better to obey God completely or offer him only what we choose?

SACRIFICING DEAREST LOVE

In due time Hannah conceived and bore a son, and she called his name Samuel, for she said, "I have asked for him from the LORD." . . .

And when she had weaned him, she took him up with her, along with a three-year-old bull, an ephah of flour, and a skin of wine, and she brought him to the house of the LORD at Shiloh. And the child was young. . . .

And she said, "Oh, my lord! As you live, my lord, I am the woman who was standing here in your presence, praying to the LORD. For this child I prayed, and the LORD has granted me my petition that I made to him. Therefore I have lent him to the LORD. As long as he lives, he is lent to the LORD."

1 Samuel 1:20, 24, 26–28 ESV

Perhaps you understand longing for a baby or a grandchild and finally holding that precious child. You do everything you can to love and protect him. In Hannah's desperation to have a son, she promised to give him to God to serve God all his life. She followed through on her promise once she had weaned her son, Samuel. She brought him to Shiloh, where the tabernacle was, to Eli, the high priest and judge of Israel, even though circumstances there were less than ideal.

Eli failed in raising his own sons to be godly. How difficult for Hannah to let her little boy live among wicked men and serve a man who could not control his own sons. But Hannah believed that God, who gave her a son, would also care for her son, and he did. Samuel grew up at the tabernacle, serving Eli and learning to know God. He became a great prophet and judge for the people of Israel.

We cannot control every moment in the lives of our loved ones, but we can trust God to protect and care for the ones we love!

LOVE FORGIVES

They were furious and gnashed their teeth at him. But Stephen, full of the Holy Spirit, looked up to heaven and saw the glory of God, and Jesus standing at the right hand of God. "Look," he said, "I see heaven open and the Son of Man standing at the right hand of God."

At this they covered their ears and, yelling at the top of their voices, they all rushed at him, dragged him out of the city and began to stone him. Meanwhile, the witnesses laid their clothes at the feet of a young man named Saul.

While they were stoning him, Stephen prayed, "Lord Jesus, receive my spirit." Then he fell on his knees and cried out, "Lord, do not hold this sin against them." When he had said this, he fell asleep.

Acts 7:54–60 NIV

Stephen, one of seven men chosen by the apostles in Jerusalem to serve tables and distribute food to widows when the church gathered, also received power from the Holy Spirit to perform wonders and signs among the people. Jewish religious leaders, antagonistic toward faith in Jesus, incited men to lie and bring Stephen before the Jewish council. Stephen's glowing appearance, his compelling defense that Jesus was indeed the Messiah, and the vision of heaven that God gave Stephen as he testified incited the council to react with violence and kill Stephen, pelting him with rocks. As he died, Stephen followed Jesus' example on the cross—with his dying breath he forgave his murderers.

Love wants the best for people, and that is heaven. Love doesn't want evil, so love forgives what seems unforgivable. Forgiving a spouse for cheating, a girlfriend for excluding you from a party, or a coworker for taking credit for your work is also difficult, especially if you must see the person often. God has forgiven us and we can read how Jesus forgave his persecutors as he hung on the cross and ask for his love and power to forgive.

LOVE AT LIFE'S END

Jesus knew that the hour had come for him to leave this world and go to the Father. He had always loved those in the world who were his own, and he loved them to the very end. . . .

After Judas had left, Jesus said, "Now the Son of Man's glory is revealed; now God's glory is revealed through him. . . . My children, I shall not be with you very much longer. You will look for me; but I tell you now what I told the Jewish authorities, 'You cannot go where I am going.' And now I give you a new commandment: love one another. As I have loved you, so you must love one another. If you have love for one another, then everyone will know that you are my disciples."

John 13:1, 31, 33–35 GNT

As Jesus faced his last hours, he spent time with his closest friends, urging them to remember his lessons and to continue loving others as he had loved them. He repeated the message in this passage a little later; it's recorded later in John's Gospel when Jesus speaks about unity.

Relationships and continuing to love others matter. Some people know their days are numbered. When we view time as extremely limited, we value the moments more and invest the hours in what matters most. But often death comes unexpectedly, so we should live each day as though it might be our last. Loving others sets Christians apart and shows the world a better way to live. Loving others reveals God and gives glory to God.

Review your interactions with people over the past few days. Did you love others? Did you speak politely, do little things like getting someone a drink of water, or really pray for someone in need? What can you do differently tomorrow?

One simple rule to guide us each day is the one rule that will make life worth living and impact people the most: love. *Love*—it's a verb, and that means action.

MIRACLES THRIVE WITH LOVE

In Joppa there was a disciple named Tabitha (which, when translated, is Dorcas), who was always doing good and helping the poor. About that time she became sick and died, and her body was washed and placed in an upstairs room. . . .

All the widows stood around [Peter], crying and showing him the robes and other clothing that Dorcas had made while she was still with them.

Peter sent them all out of the room; then he got down on his knees and prayed. Turning toward the dead woman, he said, "Tabitha, get up." She opened her eyes, and seeing Peter she sat up. . . . Then he called the believers and the widows and presented her to them alive. This became known all over Joppa, and many people believed in the Lord.

Acts 9:36–37, 39–42 NIV

Dorcas, whose Aramaic name was Tabitha, lived in the seaport city of Joppa. Probably a wealthy widow, Dorcas is the only woman specifically called a disciple in the Bible. Dorcas expressed her love for the Lord with numerous good deeds, especially helping the poor by making clothes for them. Distressed by Dorcas's death, the believers in Joppa sent for the apostle Peter, who was staying in Lydda, not too far away. The widows' tears when Peter arrived revealed how Dorcas had touched their hearts.

The Bible doesn't tell us why Peter chose to pray over Dorcas, but after he did, he spoke to her and she returned to life. The miracle caused many in Joppa to believe in Jesus. Did those faithful people in Joppa have such a strong love that they believed anything to be possible? Did they expect Peter to raise Dorcas from the dead? The passage doesn't tell us. But Peter's action reminds us that love and miracles go together.

Dorcas's life reminds us that even simple loving actions have a big impact. Her life wasn't flashy; she didn't lead any high-powered ministry programs. But her story proves that simple service can be significant.

VICTORIOUS LOVE

I've written to you, children, because you know the Father.

I've written to you, fathers, because you know Christ, who has existed from the beginning.

I've written to you, young people, because you are strong and God's word lives in you.

You have won the victory over the evil one.

Don't love the world and what it offers. Those who love the world don't have the Father's love in them. Not everything that the world offers—physical gratification, greed, and extravagant lifestyles—comes from the Father. It comes from the world, and the world and its evil desires are passing away. But the person who does what God wants lives forever. . . .

Now, dear children, live in Christ. Then, when he appears we will have confidence, and when he comes we won't turn from him in shame.

1 John 2:14–17, 28
GOD'S WORD

Television commercials, home-shopping shows, and telemarketers bombard us, enticing us to invest time and money in the next big trendy item. Girlfriends invite us to check out the latest fashions and home-decor themes. Yes, we live in the world. But we don't have to love the world.

Accumulating dozens of pairs of shoes or indulging in chocolates every day isn't necessarily wrong. But if we never feel we own enough or get enough of the things we want, we might be giving too much priority to material possessions. Check your motives—do you want more because you just never feel satisfied? When we never feel satisfied with what we own or continually want to indulge in pleasures, those are symptoms of loving the world. We're seeking something to fill the emptiness in our hearts.

In this passage, John gives us keys that help us avoid loving the world. Knowing God, knowing Christ, and having God's word within us cause us to live in the world but not belong to the world. The opposite of loving the world is having God's love in us. His love fills our hearts, fills the emptiness, and gives us confidence as women of God.

My prayer is that light
will flood your hearts and that
you will understand the hope
that was given to you when
God chose you. Then you will
discover the glorious blessings
that will be yours together with
all of God's people.
—Ephesians 1:18 CEV